STUDIES IN ENGLISH LITERATURES

Herausgegeben von Koray Melikoğlu

David Ellis

Writing Home

Black Writing in Britain Since the War

STUDIES IN ENGLISH LITERATURES

Herausgegeben von Koray Melikoğlu

ISSN 1614-4651

1   *Özden Sözalan*
       The Staged Encounter
       Contemporary Feminism and Women's Drama
       ISBN 3-89821-367-6

2   *Paul Fox (ed.)*
       Decadences
       Morality and Aesthetics in British Literature
       ISBN 3-89821-573-3

3   *Daniel M. Shea*
       James Joyce and the Mythology of Modernism
       ISBN 3-89821-574-1

4   *Paul Fox and Koray Melikoğlu (eds.)*
       Formal Investigations
       Aesthetic Style in Late-Victorian and Edwardian Detective Fiction
       ISBN 978-3-89821-593-0

5   *David Ellis*
       Writing Home
       Black Writing in Britain Since the War
       ISBN 978-3-89821-591-6

FORTHCOMING (MANUSCRIPT WORKING TITLES)

Lance Weldy
Seeking a Felicitous Space
The Dialectics of Women and Frontier Space in *Giants in the Earth*, *Little House on the Prairie*, and *My Antonia*
ISBN 3-89821-535-0

Wei H. Kao
Inclusions and Exclusions in the Irish Literary Canon in the Mid-Twentieth Century
ISBN 3-89821-545-8

Paola Baseotto
Spenserian Views of Death
ISBN 3-89821-567-9

Melanie Ann Hanson
Decapitation and Disgorgement
The Female Body as Text in Early Modern Drama and Poetry
ISBN 3-89821-605-5

Kevin Cole
Levity's Rainbow
Menippean Poetics in Swift, Fielding, and Sterne
ISBN 3-89821-654-3

Shafquat Towheed
New Readings in the Literature of British India
ISBN 3-89821-673-X

David Ellis

WRITING HOME

Black Writing in Britain Since the War

ibidem-Verlag
Stuttgart

Bibliografische Information der Deutschen Nationalbibliothek
Die Deutsche Nationalbibliothek verzeichnet diese Publikation in der Deutschen Nationalbibliografie; detaillierte bibliografische Daten sind im Internet über http://dnb.d-nb.de abrufbar.

Bibliographic information published by the Deutsche Nationalbibliothek
Die Deutsche Nationalbibliothek lists this publication in the Deutsche Nationalbibliografie; detailed bibliographic data are available in the Internet at http://dnb.d-nb.de.

Cover illustration:
Crown Copyright
Catalogue reference: PRO/BT26/1237

∞

Gedruckt auf alterungsbeständigem, säurefreien Papier
Printed on acid-free paper

ISSN: 1614-4651

ISBN-10: 3-89821-591-1
ISBN-13: 978-3-89821-591-6

© *ibidem*-Verlag
Stuttgart 2007

Alle Rechte vorbehalten

Das Werk einschließlich aller seiner Teile ist urheberrechtlich geschützt. Jede Verwertung außerhalb der engen Grenzen des Urheberrechtsgesetzes ist ohne Zustimmung des Verlages unzulässig und strafbar. Dies gilt insbesondere für Vervielfältigungen, Übersetzungen, Mikroverfilmungen und elektronische Speicherformen sowie die Einspeicherung und Verarbeitung in elektronischen Systemen.

All rights reserved. No part of this publication may be reproduced, stored in or introduced into a retrieval system, or transmitted, in any form, or by any means (electronic, mechanical, photocopying, recording or otherwise) without the prior written permission of the publisher. Any person who does any unauthorized act in relation to this publication may be liable to criminal prosecution and civil claims for damages.

Printed in Germany

Dedicated to the memory of my mother, Doreen Edith Ellis

CONTENTS

Foreword: The Question of an Audience — xi

PART 1

1.0 Introduction: The First Generation — 1
1.1 Sam Selvon: The Lonely Exile — 10
1.2 George Lamming: The Natural Exile — 31
1.3 E. R. Braithwaite: The Cultural Exile — 50

PART 2

2.0 Introduction: The Second Generation — 69
2.1 Wilson Harris: Unlikely Fiction — 77
2.2 Andrew Salkey: The Middle Man — 103
2.3 Linton Kwesi Johnson: Creation Rebel — 126

PART 3

3.0 Introduction: The Present Generation — 143
3.1 Joan Riley: Caribbean Conversations I — 151
3.2 Caryl Phillips: Caribbean Conversations II — 173
3.3 David Dabydeen: Caribbean Conversations III — 195

Bibliography — 209

Foreword: The Question of an Audience

> You say no-one arrives back,
> for the breath once mixed becomes
> an eternal entanglement
> – Berry, *Chain of Days* 49

This book is concerned with the literature that arose from the post-War emigrations from the Caribbean to Britain, tracing its development through the discussion of selected writers until the present day. The focus throughout will be on writers who were either born in the Caribbean or are of Caribbean parentage, and on those texts that primarily deal with life in Britain. The writers selected are those whose body of work facilitates a sense of historical progression within the corpus as well as comparative analysis. The book aims to establish black British writing as a coherent literary tradition, and to suggest some conceptual tools with which to approach it.

There are three sections: each deal with writers whose British-set texts may be associated with certain broad sweeps in the contours of post-War Caribbean immigration into Britain. Thus, Part One focuses on Sam Selvon, George Lamming and E. R. Braithwaite as writers whose works were among the first to come out of the experience of emigration. Part Two features Wilson Harris, Andrew Salkey and Linton Kwesi Johnson and the negotiation of the establishment of the black British as a permanent part of a multicultural population. Finally, Part Three discusses the appraisal of a split black British and Caribbean heritage through the work of Joan Riley, Caryl Phillips and David Dabydeen.

Each chapter is prefaced by an introduction that describes the social, cultural and political milieux particular to the textual analyses. The object of this foreword is thus to provide the conceptual overview which has organised the study of these texts and to consider some of the problematics associated therein.

* * *

The first point to note is that of terminology. The term 'black British' as it will be used here is both inclusive and exclusive. For example, is Sam Selvon a Caribbean writer when discussing *A Brighter Sun* (1952), but black

British when discussing *The Lonely Londoners* (1956)? Should the term black British writing include work by British Asian authors such as Hanif Kureishi? Is his Asian heritage more important than Selvon's when neither, after all, was born in the Indian subcontinent? And what of the term 'black'? Selvon and Harris both have South Asian ancestry; Oku Onuora (formally Orlando Wong) has a half-Chinese father, whilst others have the more common descendence from the African diaspora. Furthermore, as Dabydeen and Wilson-Tagoe put it, "[d]oes black denote colour of skin or quality of mind? If the former, what does skin colour have to do with the act of literary creation? If the latter, what is 'black' about 'black'?" (Dabydeen and Wilson-Tagoe 10). Even if these questions can be satisfied, can the continued use of this term be justified, or does it serve to circumscribe such writing and writers within the parameters of an imposed genre?

The present state of black publishing in Britain reflects these concerns. The success of X Press with Victor Headley's *Yardie* (1992) has served to illustrate the continued marginalisation of black writing in Britain. Written, printed and marketed without the support of an established publisher it highlights, as an article in *The Guardian* put it,

> the consensus within the (publishing) trade [. . .] that, with the exception of authors who are already established as bestsellers in the US [. . .] "black" books can't be sold outside of the major conurbations and even then they can only be sold in relatively small numbers. (Mike Phillips 4)

The clear assumption written into this consensus is that writing by black people is immediately distinguishable as being just that, and that the act of literary creation is indelibly imprinted with the writers' ethnic origin. The further assumption that the demand for such books is relatively small diminishes the number available with the inevitable by-product that those texts that are published assume an exaggerated significance as representations of the black community. Ivor Osbourne notes this potential in *Yardie*'s concentration on the drug underworld:

> When you start suggesting that gangster activities are the central issue of our lives, that it should be the central subject that black

Foreword: The Question of an Audience

writers are interested in, and that this is all black people want to read about, you're reinforcing our ghettoisation, instead of challenging cultural barriers. (Qtd. in Mike Phillips 4)

There is an element of self-fulfillment about this argument. If the publishing houses seek to develop their output of black writers, they will do so using texts that maintain a proven formula, nurturing the assumed readership base. Barbara Burford argues that this publishing, editorial and critical process forms a "cross-cultural filter" which misrepresents the black community as publishers do not "see Black people as the primary readers," but aim instead at a "white liberal academic readership" (36). Certainly, the experience of *Yardie*'s success seems to confirm this. Promoted through the black press and other cultural outlets, it subverted the usual promotion campaigns where, as Caryl Phillips notes, black faces are "few and far between" (qtd. in Mike Phillips 4). The burgeoning growth of independent black publishing houses in recent years suggests a determination within the black community to create the space to bypass the filter of the publishing industry and address itself directly. What this suggests is that the relationship between black writers and their audience is crucial to the future development of black writing. It is this relationship, furthermore, which has been a defining aspect since its very inception.

* * *

Part One of this book discusses the literature emanating from what Ramchand calls "the drift towards the audience" (*West Indian* 63). This was necessarily a (white) British audience as the writers from the Caribbean tried to escape the cultural vacuum of colonial hegemony. The literature that resulted was at once influenced by the writers' own experiences of exile and by the demands of the audience which at that time were developing a taste for Social Realism. It was also a period associated with the ideology of integration during which efforts were made to assimilate the emigrants smoothly into the labour force.

The literature that resulted thus had an educative quality about it. Selvon undertook in his Caribbean texts to acquaint the Mother Country and her inhabitants with images of life in the Colonies. In his London texts one can sense through the comedy an attempt to humanise and individualise the emigrants in response to the mass perceptions of racist ideologies, both those that had sustained the Empire and those that were a response to immigration. The early work of Lamming and Braithwaite can be read in the same way. "Writing home" at this stage thus indicates the literary representation of the Caribbean and its people to a largely ignorant host population; the writer acting as a "missionary in reverse" (Dabydeen and Wilson-Tagoe 83). It is also a gesture towards the theme in this literature of the actual correspondence between the emigrants and their families in the Caribbean. These generally emerge as rose-hued and falsely optimistic accounts of life in Britain as the emigrants tried to attain and sustain the status that such a trip merited in the islands.

The texts discussed in Part Two suggest a shift in audience. Dominated by a sense of confrontation engendered by increasing legislative, social and official racism in Britain and the influence of the Black Power movement in the US, the texts exhibit, in different ways, a determination to resist assimilation and to declare an independent cultural community. Wilson Harris and Linton Kwesi Johnson may appear to be unlikely bedfellows, but in their own ways, they both reject the colonial and neo-colonial demand to "Be British." "Writing home" here is the creation of an alternative ancestral space, be it the indigenous myths and culture of Central and South America or the spiritual homelands of pan-Africanism. Crucially, this literature was accompanied by discursive practices and ideas which the writer did not seek "to build into" British society (as Selvon did with his use of dialect), but which stood as challenges to that society.

The literature in the final part completes almost a full circle with the texts in the first part. Here, writers who represent a permanent black British population revive the sense of being British, which was the basis of colonial Caribbean ideology and also characterised the early stages of emigration. This revisiting of the theme of identity in the genre provides the space for a revaluation of the Caribbean social and cultural heritage, and its place in British society.

All three writers maintain a steady dialogue between Caribbean and British life in their texts. The effect of this is to simultaneously highlight the emergence of a black British personality distinct from its Caribbean forebears, and to be critical of that personality as part of British society. Joan

Foreword: The Question of an Audience

Riley focusses on the influence of Caribbean patriarchal traditions, and asserts the previously silenced voice of the black woman. Caryl Phillips explores the distance between the two generations of the Caribbean emigrations, and concentrates on the impossibility of return and the establishment of a cross-cultural community. David Dabydeen also argues for a polyglot British identity, which recognises the presence and value of its marginalised figures. The significance of "writing home" in this instance is clear. An unequivocal sense of a permanent presence emerges, not just from a critical appraisal of the Caribbean, but as a positive contribution to British culture and society. The new perspectives on British society which have been a defining characteristic of this literature from the start, assert themselves here as part of a self-critical, multi-cultural society.

PART 1

1.0 Introduction: The First Generation

> Mr. Lamming is, so far, the outstanding literary figure of the new West Indian movement: you can't call it a renaissance because it never had a first birth. It seems to be something more than a mere economic migration.
> – Richardson, rev. of *The Emigrants* 333

> [N]o islander from the West Indies sees himself as a West Indian until he encounters another islander in a foreign territory [. . .] in this sense, most West Indians of my generation were born in England.
> – Lamming, *Pleasures* 214

The three writers focused upon in Part One of this book are characterised by their existence as part of the first generation of West Indian writers. E. R. Braithwaite came to England in 1944, and had his first book published in 1959. Sam Selvon and George Lamming arrived together in 1950 and were first published in 1952 and 1953 respectively. This is not to say that they were among the first writers from the Caribbean to be published, but rather to emphasise the primacy given in their literature, and that of their contemporaries, to the pursuit or definition of a West Indian identity. In the ten or fifteen years that followed the arrival of these writers, West Indian literature constituted a veritable explosion upon the British cultural scene. This, however, should not be attributed to a freak generation of extraordinary literary genius, but rather to the complex processes of social, national and cultural change wrought during the post-war years. It may be said that the character of these changes had a direct informing influence upon the way in which this literature was both written and received. Some understanding of the background to this literature is thus essential to its study.

Caribbean literature was being published before the post-war period. Kenneth Ramchand (*West Indian* 3) cites Tom Redcam's *Becka's Buckra Baby* as being the earliest known work of West Indian prose fiction, published in 1903. However, it was not until the Thirties that a significant percentage of the books published (on average less than one a year),[1] were published outside the Caribbean. It was at this time that a group of men, later to be associated with a journal called *The Beacon,* began to meet in Trinidad. The importance of this group to the evolution of West Indian literature has only recently been understood. Of particular significance in this context is the ensuing work by C. L. R. James and Alfred Mendes, heralding the "decisive establishment of social realism in the West Indian novel" (Ramchand *West Indian* 65). Although short-lived (1931-1933), *The Beacon* set a precedent for the emergence of similar periodical and journals which sprang up in the early to mid-Forties. *Bim* (1942), *Focus* (1943) and *Kyk-over-Al* (1945) did not only provide organs for the publication of Caribbean writers, they were also the voice for the growing nationalism of the islands. Thus, even before the explosion of West Indian literature upon the world market, two of the most important aspects of this literature were already being established.

However, the significance of this literary background should not be over-stressed. Selvon plays down the influence of earlier Trinidadian writers such as James, Mendes and Gomes, saying, "I only knew these people very vaguely, I never mixed with them. They were a generation behind me, as it were" (qtd. in Nazareth, "Interview" 427). As will be seen, there were other, more pervasive, influences to overcome. Thus, the real significance of *Bim,* and one of the reasons for its continued success, where others have failed, may be sought in its comparative cosmopolitanism.

The island nationalism that the other journals displayed was not the project of *Bim's* editor, Frank Collymore. A schoolteacher of, and early influence upon George Lamming, Collymore recruited Lamming as a "missionary" to sign up writers in Trinidad when he moved there. This, as Lamming notes, was the first extension of the magazine from Barbados, an influence that was further extended through its connection with the *Caribbean Voices* programme started by the BBC Overseas Service in 1946. Both Selvon and Lamming pay tribute to *Bim,* not only for its existence as the first truly regional magazine in the Caribbean, but for the life line to the BBC that it represented. It served as a pool of material for the programme,

---

[1] Figures obtained from Ramchand (*West Indian* 292) show only eighteen books published between 1902 and 1928.

1.0 Introduction: The First Generation

and, as Lamming points out, "[s]ince the program went out to the entire Caribbean, *Bim* was brought to the attention of Jamaica and other places" (qtd. in Munro and Sander 9).

One might say, then, that the greatest significance of *Bim*, in particular, is that it drew the writers from the different islands together and gave them a confidence in their own work that had been absent before. Importance may be attributed to the work of James and his associates now, but at the time, as Lamming put it, "the whole idea of writers coming out of our classrooms was unheard of" (qtd. in Munro and Sander 10). By uniting the Caribbean, *Bim* served to end their cultural isolation. Furthermore, the link with the BBC provided prestige, money and, when the time came, a direction for the impulse to "get out." Henry Swanzy, the producer of *Caribbean Voices* is recognised as a significant figure in the growth of West Indian literature, and Lamming is careful to point out in *The Pleasures of Exile* (1960) the debt owed to him by all the West Indian writers.[2]

Bim thus served as a catalyst for an emerging West Indian literary culture; it operated as a point of artistic communication between the islands, and established an inter-island literary community. A consequence of this was the dissemination of the idea of emigration. As with the wider migratory movements from the West Indies, there were several "push/pull" factors in emigration. Far more than the influence of the older West Indian writers, the younger generation recognised the influence of the cultural directives of their colonial education. As will be explained more fully in the analysis of Lamming's work, the colonial experience as a whole served to undermine the acceptance of a West Indian culture in the Caribbean. The middle-classes were taught to deplore such art, while the peasant classes were excluded by a combination of illiteracy and poverty. As a result, the majority of West Indian writers at this time chose to migrate to Britain because they felt that they would be in a better position to have their work accepted. Both Selvon and Lamming claim to have left for England to "try their luck," but with no specific plans. London was, as Lamming puts it, "the literary Mecca" (qtd. in Munro and Sander 10).

---

[2] "Our sole fortune now was that it was Henry Swanzy who produced 'Caribbean Voices.' At one time or another [. . .] all the West Indian novelists have benefitted from his work and his generosity of feeling" (Lamming, *Pleasures* 67).

These emigrants cannot be dissociated from the thousands of other West Indians who left the islands in search of better prospects in a labour market starved of manpower in the post-war reconstruction boom. It was the common inheritance of all inhabitants of the British West Indies to regard Britain as the "Mother Country," and their reception there was the raw material for the literature of emigration. The difference that *may* be drawn between them is that, in leaving the Caribbean, the writers had already recognised that the West Indian islands could not maintain their existence as colonies of Britain, taking all their social and cultural praxis from that example. The emigrants learnt in practice what the intellectuals had already discovered in theory; the acceptance of British codes and practices did not make them British. It is in this way that the notion of identity became central to the literature of emigration.

* * *

The changing social and cultural situation in Britain is of equal importance to that of the Caribbean. The immediate euphoria of the Allies' victory in the Second World War served to reaffirm a belief in Empire that cast Britain as the benevolent protector of democracy. However, the Labour victory in 1945 may be seen as a result of the mood in the country that the spoils of war should be shared more equally than could be expected of a Tory government still associated with class privilege. This mood anticipated a notion of classlessness that was intrinsic to the age of affluence, which was significant in many ways to the rise of the West Indian novel.

The consumer boom of the Fifties brought with it the spread of the mass media through the increased availability of television and the cinema. The publishing industry shared in this boom. Stuart Laing notes a rise in the number of new titles published in Britain from 17,034 in 1949, to 25,000 by 1961 (123). Classlessness was closely tied to this process as the images it presented were a departure from the old class-based images of authority that had dominated previously. In particular, the literary scene was being revolutionised by the neo-Realism of the "Angry Young Men." The fetishised images of working-class life contained therein could not fail to include the figure of the black immigrant. As will be seen, even where the original text failed in this, the film adaptations that were made of many of

1.0 Introduction: The First Generation

these texts imported such images to add to the "realism." One might point in particular to the original "Angry" text, *Look Back in Anger* (1956), where John Osborne's additional dialogue for the screenplay included the Asian market stallholder, Johnny Kapoor, Jimmy Porter's empathy with whom serves to reflect and endorse his own sense of disaffection and alienation.

West Indian literature might be regarded as profiting from this obsession both with realism and a corresponding preoccupation with the idea of sex. Certainly, the early London texts of the West Indian writers, particularly *The Emigrants* (1954) and Selvon's *The Lonely Londoners* and *The Housing Lark* (1965) can be read in terms of this literary fetishism. Colin MacInnes' *City of Spades* (1957) in this sense represents a bridging point between the two writing traditions, bringing to the literature of emigration a more explicit connection between immigrant life and a sordid underworld of drug abuse, pimping and exploited homosexuality.

Commentators recognised the early parallels between the West Indian novelists and the contemporary English scene. A review of *In the Castle of My Skin* (1953) immediately situated Lamming's novel into current English trends, referring to "our more aggressive left-wing writers," and continuing,

> [a] poet like Mr. Lamming achieves distinctiveness as a writer of the people, and the English critic who hears so much echoless preaching of popular realism begins to think that this is far more likely to come from the newly articulate in the Colonies, than it is from our own tired culture. (Pritchett 460)

Maurice Richardson similarly tried to redeem *The Lonely Londoners* from being submerged into the literature of sex and violence, pointing out the appearance of drugs and sexual encounters in the text, but suggesting that it avoids the "Soho sensationalism" of the texts that surrounded it (rev. of *Lonely* 846).

Once established, and once the issues of independence and decolonisation were more firmly rooted in the public consciousness, it was these issues that became the focus for reading West Indian literature. John Hearne's *The Faces of Love* (1957) was said to display "the confidence of a new nationalism" (Allen 542), and the use of terms such as 'the West Indian novel' became more frequent. Indeed, by 1960, the notion of a West Indian novel had become so entrenched that texts were being criticised for continuing to concentrate on that theme. Writers were being asked to demonstrate that there was more to their literary imagination. V. S. Naipaul's review of Neville Dawes' *The Last Enchantment* (1960), even given his declared disparagement of anything West Indian, is characteristic of its time:

> The discovery appears to have been made that race and colour, like sex and sadism, are good commercial prospects; and while the effects of the West Indian revolution are being felt more and more [. . .] the oppressed-race theme is being worked more and more feverishly by West Indian writers. (97-98)

He ends the review with, "[n]ow he has written his Negro novel, we must hope that he will write a Jamaican one." Keith Waterhouse's review of Andrew Salkey contains similar sentiments, noting, "*Escape to an Autumn Pavement* [. . .] is notable for the fact that it isn't predominantly about the colour bar or life in exile, but rather about one man's personal problem" (63).

Thus, although West Indian literature may be regarded as receiving its first publishing impetus for its coincidence with literary trends in Britain, once it was established it was inextricably linked to the notion of West Indian identity. In doing so, however, it exposed its expression to the changing influence of British society. The notion of identity thus becomes not only mutable, but the product of a foreign environment.

It has been the opinion of many historians and commentators that the conception of a West Indian Federation, and of West Indianness as such (as opposed to island identity), was one mooted largely outside the islands themselves. George Lamming may certainly be regarded as one of the greatest exponents of this idea, saying in *Pleasures*, "[t]he West Indies is, perhaps, the only modern community in the world where the desire to be free, the ambition to make their own laws and regulate life according to their own impulses, is dormant" (34-5). For Lamming, the process of colonisation in the West Indies had been too potent to allow any other way of

1.0 Introduction: The First Generation

seeing than to accept colonial rule. Coming to England served to shake that way of seeing but then left only a vacuum. The absence of "roots," or recognisable cultural tradition, was most deeply felt when the rejection of the Mother Country left the Caribbean immigrant with no sense of national identity. It is around this national and individual dilemma that the literature of emigration revolves.

* * *

The three writers under consideration here illustrate this dilemma in very different ways. Selvon's original declared project was to put the West Indies on the map of the popular British consciousness. On coming to England he found an ignorance of his homelands in striking variance with the knowledge of Britain that was part of his colonial inheritance. His first two novels, *A Brighter Sun* and *An Island is a World* (1955), reflect his concern for the West Indies, and promote his notion of creolisation; a process whereby the national identity of the islands is born through the cosmopolitanism of their societies. The Caribbean is unique in its "racial" make-up, and it is from this very uniqueness that a national identity that is not dominated by colonial influences should be sought.

Selvon's London-set novels reflect a similar idea. The first of the cycle, *The Lonely Londoners* is a text of social integration; it is an artefact of the principal social and political aim of government for the early immigrants. He "builds" his characters into the host society in such a way as to portray them as an intrinsic part of the London landscape. The rest of his London texts, up to and including *Moses Migrating* (1983), catalogue the process whereby integration became displaced by rejection. *Moses Ascending* (1975), for instance, features the legislative and social rejection of the Seventies and the advent of Black Power as a response to this process.

Selvon's novels conceal some serious reflection upon the condition of the exile through their predominantly comic aspect. He is regarded as the least political of the major West Indian novelists, but his first text is generally credited with generating the first real interest in the West Indian novel as a distinctive literary form.

George Lamming has similar credentials. His first novel, *In the Castle of my Skin*, has been described as "the first West Indian novel to achieve classic status" (King 9). His texts display a more pronounced political intent, and are concerned with the historical processes behind the ideological maintenance of the colonial relationship. Lamming makes telling use of allegory in his texts, in many of them using the mythical island of San Cristobal as a stage to reconstruct the dramas of colonialism. His first London novel, *The Emigrants*, is split into two parts, the voyage to Britain and the life of the exiles once there. Through this structural form, he illustrates both the tentative steps towards federation as the islanders talk on the deck, and also the psychological trauma of discovering the "reality" of Britain. In *Water With Berries* (1971), Lamming, like Selvon, has progressed from the notion of the emigrant to a violent account of the birth of the black British. The relationship between Teeton (the exile) and the Old Dowager (his landlady), describes the conscious and unconscious ties of dependence still written into black/white relations.

In each of these two writers, an increasing sense of confrontation is present in their texts. Decolonisation and independence, and the various Race Relations Acts passed during the thirty years of their writing had done nothing to diminish the social friction which continued to cast blacks as outsiders. Pan-Africanism, Ethiopianism and the dream of a return to the Caribbean are indicative of the alienation and dislocation of the black individual in Britain, and his/her continued search for identity. The gesture towards the black Briton as a thoroughly integrated subject is evident in the later fiction of both writers, but finds no optimistic resolution.

By contrast, E. R. Braithwaite is often criticised for his unproblematised insertion of the colonial subject into British society. The emphasis here is on the Subject: Braithwaite's black characters display all the superlative qualities of the White Ideal – the example that the white imperialists were expected to set for the evolutionarily inferior black Other. Perhaps not surprisingly, his first novel, *To Sir, With Love* (1959) remains probably the most popular and well-known account of black experience in Britain to date. For this reason alone it deserves attention, but in this context it is a useful counterpoint to the explorations in identity that figure in the previous texts. *To Sir, With Love* inverts the usual characteristics of the colonial relationship, situating a thoroughly colonised subject into a position of authority over schoolchildren in London. The class-based aspect of colonial-

1.0 Introduction: The First Generation

ism becomes exposed in Ricky's assertion of moral values and codes of conduct.

Like *The Lonely Londoners*, it is a novel about integration, but the indices of the process are completely different. The maintenance of colonial characteristics in this text suggests the transference of such positions into the post-colonial world. This complete misapprehension of post-war society is at the root of Braithwaite's idealised account. The presence of black immigrants in British society not only signalled the end of Empire, it also demanded changes in racist ideologies. Prior to immigration, the more crass opposition of civilised White to savage Black was sustainable. Once everyday contact became more common, however, such binary oppositions became redundant. However, where Lamming uses the Prospero/Caliban metaphor to trace the continued and more subtle forms of colonisation, Braithwaite (arguably) does little more than reproduce them, trying to achieve the same point through a simple inversion.

A study of the film adaptation of Braithwaite's text shows the different ideological use to which that same character can be put. Made in 1967, the film is arguably more sensitive to social change than the novel, but the significance of the black character is noticeably different.

* * *

It should be clear, then, that the constitution of the West Indian identity as it occurs in West Indian fiction is inextricably related to the notion of exile. It should also be clear, from the way in which the literature of exile conveys the notion of identity as a mutable construct, that the influence of foreign perceptions formed in a rapidly changing society is crucial to this mutability. It is difficult to judge the point at which the emphasis ceases to be on the West Indian emigrant and switches to that of the black Briton, but it is this process that is the concern of this first chapter. The significance of the first generation of black writers in this sense is in their experience of Britain from the earliest moment of immigration up to, in the case of Selvon, the very recent past. The search for the identity of exile becomes an experiential process to be read in the continuing dialogue between the Caribbean and Britain.

1.1 Sam Selvon: The Lonely Exile

The publication of Sam Selvon's *A Brighter Sun* is taken by many critics to have initiated the birth of the modern West Indian novel. It certainly was not the first novel by a West Indian writer to have been published in Britain, but it did reach a substantially larger audience than its most immediate predecessor, Edgar Mittelholzer's *A Morning at the Office* (1950), and in such a way as to promote continued interest in the genre. Although this success may be partially attributed to the public interest stimulated by decolonisation and immigration,[3] a greater significance of this text lies in Selvon's concern to reconcile two contrasting cultural traditions.

Selvon, like many of his contemporaries, was heavily influenced by both the intellectual heritage of a colonial education and by the popular culture and folklore of the islands. The reconciliation of these two conflicting influences may be said to characterise not simply the West Indian literature under consideration here, but also the notion of the West Indian identity as it was expressed in the post-colonial era. Individual and national identity, arguably, is from the relation between the individual and his/her culture, and between that culture and other cultures. The importance of Selvon's work, and that of the whole generation of writers discussed in this chapter, is that the individual and national identities described therein were conceived in exile.

Two processes may thus be observed in Selvon's work. The learning or promotion of a West Indian identity; what he calls the Caribbean man. And the unlearning of the image of Britain and the British; the dominant culture against which any expression of West Indian identity would have to be measured. These processes may best be perceived through an examination of Selvon's London novels, but first it is important to establish Selvon's own position on these issues. Some biographical notes are thus necessary.

Selvon was born in South Trinidad in 1932, the son of a Madrassi merchant and a half-Scottish mother. He received no formal education after

---

[3] "Extra-literary factors probably help to explain the impact of *A Brighter Sun*. Selvon's book appeared, after all, in the first half of the 1950s when the argument for decolonisation was beginning to catch on the world over" (Birbalsingh, "Samuel Selvon" 13).

1.1 Sam Selvon: The Lonely Exile

high school, and joined the local branch of the Royal Naval Reserve as a wireless operator in 1940. The dominating influence of his early life was the multi-cultural aspect of his local environment. His religious training in Hinduism was not rigorously pursued, and thus, as he later wrote in *The Trinidad Express*: "By the time I was in my teens, I was a product of my environment, as Trinidadian as anyone could claim to be, quite at ease with a cosmopolitan attitude, and I had no desire to isolate myself from the mixture of races that comprised the community" (23 Sept. 1979: 2; qtd. in Pouchet Paquet, "Samuel Dickson Selvon" 439-40).

There are two important strands to be drawn out from this statement. First is the way in which Selvon conflates the terms 'Trinidadian' and 'cosmopolitan.' For him, the essence of Trinidadian society was not in the way in which the diverse cultures managed to retain their relative autonomy, but rather in the way in which these cultures interacted with, and affected each other. National, or at least island identity, for Selvon, then, was the result of a mixed community. The second point is the way in which the individual is regarded primarily as a product of his/her society. Selvon has said elsewhere that notions of "ancestry and going back and tracing things like that" are of no interest to him (qtd. in Pouchet Paquet, "Samuel Dickson Selvon" 441). It is thus clear that he places greater emphasis on the operation of culture and ideology in the formation of identity.

These two points are brought together in his concept of the Caribbean man. Stepping outside of a specifically Trinidadian context, this idea unites the Caribbean through the process of creolisation. He says, "I am always going to be writing as Caribbean man [. . .] you become creolised, you not Indian, you not Black, you not even White, you assimilate all these cultures and become a different man who is Caribbean man" (qtd. in Pouchet Paquet, "Samuel Dickson Selvon" 441). The "even" is significant because, although Selvon undermines the importance of cultural tradition in the formation of identity, he replaces this with a legacy of colonial rule and the White presence as the homogenising factor in the formation of the Caribbean man.

In a discussion of the colonial relationship portrayed in *Those Who Eat the Cascadura* (1972) he says, "[i]t's more than racial [. . .] I mean it goes right back to the whole idea of being colonized, of the feeling that White is supreme, of looking up to the White man as if it is a goal to be attained" (qtd. in Pouchet Paquet, "Samuel Dickson Selvon" 444). The black population of the Caribbean is thus united by the experience of White rule and exploitation: "The comedy element has always been there among black people from the Caribbean. It is their means of defence against the sufferings and tribulation they have to undergo" (Nazareth, "Interview" 423-4).

Selvon situates himself as a writer within this common identity of the Caribbean man. It should be remembered, however, that many of the remarks quoted above were made in 1986, and thus raise questions as to the extent to which such ideas are those of the exile. One is reminded here of George Lamming's assertion that most West Indians of his generation were "born" in England (*Pleasures* 214). In this way the idea of an identity being learnt in exile becomes more apparent. This is an aspect of exile of which Selvon is himself aware. Speaking in 1982 to Ramchand, he refers to the dream of a "strong human bond" between the blacks and the Indians in the Caribbean, and says: "I feel it is easy to keep the dream alive because I spend most or all of my time living abroad [. . .] In other words, if I had remained on the island experiencing the realities of what I hear is happening, then the dream would turn nightmare" ("Sam Selvon" 57).

The question that is implicit in Selvon's formulation of the Caribbean man is in the space that it leaves between the Caribbean man as he is viewed and portrayed by the exile, and the exile himself, now regarding himself as West Indian. In other words, can the West Indians who were "born" in England regard themselves as the same West Indians who remained in the islands? Or, in Selvon's terms, is the dream of a Caribbean identity something that exists for the exile, or something that exists within the exile?

*   *   *

More than the work of any other Caribbean writer, Selvon's fiction is characterised not only by its continuing Caribbean focus, but also by the way in which this focus is transferred to the London metropolis. As a glance at his bibliography will show, the production of the Trinidad and London novels is interspersed, suggesting that the development of the West Indian and emigrant characters were contemporaneous. It is the relationship between

1.1 Sam Selvon: The Lonely Exile

these two identities that is of interest here. There are, however, certain factors that need to be taken into account before any analysis may begin.

Most importantly, it would be a mistake to read the texts without taking into account their production over a period of more than three decades. The point has already been made that Selvon's remarks on the concept of the Caribbean man were made ten years before his death in 1994. And, although his early novels, in particular *A Brighter Sun* and *Turn Again Tiger* (1958) do serve to bear out his later reflections on the process of creolisation, it is also true that he denies this was part of his project at the time. The relationship between Tiger/Urmilla and Joe/Rita is usually read as emblematic of the "emergence of the Indian peasant in a creolised culture" (Rohlehr, "Samuel Selvon" 153). For Selvon, however, "the fact that Joe happened to be a Black man was quite incidental" (Ramchand, "Samuel Selvon" 58). The author's own intentions during the act of writing may themselves be regarded as quite incidental to the forces that surround literary production and reception, but it is also true that, as Selvon's writing career progressed, he claimed a greater awareness of the political issues inherent in his subject matter. One should be careful, then, not to make false comparisons between texts, assuming that because they are by the same writer, due account need not be taken of their time of production.

Similarly, one should note the increasing use of "bad" language and sexual explicitness in Selvon's texts. This may be explained in terms not simply of Selvon's evolving narrative technique, but also in relation to the relaxation of publishing restriction during his writing career. Black writing in this sense may be regarded as a monitor for race relations in the post-Windrush era, as the notion of what is acceptable to a predominantly white reading public may be discerned in the content of these texts. The increasing acceptability of the black male as a legitimate sex figure will be noted in each of the writers in this chapter.

With these reservations in mind, Selvon's novels may now be approached. It is Selvon's role as the exile that is of the greatest interest here, and thus it is his London novels that will receive the fullest attention. However, it is only by bringing the Trinidad texts to bear that the notion of identity can be fully explored. This is particularly important given Selvon's place as a black writer in Britain for almost the entire post-war period of immigration. A useful point of departure is in the use of dialect in these texts.

It is largely Selvon's use of dialect that has attracted critical attention to his work. This, together with his "ballad" prose style and concentration upon working-class experience, has earned him the titles of "folk-poet," "Runyonesque," the "Steinbeck of the West Indies" and the "successor to Naipaul." As this labelling activity suggests, the main concern of the critics has been either to situate Selvon within previous literary traditions, or to suggest how his use of dialect and the ballad form serve to explode such traditions.

For the most part, early reviews concentrated upon narrative technique. *A Brighter Sun* was described as "not so much a novel as a series of portraits strung together" (*Times Literary Supplement* 1972: 145). V. S. Naipaul (perhaps wary of his "successor") makes a similar, if rather more critical, assertion in a review of *Turn Again Tiger*: "Mr Selvon is without the stamina for the full-length novel, and he has here found the undemanding form which suits his talents best" (826-7).

Later, more academic, reviews saw his technique in a rather different light. F. Gordon Rohlehr in "The Folk in Caribbean Literature" (qtd. in Pouchet Paquet, "Samuel Dickson Selvon" 447) locates Selvon within the "oral and scribal traditions" of the Caribbean, while Michel Fabre saw in *Moses Ascending* "a unique attempt to unite the iconoclastic traditions of mainstream post-modern fiction with the iconoclastic techniques of the calypso" ("Moses" 390). In most cases, though, such scholarship has served to maintain the division of the Trinidad novels and the London cycle, particularly with regard to the use of dialect and the narrative voice. It is this methodological division that needs to be challenged if issues of identity and exile are to be approached.

To look initially at the use of dialect and the narrative voice in the Trinidad novel, since this is taken to be a fairly unproblematic use, one is immediately struck by the sheer variety of voices in the novel. To use *A Brighter Sun* as an example, there is the Standard English of the narrative voice, and a number of variations on this. For example, Rita's African-Caribbean patois ("Get out me blasted chair [. . .] Get out de house, yuh worthless bitch! Yuh have a nasty coolie mind! Dat poor girl does only be

1.1 Sam Selvon: The Lonely Exile

tinking bout you all de time" [143]) is recognisably different to the speech patterns of the older East Indians: "Since I come Trinidad side, ah little boy. Work in canefield. Grow big man. Nutting man, nutting. Old carat hut, leaking. Garden which side Barataria. Plenty rum" (116). To demonstrate the continuing evolution of Caribbean language use, there is the wartime impact of the Americans: "Let me tell you something about these customs, John [. . .] most of it is just plain dumb" (116).

These linguistic characterisations do not merely add colour and authenticity to the novel; they also provide a discursive picture of pre-creolised society against which the progression of Tiger as the symbol of the creolised peasant may be plotted.

Rohlehr suggests that the "use of Tiger's language serves to signify his shift from a 'folk' to a semi-urban situation" ("Samuel Selvon" 153). However, there is rather more going on than this. Tiger's search for (ontological) maturity is not satisfied by the traditional indices of supporting a family that his father accepts: "Tiger's bap seemed to take it that marriage had turned him into a man right away" (44). For Tiger, literacy is a greater signifier of manhood. When he finds out that Joe is illiterate, he is shocked:

> 'You mean a big man like you can't write?'
> 'Wat happen for dat? Yuh talking like you cud write?'
> 'No, but I mean, I smaller than you. And too, besides you come from Port-of-Spain, and I from the country.'
> But he was glad Joe couldn't write, because Joe was a man.
> (42)

Tiger's determination to learn to read and write is prompted by his belief that the knowledge available in books can accelerate and supplant the wisdom of experience. This is very much the attitude of the exile who finds island life, and the traditional Indian aspirations/expectations of raising boy-children and subsistence farming profoundly unsatisfying. In failing to leave the island, Tiger becomes trapped into the colonial stigma of basing his ambitions upon aping White praxis. Book experience thus leads Tiger to attempt to learn to speak "correctly" through the use of dictionary meanings. Talking to the Americans building the road, he says, "[m]y humble abode is not a massive structure [. . .] but I going to construct a building as soon as financial embarrassment over" (166). Similarly, he tries to impress/intimidate Urmilla with the same technique: "If you don't have education, people could always tie you up. All the time I did think a fish was just like you say, but now I find out for truth what it really is! Look, hand me my small cylinders of narcotic rolled in paper" (160).

The problem here is that Tiger forfeits a sense of (national) self in accepting the supremacy of Whiteness through education. It is the same process that will be shown to be evident in E. R. Braithwaite's *To Sir, With Love*, as colonial rule is perpetuated by a hegemonic education system. The other West Indians working on the road "called one another Joe and imitated the Yankee drawl" (158), while Tiger misinterprets – by seeking literal translations – slang terms such as 'swell' (168). The struggle that is occurring here is the point at which creolisation becomes secondary to the norms of the White example. For Selvon, the opening out of the Indian community should not devolve into a quest for ontological Whiteness, but be part of the creolisation process which, in this case, is signified by the West Indians' assimilation of American slang into their existing discourse.

The use of the dictionary thus serves two purposes. Most obviously it suggests that trying to completely emulate the norms of White behaviour is not the way forward for the formation of a West Indian identity. Secondly, it challenges the myths of these dictates. As Selvon's earlier comments on the colonial relationship suggest, the goal of Whiteness is something that impedes creolisation, and thus he uses his position as an exile to undermine that goal, again through the use, or recognition, of dialect.

What the use of Tiger's dictionary English also illustrates is that "correct" English does not exist as a spoken language, and thus the place that this concept occupies in the operation of colonial hegemony is a false one. Speech patterns such as these, with their implications of education, still functioned, however, as criteria for the stratification of West Indian society. In *Turn Again Tiger*, Tiger's position in the village is enhanced by his literacy and even his father gains credit by association (54-5). Selvon is addressing here the dual operation of education as a means of continued subjection, but also as the only route to political and social freedom. By undermining the authority of "Queen's" English, he is giving authority to

1.1 Sam Selvon: The Lonely Exile

creolised speech. His experience as an exile in Britain can be seen to have a bearing on this.

Just as many of the first immigrants experienced shock at seeing white manual labourers at the docks, so there must have been a similar shock to find not all whites shared the accent of privileged education. More than this, Britain was about to enter a virtual cultural revolution in which the maintenance of its own class structure upon the demonisation of regional accents was being challenged through television and the cinema. Selvon cannot fail to have been affected by this; indeed the transmission of his and other West Indian literature on the radio owed much to the same process. It is thus that he was able to point out in an interview with Ramchand that

> a lot of people forget [. . .] that Standard English or 'proper' English is also used as part of our dialect in certain phrases or words. For instance, if I rudely interrupt a creolised Trinidadian and he or she turns to me, looks me up and down and says in the Queen's English 'I beg your pardon,' I would consider that to be part of the Trinidad dialect. (Qtd. in "Sam Selvon" 60)

By 1982 at least, Selvon could see the West Indies as having claimed the language for its own.

To consider this idea in terms of the London cycle, one can see that a completely different set of criteria was operating during the act of writing. What is true is that Selvon maintained the ballad format, although arguably in a far more fragmented style than that employed in the Trinidad novels. Initially one might read this in the same manner as the sense of fragmentation that dogs the immigrants in Lamming's *The Emigrants*. However, as one contemporary reviewer for *The New Statesman* said of the short stories in *Ways of Sunlight* (1957), "we see them (i.e. the various characters) not partially, as coloured men in London, but wholly – as men expelled from the deadly deserts of the West Indies" (Richardson, rev. of *Ways* 546). Certainly it is true that, despite Moses' continual assertion that there are no "ease-me-ups" among the boys in Britain, all of the London novels display a strong sense of group cohesion. As one reviewer of *The Housing Lark* significantly put it, "this book seems to be written *at* the English in more ways than one" (*Times Literary Supplement* 1965: 249). It is from this assertion that the use of dialect may be approached.

First, it should be noted that at the time of writing his first London novel, *The Lonely Londoners*, Selvon was aware of writing for a different audience. The critical response emphasised the dialect Selvon employed. As Selvon later said of the book, "apart from Vic Reid's *New Day* I was the only other West Indian novelist to write a novel in which both narrative and dialogue were written in dialect" (Ramchand, "Sam Selvon" 60). Also, as many other writers have pointed out, the dialect used was not a "true" Caribbean dialect, but a modified one. As Selvon later explained: "My intention was not to be realistic and to differentiate between the several West Indian groups." He continues, "I only resorted to a modified Trinidadian dialect because [. . .] it is close to correct spoken English, and I thought it would be more recognisable to the European reader" (qtd. in Fabre, "Moses" 387).

Clearly, Selvon thought that he had to address a European audience differently when using a London setting. Indeed, one might go further than that and suggest that it is only when he is dealing with the emigrant identity that he finds the use of such dialect appropriate. As Fabre points out, in *Moses Migrating* (in which the characters return to Trinidad), "he continues to use 'fabricated dialect' instead of adopting, as might have been justifiable, a form of speech more akin to real Trinidadian" ("Moses" 390).

The point here is that it was not the audience that had changed, after all, each of Selvon's first three novels were published in London by Wingate, but that the sense of West Indian identity had. There are clearly two forces at work in the formation of this identity: first, Selvon's own perceptions as the exile, and second, his own idea of how such an identity could be moulded into British society. In *The Lonely Londoners* at least, Selvon's project may be said to be that of extending the creolisation process to Britain. As he explains in his interview with Fabre, "[i]f I ever write about Blacks in Canada, I'll build the writing into society at large; *I'm going to build it in as I did in The Lonely Londoners*" (qtd. in Fabre, "Moses" 387; my italics). An examination of the West Indian identity as it is portrayed in *The Lonely Londoners* with regard to the characterisations of the Trinidad novels may thus be used to expose the indices of exile. Then, a further

1.1 Sam Selvon: The Lonely Exile

comparison with *Moses Ascending* and *Moses Migrating*, will afford a picture of the continuing success, or failure, of creolisation in Selvon's Brit'n.

* * *

As noted above, *The Lonely Londoners* received wide acclaim for its use of dialect in the narrative voice. This is not, as is the case with dialogue, a constant use, but rather it varies according to the use to which the narration is being put. As Selvon later said, "[y]ou don't want to describe a London spring in dialect, this is straight poetry" (qtd. in Fabre, "Moses"). There is, however, a very clear and immediate difference between, "[o]n New Year's Day, 1939, while Trinidadians who had money, or hopes of winning money were attending the races in Queen's Park" (*A Brighter Sun* 3), and "[o]ne grim evening when it had a kind of unrealness about London [. . .] Moses Aloetta hop on a 46 bus" (7). In the latter opening to the novel, the reader is drawn into the narration – and vice versa. Phrases such as "a kind of unrealness," invite the implied reader into an active reading role, through their assumption of shared understanding. At the same time, other phrases such as "hop on a 46 bus" locate the narrative voice into the same discursive terrain that the dialogue comes to occupy. Through this technique, and others like it, both the reader and the narrator lose the objectivity of the Trinidad novels and become "one of the boys."

Immediately, then, one of the ways in which the diversity of Caribbean society is illustrated in the Trinidad novels is reversed here to project a unitary identity. This technique is reinforced by the operation of a modified dialect. There is no discernable, sustained difference between the discourse of Moses, the Trinidadian exiled in Britain for ten years, and Galahad, the newcomer, and between either of them and Tolroy, the Jamaican. This similarity becomes apparent in the way in which certain figures have their difference characterised by altered speech patterns. For example, the Nigerian, Cap, a veritable confidence trickster, is said to have "the sort of voice that would melt butter in the winter, and he does speak like a gentleman" (23-4). There are also Harris' attempts to break into polite white society; "[m]an, when Harris start to spout English for you, you realise that you don't really know the language" (95). This alterity is only made possible by the homogeneity of the other characters, and the narrator's speech. As

Ramchand notes, "[by] the end of the text, the boys have become blended into a chorus to match the Tiresias role that Rohlehr attributes to Moses" ("Song" 653).

This is not to suggest that Selvon reproduces a series of happy-go-lucky immigrants to try and dispel the myths of racism being propagated at the time of the novel's production. What he does do, though, is suggest a core character: an identity against which deviance may be measured. The account of Galahad's appearance at the Employment Exchange is representative of the process of creolisation present in this text. Moses and Galahad, sharing the discourse of the West Indian identity, discuss the merits of living on the Welfare State. Galahad refuses, saying, "I don't want to start antsing on the State unless I have to. Me, I'm a born hustler." To which Moses replies, "I wish it had plenty other fellars like you [. . .] but a lot of parasites muddy the water for the boys, and these days when one spade do something wrong, they crying down the lot" (25).

Here is the thrust of Selvon's project. Not to pretend that all immigrants are paradigms of honest living and hard labour, but, at the same time, to suggest that they are not all lazy, deceitful and amoral either. By using Cap as an exemplar of these traits, albeit in a rather modest way, and distancing him linguistically from the rest of the group, Selvon makes the point that such characters are in the minority among the immigrants.

It may be said, then, that the East Indian identity that Selvon constructs finds its characteristics in response to the White presence. Just as the process of creolisation in the Caribbean is concretised by this presence and the colonial legacy, so a similar process is at work here. The cultural differences that have characterised creolisation in Trinidad have been erased here in favour of addressing specifically British issues. The most obvious absence here is that of the East Indian. Before, the relationship between blacks and the Indians provided the main thrust of the Trinidad novels. Here, this relationship is dissolved, and Selvon writes instead as an African-Caribbean through the narrative voice, particularly in the way this voice collides with Moses.' As he later explained, "[i]n Trinidad you were a citizen of that country, but here, in England, you are a black man as opposed to a white man and a white society" (qtd. in Nazareth, interview 436). Thus, if *The Housing Lark* was "written *at* the English in more ways

1.1 Sam Selvon: The Lonely Exile

than one," it was following in a direct line from *The Lonely Londoners* in this respect, as the novels and the West Indian identity inscribed therein enter into the ideology of integration that was current at that time.

* * *

By 1975, however, the optimism that was implicit in Selvon's promotion of creolisation in Britain was not so apparent. *Moses Ascending*, despite its apparent operation as a sequel to *The Lonely Londoners* presents a very different picture of immigrant life in Britain. This is not very surprising as, by the time of its production, the issues were more those of the black British: the generation of blacks born in Britain, and of immigrants from East Africa and the Indian subcontinent. This difference manifests itself in the text as discord and disruption as Selvon's attempts to project an (exiled) West Indian identity had been overtaken by racist ideologies that had long since defeated any hopes of integration. Again, Selvon uses a modified dialect in dialogue and narration, but in this case the dialect is based on more than just the Trinidadian. Rather, it is a riot of voices that reflect the discord within the black community and Selvon's own disillusionment with the process of integration in Britain.

Moses remains the central character in the text, occupying a rather bewildering position of author/narrator/character that allows him to simultaneously take part in the action, narrate the events and discuss the writer's role in this process through direct address to the reader. In this sense, the character has been developed from the earlier text with apparently greater control over the action. However, what this text illustrates is his loss of control over the group; as the power of Tiresias recedes, so the chorus splits into individual voices.

The disintegration of the group is made clear from the start. Tolroy, one of the characters to survive from the first novel is planning to return to the Caribbean, and Moses, in buying Tolroy's house, plans to leave Galahad and his associates behind; "[w]hen I leave here, my past will be behind me, you inclusive," he tells him (2-3). However, it soon becomes evident that rather than shedding his past existence, Moses remains out of step with new social realities. During the same exchange with Galahad, Moses is still talking in terms of training him for "the London jungle," and reaping the

21

harvest of "the years of slavery I put in in Brit'n." Galahad, by contrast is concerned with "current events," and "the new generation of black people" (3-4).

This divergence of the two central characters is marked out discursively. Moses, assuming the persona of a retired gentleman of letters, employs an archaic discourse wherever possible, but the falsity of it becomes as apparent and deliberate as that of Tiger in the Trinidad novels: "I longed to get back to my philosophizing and rhapsodizing, decorating my thoughts with little grace-notes and showing the white people that we, too, could write book" (100-101). In times of stress, too, this mode of speech eludes him. Recounting his arrest at the demonstration in Trafalgar Square, he says, "[i]f I had had time I would have said 'Unhand me, knave,' but instead I say, 'Let me go, man, I ain't done nothin'" (36). In effect, then, the new identity that Moses is trying to assume is based too much on the White model, and remains unsustainable. The profusion of voices present in his discourse is a signifier for a confused identity following the collapse of the West Indian identity as it was defined by the exile. This process results in isolation: "I didn't have anything to do with black power, nor white power, nor any fucking power but my own" (14).

Galahad's discourse presents a profound contrast to this, and thus signals his active participation in the present. He arrives at Moses' house in his "Black Power glad rags," and opens with "[p]eace, brother. Black is beautiful [. . .] How you like the rags, man? You dig, or you don't dig?" Then, in the next sentence, as he tries to enlist Moses' support for the movement, he assumes the voice of classic revolutionary Marxism: "It is only right that you should contribute to the cause. We need financiers. Without the black gentry and nobility on our side, it is a losing battle" (11). Galahad, then, has also assumed new discursive models, but where Moses' signifies regression, Galahad's is a signifier for an engagement with the present.

In this way, Selvon suggests that the identity of the exile/immigrant has been supplanted by the identity of the black British, but that this has not been accompanied by a corresponding acceptance of black people into Britain. Thus, the conciliation of *The Lonely Londoners* is replaced by a greater sense of confrontation and challenge. In particular, where, in the first London text, Selvon avoided the presentation of conflict with author-

1.1 Sam Selvon: The Lonely Exile

ity (as demonstrated in the Employment Exchange), in this text, confrontation with the police remains an ever-present fact of life for the black community. Moses' arrest in Trafalgar Square, the raid on the Black Power meeting and subsequent arrest of Galahad and Brenda (90-95), and the surveillance of Moses' house (31) all suggest a wider tyranny that is both unjust and unjustified. Furthermore, remarks such as, "[h]e's illiterate but being as he's white, we say he's suffering from dyslexia" (137), and the Asians' fear that Bob was a skinhead and would "bash" them (96), all demonstrate the depth of popular racism in Britain at this time.

However, what seems more at issue with Selvon in this text is the fragmentation of the black community, and the ways in which this enabled its continued oppression. Here, the situation in Britain is more akin to the multi-cultural aspect of the Caribbean that Selvon concentrates upon in his Trinidad novels. The suggestion, though, is one of continued division despite the increasingly violent presence of White society. The Black Panther's theft of the Party funds is an obvious example of this division, but more telling is the black characters' ignorance of the Indians and Asians. Selvon has a Jamaican asking for pork in a Halal butchers (52), and Moses describing Farouk starting up "an oriental chant in one of them strange tongues, Urdu or Punjabi or something" (55). The illegal immigrants themselves practice segregation upon one another in Moses' room: "They are standing around in little groups glaring at each other," we are told (74), while Galahad castigates Moses for his involvement: "[i]f you had stuck to your own kind, you wouldn't have been in this shit" (78).

The discursive diversity of this text thus reflects and compounds the division that had grown up in the black community in the years separating this text from *The Lonely Londoners*. As a result, the West Indian identity that provided the unity of the boys in that text and *The Housing Lark*, and kept the loose, episodic form of those texts coherent, is absent here. The constant refrain of the Trinidad texts, starting in *A Brighter Sun*, which signals disunity between elements of the non-white population as the cause of their continued submission, "[y]ou don't see why it is that black people can't get on in this country at all at all" (189), is thus revived in *Moses Ascending* with increased pessimism:

> I don't know if I can describe it properly, not being a man of words, but I had a kind of sad feeling that all black people are doomed to suffer, that we could never make any headway in Brit'n [. . .] no matter how hard we struggle, or try to stay out of trouble. After spending the best years of my life in the Mother Country it was a dismal conclusion to come to, making you feel that one and one make zero. (35)

Selvon's dream of the emergence of the West Indian identity in Britain is thus shown to have failed. More than this, a full circle has turned as the unity of the West Indian exile is supplanted by a kind of diversity that prompted Selvon's dream of creolisation in the first place. It is perhaps, then, no surprise that the final novel in the cycle, *Moses Migrating*, takes the action back to Trinidad, and no surprise also that three years after the publication of *Moses Ascending*, Selvon himself migrated to Canada.

* * *

In the last book of the London cycle, *Moses Migrating*, a different set of criteria are in force. As noted above, by the publication of this novel Selvon was no longer an exile in England, but had moved to Canada. As an interview recorded in Iowa shortly after Selvon had finished the first draft suggests, his reasoning during the act of writing had changed significantly. Some examination of his remarks is thus pertinent to a reading of this text.

Selvon begins the interview by reaffirming the thought processes that lay behind the discursive structure of *The Lonely Londoners* and *Moses Ascending*. His use of a modified dialect in the first, with the addition of an archaic English form in the second to describe the assimilation of English culture by the black immigrant makes clear his commitment to write with an English audience in mind; "[i]n my writing I always had the feeling, 'Would these people understand what I am talking about?' When I say 'these people' I mean the English people" (qtd. in Nazareth, interview 436). In *Moses Migrating*, though, Selvon has "consciously turned away from the English reader,"[4] and tried to relocate Moses into the Caribbean.

---

[4] Selvon's remarks are confused here. The full quotation is, "I have really and truly never thought in terms of writing for Trinidadians as such or *people in the Carib-*

1.1 Sam Selvon: The Lonely Exile

He says, "if one compares it with *Moses Ascending* one could see, well, no this isn't the kind of language that he uses, really, in *Moses Ascending*" (qtd. in Nazareth, interview 425).

The hesitation in this last sentence is indicative of Selvon's uncertainty of the success of this project. At the time of the interview, the text had not gone to press and he readily admits that this "is one novel I might have to revise" (424) The question as to the extent to which Selvon was successful in rewriting the discursive pattern of the novel will be discussed later, but the most important idea to note immediately is the changed target of his writing. Selvon implies that *Moses Migrating* was the first in which he wrote consciously for the Caribbean reader, but the text itself invites a different audience. The suggestion here, then, is that *Moses Migrating* was written at the black British, and in this sense represents the ultimate text of exile.

It may be noted first of all that the notion of returning Moses to the Caribbean contains a logic, not only as a sequel to what may be termed the 'Moses trilogy,' but also within the growing tradition of the West Indian and black British novel. One of the recurring themes of black British fiction in the 1980s, as will be seen in the final chapter, is that of return to the islands. This much is characterised particularly by the work of Caryl Phillips and Joan Riley.[5] Thus, in writing this text, Selvon is participating in a wider literary tradition than his own. What differentiates Selvon's text particularly is Moses' existence as a long-term, adult emigrant, where the other texts frequently feature a child, or youth as the central character. This difference expresses itself through Moses' total cultural dislocation. The importance of this novel, then, may be seen not only in the (by now) cli-

---

bean except for my latest novel, which I have just completed, which is a kind of sequel to Moses Ascending. And yet I have difficulty now because I think that I have consciously turned away from the English reader in the Caribbean" (Nazareth, interview 424; my italics). I have shortened the quote in such as way as to clarify its meaning commensurate with Selvon's other remarks.

[5] I am thinking here of texts such as Phillips' *A State of Independence* (1985) and *Strange Fruit* (1981), and Riley's *A Kindness To The Children* (1992), all of which are concerned with the theme of return, and which will be dealt with in greater detail in the final chapter.

chéd notion of dispelling the myths of exile, but also in the way in which Selvon uses this device simultaneously to express Moses' continued alienation within British society.

Moses' isolation had already been established in *Moses Ascending*, first triumphantly in his "penthouse," and then ignominiously as he is forced into the basement room after his association with Jeannie. His suggested epilogue of a restitution having similarly embarrassed Bob does not come to fruition in this next novel, and Selvon picks up the character very much where he left off: underdog to both the white couple, and Brenda and Galahad's Black Power militants. In this sense, the first section of the text serves to re-establish the main characters into the roles of the previous text in a way that is not attempted in *Moses Ascending*, where a deliberate effort is made to distinguish between the emigrants of the Fifties and the black communities of the Seventies. What Selvon is clearly trying to do, then, is take a known character back to the Caribbean in order to emphasise the contrast between the two identities of the black British subject (as Moses now regards himself,) and the returning Caribbean exile. As a transition between these two states, Selvon uses the "middle passage" of the sea-voyage to the Caribbean.

Although the notion of a middle passage is common enough in Caribbean literature, Lamming's *The Emigrants* does provide an interesting contrast to the voyage featured in Selvon's text. In both cases there is a strict division between the first-class travellers and those on the lower decks. In Lamming's text this voyage provides an opportunity for the islanders to cohere into a group with a common social inheritance, and, furthermore, anticipates the reductive perceptions of racism that await them in Britain. In Selvon's text, this strict division is also evident, but he uses this to simultaneously demonstrate Moses' continued isolation and also to typify the continued premises of racism.

As in *The Emigrants*, the first-class passengers are predominantly white, amongst whom Moses claims to feel more comfortable (27). However, his presence on the upper deck is at first challenged, and then only countenanced upon certain assumptions. In his first effort to cross the barrier alone he is immediately stopped, and when he explains that he is looking for a friend, he is told to try Deck C (43). On sight, he and all black indi-

1.1 Sam Selvon: The Lonely Exile

viduals, as it is assumed that his friend would also be black, are designated as literally third-class citizens. His subsequent entrance to the upper deck is secured by Jeannie's appearance for two reasons; first, because she is white, and second, because of her overt sexuality. Once in Jeannie and Bob's cabin, Moses' presence goes unremarked by the stewards, and while Moses puts this down to good training (39), it slowly emerges that he is considered to be there as a gigolo (54). On deck A, then, Moses falls prey to the kind of popular racism that assumes that the black man is there to perform some physical duty or duties. This reduction of the black man as body is compounded by Bob's designation of Moses as their chauffeur and handyman (52).

On Deck C, where, in Lamming, new loyalties are forged that overcome inter-island rivalry, Moses resurrects these sentiments. The first of his cabin-mates that he meets he dubs Dominica after the island of his birth, despite the fact that he is now living in London. Owen, a scholarship student, makes up a familiar trio in the literature of emigration, but this familiarity is interrupted by the inclusion of a white man, Walter. Walter's presence excludes the potential for the ship to act as a space for reconciliation. Instead, he is a goad for Moses' exaggerated patriotism, resulting in Moses' alienation as he disdains his black cabin-mates and attempts to use Walter as a prop for his missionary zeal. The irony of the situation is that while Moses devotes himself to his self-appointed role as ambassador of British manners and gentility, the odd trio that make up his cabin do find a common ground, and have exchanged addresses by the end of the voyage.

Moses' social isolation is thus accentuated by the spacial structure of the ship. Lamming's microcosm of West Indian federation exists in Selvon as a metaphor for Britain's ideological and legislative racial divisions. The difference between the Moses described in *Moses Ascending* and the one who lands in Trinidad, is that the affectations of the gentleman-at-leisure featured in the previous text have become the patriotic bigotry of the colonialist. That he is an outdated figure is implicit in his (lack of) interaction with Cabin 13B, and becomes explicit in his masquerade as Britannia in the Trinidad carnival. Selvon then pits this identity of the exile against the more traditional image of the prodigal son, using the theme of the masquerade to explore the true identity of the exile.

As soon as the ship docks, Selvon is at pains to deflate any sentimentalisation of the return to Moses' homeland: "When we sighted the tips of the Northern Range dappled in morning sunshine, did I stand at the rails with conflicting emotions to get my first glimpse of my native land after the years? [. . .] None of that shit. I was sound asleep, having drunk myself into a stupor the night before" (57-8). This process is affirmed as Moses ignores an old acquaintance at the docks in order to avoid "spongers" (59). Once in The Hilton, the textual equivalent of deck A, Moses begins to think of his role as the prodigal, using archaic images of getting ice from a shop, and chasing fowl down the yard (61). When this role becomes actuality, as Moses sees his Tanty still occupying the same position on the Savannah as thirty years previously (and Selvon is quick to point out the unreality of this situation), Moses experiences an uncertainty of identity: "I began to rue my impulsive dash from the hotel. Not that I wasn't please to see Tanty, but it was as if out here by the Savannah I lose my identity and become prey to incidents and accidents [. . .] I wish Bob and Jeannie was with me, they would of sustain me with their presence" (65).

Moses' crisis of identity is made apparent in terms of his speech patterns. Tanty notes, "[y]ou sounding strange, Moses. You learn to talk like white people?" To which he replies, "God forbid" (65-6), and thus, for a moment, his promotion of the British Way of Life is forgotten. His hasty retreat to the safety of the hotel places him in the company of Lennard, the reporter from *The Trinidad Guardian,* and thus reminds him of his role as ambassador, leading to the idea of his playing Britannia in the Carnival. In the first two scenes, then, Selvon has set up the oppositionary personas of the exiled identity, and the remainder of the novel is an exposition of the struggle for authenticity between these two personas.

Meeting Tanty Flora does have a marginal effect upon Moses' relation to Trinidad. A sign of his increased involvement may be recognised in the adoption, both in his speech patterns and the narrative voice, of the dialect form, "de-Hilton" (as opposed to The Hilton); a usage introduced to the text by Tanty (64). Other than this, until he meets Doris, the text serves to confirm a widening gulf between Moses as the retrograde individual, and Trinidad as a developing society. As a personal gulf, this is typified by Moses' frustrated search for mauby (a drink now consigned to sidestreets)

1.1 Sam Selvon: The Lonely Exile

(81), his assumption that Lennard worked for *The Manchester Guardian* (68) and his own admission that he "was scared stiff to refamiliarise myself with anything, I should have kept my arse quiet in de-Hilton, safe and secure among the foreigners and visitors" (84). In a wider context, this gulf is illustrated by the conflict between Moses' estimate of Britain as a still powerful nation, and the repeated references elsewhere in the text to the Oil Crisis and Britain's economic collapse. His alienation in this respect is so complete that it involves not only his relation to Britain and the Caribbean, but, as the editor of *The Guardian* says, puts him "contrary to world opinion" (78).

Meeting Doris, however, changes all of this. Selvon anticipates this change of mood as Moses' journey through John-John serves to recall the scenes of his childhood and encourages a greater feeling of homecoming. When he meets Doris his Anglophilia subsides into a eulogy on Caribbean womanhood:

> I will say one thing for the pot-pourri mixture of races that populate the island, sometime out of the brew you get a species called high-brown, and the females of that concoction is some of the most beautiful creatures in the world, a glorious composition of sperms and ovaries that create the best of the first, second and third world. (87)

He soon learns that the best way to impress Doris is to display an affinity with island characteristics, and thus he "subtlety emphasises" the "ours" when referring to blue-back crabs (103). His final seduction of Doris is achieved when he delivers an ultimatum to her using a Trinidadian mannerism: "'Doris,' I say, 'you going to play Jouvert with me, or else we blow off right here.' And I put my thumb on my cheek, spread out the other fingers and wiggle them, and blew out, which signified that I would have nothing more to do with her" (162).

As has been noted elsewhere, "[r]everting to dialect is a strategy which Selvon's characters use frequently either to establish a sense of shared identity or to recover a former closeness" (Bernhardt 273). In this instance it works and the two of them become immersed in the mass hysteria of Jouvert, their proposals of marriage becoming submerged and interrupted by calls to "play mas." When Moses awakes the next day, Doris has gone and Lennard is there to hurry him into the part of Britannia, and thus his masquerade as the prodigal son is over.

In the end, the struggle between the two identities comes to no resolution. Doris represents the paradigm of Caribbean womanhood, a masquerade itself in its exaggeration, but Moses cannot return there. He decides to return to Britain, although there is no positively expressed reason given for this, and, on returning with his trophy as a symbol of his pro-British patriotism, he is still left waiting on the suspicious bureaucracy of immigration control. As Selvon says in his interview with Nazareth, "[i]t's all very well and good to appreciate what the world is like and what people are like, but, who the hell am I? And where do I fit into it, have I got roots, am I an Indian? Am I a Negro? What am I? What is a Trinidadian?" (qtd. in "Interview" 426). In this context, Moses might have seen himself in the *soucouyant* that he and Doris discover on the way to Jouvert (163-4): he has shed his skin in leaving Trinidad, and cannot now put it back on.

1.2 George Lamming: The Natural Exile

Comparisons between Selvon and Lamming are frequent in the secondary material surrounding West Indian literature. Their arrival in Britain aboard the same ship in 1950 and continued concern with the constitution of the West Indian identity provide ample opportunity for comparative analysis. The parallels drawn between the middle passages of *The Emigrants* and *Moses Migrating* illustrate how such an analysis can remain meaningful (indeed gain its meaning) despite the disparity in publication dates. There is, however, an important difference in the expressed objectives of the two writers that demands a different approach to their work.

In his interview with Nazareth, Selvon claims that he "started out with the ambition to project my part of the world onto the map" (qtd. in Nazareth, "Interview" 424): he was, as Lamming put it, "the least political of us all" (*Pleasures* 43). By comparison, Lamming's objective was a sustained, political assault upon a learned way of seeing. His texts contain a much stronger allegorical content than Selvon's, and continually refer back to the ideological and material inheritance of a colonial past. He is thus much more outspoken about the thought processes that inform the writing of his texts, and these writings themselves have to be considered in conjunction with any analysis of his fictional work. In particular, *The Pleasures of Exile*, Lamming's commentary on the Caribbean writer-in-exile, serves to highlight an important distinction between Lamming's and Selvon's thoughts on the formation of the West Indian identity and reveals certain basic principles behind Lamming's political aesthetic. Some discussion of the growth of this aesthetic is essential to an understanding of his fiction.

Lamming traces his recognition of the political role of the artist back to an early age. Born in Barbados in 1927, he came from a poor family, but one in which he recalls a "tremendous respect for education" (qtd. in Munro and Sander, "Interview with George Lamming" 5). This is hardly surprising in a society in which skin tone and education were the main criteria for social advancement. Lamming soon realised that both criteria effectively represented a tacit acceptance of a White Ideal and ideals. He says,

> [t]he West Indian's education was imported in much the same way that flour and butter are imported from Canada. Since the cultural negotiation was strictly between England and the natives [. . .] it is to be expected that England's export of literature would be English. Deliberately and exclusively English. (*Pleasures* 27)

The inevitable outcome of this negotiation was a way of seeing for the (educated) West Indian middle-class that privileged the Great Tradition of English Literature, and deplored any attempts at an indigenous culture. It was clearly only one aspect of the wider social process of colonisation that was to develop into the cultural hegemony of post-colonialism. For Lamming, however, it assigned to the Caribbean artist the crucial role of undermining this way of seeing, and he identified three main functions which characterised this role.

Firstly, by interrupting the flow of ideas from the colonising country, the West Indian writer could make a pioneering contribution to "decolonizing the intellectual life of an area" (qtd. in Munro and Sander, "Interview with George Lamming" 14). He thus assigns to the native writer the ability to write "a history of an area, as opposed to a history imposed upon an area" (13). Secondly, the native writer can contribute to the expression of a national identity; he cites just three important events in British Caribbean history, the third of which is "the discovery of the novel by West Indians as a way of investigating and projecting the inner experiences of the West Indian community" (*Pleasures* 37). In these terms, he says, "[i]t is the West Indian novel which has restored the West Indian peasant to his true and original status of personality" (38). Thirdly, the writer can combine these two functions through the symbolic role of the priest, or *houngan* at the Haitian Ceremony of the Souls. In this recurrent motif running through Lamming's texts, the past and present are reconciled as, each year, the natives of Haiti undergo a dialogue with the dead, on the one hand to release them from their state of purgatory, and on the other to discover any need for forgiveness from the dead. Lamming explains, "[i]t is not important to believe in the actual details of the ceremony. What is important is its symbolic drama, the drama of redemption, the drama of returning, the drama of cleansing for a commitment towards the future" (qtd. in Pouchet Paquet,

1.2 George Lamming: The Natural Exile

Novels 2). The writer exists for Lamming as the medium which reconciles the past and the present, or, as Pouchet Paquet puts it, "he provides historical continuity: and he liberates a new generation from a cycle of 'spiritual dispossession and self-mutilation'" (*Novels* 4).

Effectively, these three functions of the writer all combine to create the singular task of projecting an alternative way of seeing. In particular, the function of the exiled writer is to undermine what Lamming calls the "idea of England [the] knowledge acquired in the absence of the people known" (*Pleasures* 25). This may occur on the fundamental level of informing both sides of the colonial relationship of each others' day-to-day existence, undermining the racist ideologies that produce distorted and stereotypical images of black/white characteristics. More interesting, though, is his recognition of language as a site of struggle in the process of decolonisation. Using the Prospero/Caliban opposition to describe colonial relations, he says:

> Caliban received not just words, but language as symbolic interpretation, as instrument of the exploring consciousness. Once he had accepted language as such, the future of his development, however independent it was, would always be inextricably tied up with that pioneering aspect of Prospero. Caliban at some stage would have to find a way of breaking that contract, which got sealed by 'language' in order to restructure reality for himself.
>
> (Qtd. in Kent 88-9)

This is the same notion that Lamming applied to the rewriting of the histories of colonisation. Escaping the idea of England simultaneously implies escaping an idea of the colonised self, as the two concepts find their meaning only in relation to each other. The Caribbean writer, in wresting the meaning of language from a state of colonised awareness may thereby assert an independent national identity through both its content and expression. The role of the West Indian novel in this respect is to challenge the monolithic culture of England, not just for the fact of an indigenous culture as a fetishised article, but in the space it offers for an independent cultural ethos in the Caribbean. In these terms, as Stuart Hall puts it, "The West Indian novel has two functions to perform: to dramatise and evaluate. It must

33

give us an eye with which to see our society, and an eye with which to measure ourselves in our search for our identity" (172).

Lamming is thus keen to distinguish between the emerging literature of the West Indies, and the social function that it performs, and the role of the English novel. He refers in *Pleasures* to the then current trend in English literature for the working-class realism of the "Angry Young Men": "The English novel, from its beginnings to its present exercises in anger, has always been middle-class in taste, and middle-class by intention" (44). This, he says, is because the English novelists have become removed from the "peoples' speech, the organic music of the earth." English literature he thus dismisses as a sterile form limited to the "intellectual stammering which reverberates through the late night coffee caves" (*Pleasures* 45). In effect, the West Indian writers are struggling, not so much against the culture of colonial tradition, as rediscovering an authentic culture that preceded it. It is notable that Lamming talks of '*re*structuring' some alternative reality, and this notion of an earlier, and more pure form of expression is apparent in the terms he uses to describe the value of the work of Selvon and Reid: "The peasant tongue has its own rhythms which are Selvon's and Reid's rhythms; and no artifice of technique, no sophisticated gimmicks leading to the mutilation of form, can achieve the specific taste and sound of Selvon's prose" (*Pleasures* 45).

The Prospero/Caliban opposition provides some clue to Lamming's thinking on this point. Just as the island in *The Tempest* may be regarded as an Arcadian location prior to the arrival of Prospero, a place of "Nature" corrupted and perverted by an "unnatural" magic, so one can detect similar values encoded into Lamming's estimate of the emerging West Indian literature. Lamming's celebration of the "peasant" in this literature must be read, not simply in terms of class, but in terms of individual and societal authenticity.

The Caribbean in this respect constitutes a space where Nature has maintained a foothold against Culture, and this is manifested in the opposition between the peasant (Nature) and the colonial middle-class (Culture). Although the class aspect is clearly important, it is a class distinction that is based upon the internalisation of foreign, and thus inauthentic, social praxis. The exile of the West Indian writer has been initiated, as Lamming

1.2 George Lamming: The Natural Exile

says, by the fear that "they will be ignored in and by a society about which they have been at once articulate and authentic" because of just such an internalisation (*Pleasures* 46).

This is clearly the perspective of the exile, and it is a hidden influence that pervades Lamming's work. Sam Selvon has spoken of the dream of a "strong human bond" existing in the Caribbean, but admits that it is a dream sustained by his absence from the reality of the islands.[6] Lamming's absence, and more importantly, his presence in Britain have served to shape his views on the function of literature and the operation of culture. The evolution of the West Indies as a potential Arcadia, smothered by the trappings of colonialism, becomes clear as Lamming discovers the "reality" of Britain. Tornado's description of the Mother Country in *The Emigrants* is symptomatic of that reality; "the way the houses build was that people doan' have nothing to do with one another. You can live an' die in yuh room an' the people next door never say boo no matter how long inhabit the place" (76). This may be compared with Lamming's assertion in *Pleasures* that "it is not at all by chance that so much of the action in West Indian novels takes place outside, in the open air" (*Pleasures* 45).

It is this kind of statement which lifts an understanding of Lamming's work out of the context of merely class-based oppositions, and situates it within the Nature/Culture theme that can be seen to affect a far wider spectrum of issues involving the black writer in Britain. Notably, after the publication of *Water With Berries* in 1973, Lamming was still using the language of an organic culture suppressed by a society that has cut itself off from its roots:

> In contemporary England, the world to the creative imagination is very *atomized*. The literary imagination is concerned with explor-

---

[6] Selvon is actually talking here about the dream of a bond between the blacks and the whites in the Caribbean. He says, "I feel it is easy to keep the dream alive because I spend most, or all of my time abroad, but whenever I come back to Trinidad and I listen and I hear about what is happening, my disillusionment is fuelled. In other words, if I had remained in the island experiencing the realities of what I hear is happening, the dream would turn nightmare" (qtd. in Ramchand, "Sam Selvon" 57).

ing and explaining [. . .] the disintegration of an individual, and it goes on in the restricted world of a few bars, but with no informing influence from the subsoil of life outside. (Qtd. in Kent 90)

The language used is reminiscent of that employed to describe the "coffee caves" in *Pleasures* thirteen years earlier, and thus this notion of a suppressed Nature can be seen to be an enduring theme running throughout Lamming's work.

An important distinction may thus be drawn between the thought of Lamming and Selvon on the formation of the West Indian identity. For Selvon, the process of creolisation is something that is self-determining; it is the result of the diverse cultural traditions that make up West Indian societies. Although this is clearly the result of slavery and imperialism, the triumph of creolisation is that it generates a new collective identity from a dismembered past. For Lamming, however, the West Indian identity is formed through continuous reference to a past in which unity is achieved as a point of collective opposition to the white oppressor. Lamming's aesthetic is thus one that is built upon antitheses. Prospero and Caliban, coloniser and colonised; these are terms which should not be abolished in the post-colonial world, but should have their continued effect recognised and challenged. Of particular interest here is the opposition, remarked upon above, of Nature and Culture. It is through inverting the popular significance of these terms in racist ideologies that Lamming can wrest the constitution of the West Indian identity from the dominant perceptions of white society.

* * *

The notion of a Nature/Culture opposition has already been discussed in reference to the insertion of a West Indian literary tradition into the Great Tradition of English literature. As noted there, Lamming implies an Arcadian culture which pre-dates the corruption of colonial society and the rediscovery of which is essential to the reconstitution of the West Indian identity. In his fictional texts, sexuality provides the most effective medium to suggest a "lost innocence," and thus it is through this theme that the Nature/Culture opposition may best be discussed.

1.2 George Lamming: The Natural Exile

The first aspect to note when discussing sexuality in the work of Lamming is that his is an extremely conservative view. Speaking in 1973 about *Season of Adventure* (1960) he says,

> [t]he intention at work there is to suggest that if the man/woman relationship is aborted, is perverted, there will be a corresponding perversion in the relationship between the man and what he calls his work or his conception of fulfilment. The other aspect of that is that the relationship between the man and the woman will always be characterised by the prevailing concept of the man/woman relationships held by the society in which the individual relationships are taking place. (Qtd. in Kent 90)

Although Lamming does recognise that sexual practices are very much determined by the social mores of their situation, this does not shake the potency of such mores as an aspect of social control. What is most important in this respect is that although Lamming does recognise the arbitrariness of such social concepts, he does not question the fundamental unit of the male/female relationship. Given this basic assumption, there is a greater significance to be found in his casual use of such terms as 'aborted' and 'perverted.' There is the suggestion here that Caliban is still using Prospero's language, and the importance of this lies in the way in which racist ideologies have been thoroughly sexualised from their earliest expression. Some understanding of this process is necessary before the significance of the Nature/Culture divide can be approached.

Assigning an overrated sexual capacity and appetite to the black male was part of the early racial mythologies designed to maintain a sense of difference between the "civilised" whites and the more "animalistic" black. This was adapted to the ideology of slavery as a justification for further repression and oppression, as any number of brutal and savage acts could be carried out in the name of protecting the white female's "honour." The black body at this juncture arguably, was thoroughly demonized.

By the time of the post-colonial era, the envy, excitement and repression that inevitably accompany this demonisation had become more apparent. There was then a switch to the fetishisation of the black body, with the myth of black male potency. The result of this change from demonisation to fetishism was merely to produce a more subtle form of oppression to which Lamming in his texts is acutely sensitive. It remained part of a reductive way of seeing which continued to focus on the black as body; a pseudo-liberal view which grudgingly allowed an admittance of admiration for the blacks' ability in the dance-hall, sportsfield or bedroom, but contained them within the realms of the physical/animal, and at a remove from the intellectual/(white) human.

The so-called sexual revolution of the Sixties served to accelerate this process of fetishisation at a crucial moment in the history of emigration. The increasing influence of American culture through popular music and the screen introduced the black as sex idol to the populace. Figures as diverse as Sidney Poitier and Jimi Hendrix served to legitimate black sexuality, and to simultaneously present them as threat.

Clearly this would be an issue in the literature of the exiled writer, as much of the anti-immigration propaganda was based upon the image of the black man as threat: to jobs, to housing and to the white female. The first large-scale arrivals from the Caribbean were predominantly male and the sight of "mixed" couples added fuel to the myth of black potency. Selvon makes light of this issue, and his London novels are littered with outrageous characters devoting their lives to "pussy-hunting." Lamming, however, is more sensitive to the implications of such myths, recognising in them the source of a continued oppression, and thus, in his texts sexuality takes on a greater allegorical significance. This is an avenue through which Lamming's fiction may be approached.

The Emigrants picks up more or less where Lamming's first novel, *In The Castle of My Skin* left off, the transformation being, as Lamming puts it, "that where the boys of *In The Castle* are held to one particular territory, the men are drawn from all territories of the Caribbean" (qtd. in Kent 96). In the first part, "The Voyage," the Golden Image winds through the islands picking up passengers before starting the sea crossing proper. Very nearly half of the text is thus set outside Britain. In this first half, the treatment of sexuality is very different from that described in the latter half. The opening passage is symptomatic of what is to come. The men sit around talking: "The women in the town were very pretty and curious, and it would appear inexpensive. One man said he had ridden a mam'selle

1.2 George Lamming: The Natural Exile

sixty to the minute without paying a blind cent. He was sure he would do it all over again before sundown" (10). Sexuality is given public status in this part of the text, and although there is always a potentially oppressive aspect to the males' continual pursuit of the women, the very nature of this pursuit as a casual, public activity disarms it. Lamming's women at this stage of the narrative are very much in control of their sexuality and Queenie and Lillian accept and reject suitors with practiced ease. One is reminded here of Selvon's women grouped around the stand-pipe, washing, in the kind of recurrent scene in Caribbean literature that reflects back upon the neurotic privacy of Britain. In much the same way, the almost ritualistic seduction scene between the Governor and the Martiniquan woman, quite apart from being characterised by the equality with which it is carried out, is also notable for the way in which the other passengers recognise their own part in the ritual, and move away from the main actors (29-30).

Life on the ship may thus be regarded as a continuation of life on the islands and properly so, as its textual function is to operate as a microcosm of the islanders merging into West Indians. The emphasis is on the communal nature of life in the West Indies. The dormitory arrangements below decks not only reflect back on conditions in the middle passage of the slave trade, but also on the urban "yards" (a recurrent setting established by James' *Minty Alley*) the ramshackle nature of which prohibits any sense of privacy.

Sexuality thus emerges as an essential part of island life, influenced by the public nature of lived existence there. This element is emphasised by the dance at the end of the voyage as it overrides and expels the sounds of the more genteel dance on the upper deck. The calypso dance is assigned an explicitly sexual function as the "part of the body below the waist seemed to detach itself in a wagging performance, distinct and isolated from the upper part of the body which remained a tense, quivering erection" (93). This may be considered in the context of the controversy at the time in Britain over the "explicitness" of rock'n'roll.

For all this, though, the pattern of relationships that emerges from Part One, "The Voyage," is built along essentially homophobic lines. Lamming's drive towards an open and "natural" sexuality precludes any notion of "deviance." This much is reflected in the pronounced genderisation of the most influential characters. The Governor is described as "excessively muscular [. . .] every limb seemed a loud assertion of masculinity" (49), while his female equivalent, Queenie, is "like a leopard [. . .] or some kind of majestic animal" (97). This is further endorsed by the groups' perceptions of Tornado and Lillian:

> They knew the relationship between herself and Tornado, and they knew Tornado [. . .] Lillian reticent and gentle as she seemed most of the time showed an elemental savagery that was frightening. She and Tornado were a match in aggressiveness. They looked so strong together. (49)

This elemental nature is recurrent throughout the voyage, from Queenie's leopard-like aspect, to Tornado and Lillian's "petting session" (50).

In this Arcadian vision of sex and nature, in which freedom may be compared to a penis,[7] sexual relations take on a tone that invites comparison to the "naturalness" of animals mating, but in a way that avoids racist perceptions; which seek, in this comparison, a sense of evolutionary superiority. It is notable, in this respect, that when there is an instance of sexual transgression on the voyage (the union between Lillian and the Governor), it is not only carried out in private, but also conveyed through the mechanistic, and therefore unnatural, imagery of the motion of the ship's engines. Through such means, then, the function of the first part of the text is to establish the emigrants as liberated from the perceptions of white society, and achieving a state of "Nature."

The comparison is stark when the emigrants arrive in England. The semi-lyrical passage which describes the journey from the port to Paddington also conveys a metaphysical journey during which the emigrants are hurried from their state of Nature into the heart of the city: "Look. Changes very quickly. From the land down yonder where everything was clean, cultivated, to this. Now only buildings [. . .] too many buildings" (120). The passage is punctuated with instances of misunderstanding that induce a

---

[7] "I felt this freedom. It was a private and personal acquisition, and I used it as a man uses what is private and personal, like his penis" (*Emigrants* 13).

1.2 George Lamming: The Natural Exile

subtle sense of threat, as the emigrants become increasingly the subject of English perceptions. The sense of the West Indian self, tentatively formed on the ship, begins its disintegration here, as Tornado's inability to see through the smoke indicates the start of a theme in which blindness becomes a signifier for the emigrants' collapse under the weight of such perceptions.

The corollary of this blindness is the English way of seeing, through which the West Indian personality becomes built over in much the same way that the (natural) countryside has been obscured by industrial and urban development. As Pouchet Paquet notes, "[a]ll points of contact with the English world are negative. In each case the emigrants and the English are trapped by inherited colonial values and postures, and the result is invariably destructive to the emigrant psyche (*Novels* 40). What is also notable is that in all the instances she cites, the damage to the emigrant psyche is communicated through reference to sexuality.

The fall of Dickson proceeds from his reduction to a sexual object by an English matron and her sister. Previously he had always defined his identity through reference to his education: "I am not a cook [. . .] I am a trained teacher with a degree and a diploma in education" (55). This notion is reflected in his "obsession with the principles of language [he] wouldn't at the point of peril end a sentence with a preposition" (59). Even as he is anticipating the seduction ahead, Dickson attributes his situation to his education as something that has transcended colour difference; "out of all of them she chose me I here she there the common language of a common civilisation" (225).

Dickson is the victim here of fetishisation. It is an episode similar to that recounted by Lamming in *Pleasures*, in which a Jamaican continually has his jacket lifted up by factory girls hoping to catch a glimpse of his 'tail.' As Lamming points out, this was no reduction to ape status. Rather the girls were "curious to see his prick in order to get eye evidence of its size" (78). However, what Lamming does add to the account in *The Emigrants* is a greater sense of voyeurism, of sexual perversity. He draws out the seduction scene between the two: the light is turned out, Dickson's body is "spouting its need," and then two women enter:

> I don't understand. Come in. Your sister *too*.
> And he heard her say: I beg your pardon. She only wanted to see what he *looked* like. He was lying on the divan, his clothes uncouthly thrown in one corner, and he sat up, rigid and bewildered, in his vest. The women were consumed with curiosity. They devoured his body with their eyes. It disintegrated and dissolved in their stare, gradually regaining its life through his reflection in the mirror. (226)

The women's curiosity is one based on sexual rather than anatomical fetishism, and Dickson's subsequent breakdown becomes most unbearable when Collis, in his own traumatised vision, introduces the notion of the effect of this on the sexual act (265).

A more clear account of the corruption of the emigrants' existence through sexual transgression is apparent in the part that Peggy and Frederick play in their lives. Frederick had already obliged Miss Bis to leave the Caribbean through his desertion of her prior to the narrative proper. In England they have both assumed new identities; Frederick is now impotent, and in the company of the bi-sexual, Peggy. This partnership touches the lives of almost all the emigrants. Higgins is arrested as a dope peddler when he is actually carrying an aphrodisiac prepared for Frederick by Azi. Both Azi and Collis take part in further acts of voyeurism in Frederick's attempts to regain his sexual potency. However, it is Peggy who has the most devastating effect, as both Miss Bis and Queenie are drawn into her sexual activities. The result is such a complete physical and moral collapse in the former that she is unrecognisable to Frederick, and murders Queenie in order to secure the maintenance of her new identity as Una Solomon.

The passages that surround the seduction of the black characters endow the whites with a vampiristic quality. Their white skin becomes a signifier for a lost vitality, literally drained of life. Peggy's hand is a "white inert feeler that lay flat and open on the table," while Frederick's white flesh is "wrapped around him like dead nature" (216) As a result of their association with them, Miss Bis is left "ravaged" and "pitiably thin" (237), while the last image of Queenie lying on the floor in a drunken stupor bears little

1.2 George Lamming: The Natural Exile

resemblance to the "majestic animal" the Governor encountered on the ship.

Images of sexuality are thus intrinsic to the general demise of the emigrants after they arrive in England. There seems to be a dual purpose inscribed into the way Lamming uses this notion in the text. Firstly, there is a clear opposition between the "natural" black sexuality as it is displayed on the ship, and the "corrupt" and corrupting sexuality of the whites. The cameo scene of Frederick "staring hungrily" but impotently on as Azi effortlessly brings Peggy to a climax, is emblematic of a wider opposition running through the text. Lamming thus redefines the significance attached to the black body by racist ideologies, using the process of fetishism in order to claim not only a physical superiority over the whites, but a moral one too. Secondly, there is the corresponding suggestion of the Caribbean Arcadia. As Munro notes, "[o]f the twenty-two scenes that follow their arrival in Britain, only two occur outside" (131). There is an unmistakeable suggestion that it is this "compulsive privacy," so at odds with the public nature of Caribbean life, which encourages this.

In this text, then, the relationship between the sexual and the political is very much based upon Lamming's notion of overcoming the "way of seeing" that he later develops in *Pleasures*. His project here is an educational one in much the same way that Selvon builds up a set of characters that implicitly undermine contemporary myths concerning, for instance, immigrants and the Welfare State. In a similar way, Lamming could be said to have taken on the issue of sexuality, not simply to challenge the notion of a black threat to white sexuality, but to actually reverse it by using the structure of the text (i.e. the division into the voyage and life in England) to present a natural black sexuality that is corrupted by white perceptions.

This is a complex issue, though, as, in positing notions of the "natural" and the "perverse," Lamming is obliged to introduce such unlikely characters as Azi, Frederick, Peggy and Miss Bis, and what Hall refers to as "inexplicable Freudian complications" (176). The use of such binary oppositions insists upon a sense of closure, and in order to achieve such a resolution, Lamming resorts to some bizarre twists of Fate. Azi's appearance as an eccentric don at Cambridge, the convenient disposal of Queenie's body by her landlord and the unwitting reunion of Miss Bi and Frederick are all examples of this. Instead of providing closure, they distract the reader from following a truer allegorical path. In *Water With Berries*, however, Lamming concentrates on a much smaller core of characters, and thus the relation between the sexual and the political achieves greater clarity.

* * *

Arguably, the main thrust of this text lies in the relationship between Teeton and the Old Dowager. Lamming is explicit in his explanation of the metaphoric roles that exist within this relationship. The Old Dowager is the symbol of a contracted imperial power; unable to maintain the aggressive expansion of a past age, she is now left only with the "memories of a great past, of a great ancestral root" (qtd. in Kent 91). Teeton exists as a tenant in her house, still colonised by the imbalance of the relationship that manifests itself in the "maternal concern" that the Old Dowager displays towards him. Ultimately, the only way that Teeton can break out of the subjugation inherent in this relationship is by killing her: symbolically, by violent revolution.

The seeds of this thought can again be seen in *Pleasures*, as Lamming warns against the lethargy, the lack of consciousness amongst West Indians, when he says: "numerical superiority has given the West Indian a certain leisure, a certain experience of relaxation amongst white expatriates, for the West Indian has learnt [. . .] to take that white presence for granted. Which is, precisely, his problem" (33).

There may be seen, then, a development in Lamming's thought from that apparent in *The Emigrants*. There, a corrupt sexuality was a signifier for the very extreme and immediate effects of encountering the reality of England, and the polarised black images that it presented. In *Water*, the presence of the emigrants in the country for seven years presents a less explosive relationship between the coloniser and the colonised, in which the way of seeing (with which Lamming was previously concerned) has now become a two-way perception embodied in the Teeton/Old Dowager relationship.

Although Lamming chooses to emphasise the maternal aspect of this relationship, the first part of the text, "The Fall," is punctuated with instances of the Old Dowager becoming young again through her interaction with

1.2 George Lamming: The Natural Exile

Teeton. Although this might be read as indicative of a rejuvenated power springing from Teeton's domestic dependence (and one might like to relate this to the idea of the vampire in *The Emigrants*) the language, again, is sexualised.

As the Old Dowager's lingering colonialism is described through her control of her garden, Teeton sees her "[b]ending low, her hands in a tender hug round the head of the stalk. And he saw her lips move." This "effortless intercourse with nature" becomes conflated with an "instinct for authority" and "habits of command" (39). There are many other references to the Old Dowager becoming young again, but none as explicit as when she is preparing herself for the ill-fated lunch to celebrate her sale of Teeton's paintings. In waiting, she becomes "like a girl again, struggling against the first warning of excitement; fearing that there might be some flaw in her self-restraint; some brigand of emotion was about to ransack her secrets, expose her delights" (162). Her anticipation is strongly reminiscent of Dickson's emotions under similar circumstances; "[s]o nice of Teeton. To choose me. Of all people" (162).

The fetishism is the same in both cases, but the role of the emigrant changes. Thus, Dickson reads his seduction of the Englishwoman as a consequence of his embodiment of English culture, but still finds that is a victim of an oppressive way of seeing. Teeton, by comparison, comes to realise that he has been complicit in his own oppression by allowing himself to fall into a relationship with the Old Dowager that has circumscribed his freedom.

This becomes clear when the ritualised aspect of their relationship is interrupted by Nicole's death and their subsequent flight to the Orkneys. Once there, the implicit imbalance in their relationship becomes evident as Teeton's dependence upon her is accentuated: "The Old Dowager was his only certainty. Now she looked so much stronger than he had ever seen her: and somewhat younger" (175). There is a corresponding heightening in the explicitness of the Old Dowager's sexuality, and it is this that alerts Teeton for the first time to the extent to which his thoughts and actions had been inhibited by the Old Dowager's attentions. As she "turned her gaze on Teeton, and let her eyes travel slowly, playfully over his body," and likens him to her husband, Teeton becomes "embarrassed by this association," but then realises that "he felt no impulse to show any displeasure; it struck Teeton that there was a sense, deep and subtle and even dangerous, in which she had achieved some powerful hold over the roots of his emotion" (186). With this, Teeton comes to realise that he must break out of the relationship, and this revolves around his ability - under question from the first page of the text: to tell the Old Dowager that he plans to leave England. It is this determination that ultimately leads to her murder.

A relationship that is thus intended to represent the post-colonial condition, through a mother/son metaphor, is perverted by the covert introduction of a sexual aspect. When this sexualisation becomes overt, there is a violent break in that relationship which results in the collapse of a social/political process - the return of The Gathering to San Cristobal. Lamming explains that the conclusion of the narrative, with the suspension of this planned return was intended to suggest the concern with the "new reality" of the "increasing world of Blacks in England" (qtd. in Kent 95). This suspension can be regarded as the outcome of a break in previous social relations conveyed through a sexualised individual relationship.

What Lamming achieves with the sexualisation of the relationship between Teeton and the Old Dowager is to set the metaphoric significance of the relationship within the sexualisation of the colonial process that it embodies. Teeton, like Dickson, is a fetishized physical presence for the Old Dowager. But where in *The Emigrants* this is an overt process that results in individual trauma, the drama that Lamming is recounting here is more insidious. Thus, although the main crisis point of the novel (Teeton telling the Old Dowager of his decision to leave) is present from the first page of the text, it is not until the final scenes that Teeton realises what is preventing him from action. Lamming throws this subtle process into sharp relief with accounts of the overt colonialism on San Cristobal.

Here, the admixture of sexual, moral and political corruption is complete. Teeton's own escape from the "justice" of the island bought through the effectual prostitution of his wife, Randa, to the American ambassador. Jeremy Rexnol Vassen-Jerme, the sinister agent of the San Cristobal government, has his own composure shaken by Teeton's reference to the German ambassador, suggesting a homosexual relationship there (99). Chaca-Chacare, a member of The Gathering, describes the death of Lady Belve-

1.2 George Lamming: The Natural Exile

dere during a secret session of flagellation (45). It is against this background that the servants' revolt on the Gore-Brittain estate must be read. The rape of Myra, and her complete sexual degradation is the direct result of a history of slavery and colonisation in which sexuality has become at once a source and target of oppression. Myra's account of her ordeal is strongly reminiscent of Mittelholzer's *Kaywana Blood* (1958), in which Cuffy's revolution is not complete until the learned taboo surrounding the white female body is broken.

The effect of this subplot is to establish a parallel between the lived experiences of colonialism and post-colonialism. For Lamming, the difference seems to be one largely of degree; Myra's rape and the Old Dowager's murder are both the culmination of the same process of decolonisation of the mind. As Lamming later said of the rape scene, "[i]t seems to me that there is almost a therapeutic need for a certain kind of violence [. . .] There cannot be a parting of ways. There has to be a smashing" (qtd. in Kent 91). What makes this parallel all the more complete is the way in which Lamming situates sexuality at the centre of the "recolonisation" of the black British, and the way in which a perverted sexuality constitutes points of crisis in the text.

What is notable is that in the first part of the text, there are two centres of interest: the relationship between Teeton and the Old Dowager, and the relationship between Roger and Derek. In each case, a sense of ritual, or routine, is established which is then broken by an interrupted male/female relationship. With Teeton it is the news of Randa's death that reactivates his sense of betrayal and desertion; with Roger it is the news of Nicole's pregnancy that triggers his fear of the half-caste. What is important is the way in which it is a routine of mind that is interrupted, and it is this routine that Lamming is concerned with as he shifts his focus from the literature of emigration to that of black Britain.

A progression is thus evident from the writing of *The Emigrants* to that of *Water With Berries*. In the former it is the shock of discovering the reality of Britain, in the latter it is the shock of rediscovering the self; of breaking out of the social roles that British society had defined for the blacks. In both cases the shock is administered through the medium of sexuality; a technique which at once recalls the history of the sexualisation of racist ideologies, and illustrates the ways in which this process has continued into modern society.

The notion of Nature against Culture has thus also changed its premise between these two texts. In *The Emigrants* and also in *Pleasures*, Lamming was embarking on a mission of education. As an exiled writer addressing a foreign audience, it is clear that he was attempting to overcome the myths of absence; the myths that accompanied the spread of anti-immigration propaganda. It was, in many ways, a simplistic, head-on assault against the main oppositionary images of racism – celebrating that which racist mythologies demonised. The result was an equally simplistic formula in which the Caribbean, and the Caribbean personality emerged as something akin to the "noble savage" of seventeenth- and eighteenth-century European fiction; his "animalism" celebrated in opposition to the corrupt white character. "Nature," in this sense was a state of innocence. In *Water*, Lamming is more concerned with the notion of "breaking the contract sealed by language"; with breaking out of an unconscious complicity with determined social roles. "Nature" in this sense means the assumption of a self-determined social role that does not imply nostalgia for a Caribbean Arcadia, but a true expression of being black British.

* * *

In *The Pleasures of Exile*, Lamming states:

> We must accept that racial antagonism in Great Britain is, after Notting Hill, an atmosphere and background against which my life and yours are being lived. Our duty is to find ways of changing the root and perspectives of that background, of dismantling the accumulated myth, both cultural and political, which an inherited and uncritical way of seeing has now reinforced. And our biggest weapon, our greatest and safest chance lies in education; education among the young; for it is my feeling that two-thirds of the parents are beyond redemption. (76)

This, for Lamming, was the project of the exiled writer.

By 1973, though, Lamming could see that this project had failed; the new generation of black British was in place, and racial antagonism had

1.2 George Lamming: The Natural Exile

not decreased. Furthermore, his own literature, and the literature of the Caribbean, had been subsumed into the literature of its European predecessors. It is perhaps, then, no surprise that just as Selvon migrated to Canada during the Seventies, so Lamming undertook his own intellectual "migration," and has not been published since *Water With Berries*. Thus, where Moses is left at the end of Selvon's last text awaiting the "justice" of the Customs officials, so the evolution of the Caribbean personality that began with the boys in *In The Castle of My Skin* has ended in *Water* with the impotent artist either dead, or awaiting trial.

1.3 E. R. Braithwaite: The Cultural Exile

For many commentators E. R. Braithwaite would stand as an anomaly in the company of Selvon and Lamming. Discussing Braithwaite's most well-known text, Kenneth Ramchand states, "[n]ot only is *To Sir, With Love* not a work of fiction. It differs startlingly in temper from those fictional works with which it has been indiscriminately associated" ("Myth" 16). For Frank Birbalsingh, too, Braithwaite's writing mainly consists of "autobiographical accounts" which have been fictionalised only in the romantic solutions that they offer, and the naive idealism that accompanies such resolutions ("To John Bull" 74).

The use of autobiographical detail is not unusual in the fiction of emigration, after all many of Selvon's characters are based upon real figures. However, what differentiates Braithwaite's texts is the way in which real experience is *not* used to essay towards a notion of West Indian identity. In Braithwaite's texts, the black characters maintain the same characteristics that one would expect from slightly superior white characters. They are not necessarily integrated, but they are not differentiated as a group in the same way that Selvon and Lamming's emigrants become isolated and physically and spiritually forced into black enclaves. Indeed, the notion of a black community as such does not play a significant part in Braithwaite's fiction. One must ask, then; how have his ideas come to differ from those of other emigrant writers?

Braithwaite is immediately distinguishable from his literary peers by the manner of his emigration. For Lamming and Selvon the urge to leave the islands was in search of what Lamming calls "a better break," during the emigration fever of the early Fifties. They were interested in the potential, the *idea* of Britain rather than following up a specific opportunity. By contrast, Braithwaite emigrated as part of his educational career having already studied in New York, and joined up with the RAF soon after his arrival. He thus preceded the mass emigrations by about ten years. As a result, the notion of an immigrant community in Britain came late to him, and his concern as a commentator on race relations has always been to express similarity rather than difference. Comparatively removed from the debate surrounding West Indian Federation, Braithwaite's writing has al-

1.3 E. R. Braithwaite: The Cultural Exile

ways reflected a continued belief in and adherence to the peculiar ties joining the British Caribbean and the Mother Country. Many of the views implicit in his fiction may be found in his essay, "The 'Colored Immigrant' in Britain" (1967).

Written in 1967, this essay is effectively a generalised account of Braithwaite's own experiences in Britain. Starting from the War and immediate post-War period, he traces a line of deepening prejudice against the black presence and covers the usual sensitive areas of housing, education, (un)employment and "mixed" relationships. As he put it, "[t]he British had welcomed these colored comrades-in-arms; colored brothers-in-law were quite another matter" (497-8). His description of British attitudes is one of a steady and increasing resentment that became written into the legislature through the Immigration Act of 1962 and an affirmed part of the political agenda by the 1964 General Election.

His estimate of black attitudes is rather more interesting. The new settlers that stayed after the War years were, he says, "relatively few in number, and mainly young, intelligent, and articulate men" (497). After that, however, these emigrants were increasingly joined by "illiterate peasants and others, in spite of their claims, completely unskilled according to British standards and even lacking the basic educational requirement necessary for training in new skills" (498). There is no doubt in his writing that Braithwaite condemns the failure of the British government to integrate the migrant workforce into the community, but there is definitely a sense implicit in "in spite of their claims" and "even lacking" that suggests a condemnation also of these migrants and their "disorganized flood of thousands." Thus, when Braithwaite goes on to discuss the "very little contact between the immigrant workers and either the professional elite or the students," there is little doubt on which side Braithwaite would place himself (500).

Throughout, Braithwaite seems to distance himself from the majority of West Indian migrants and sees himself as removed from the black ghettoes, having already passed into white society. He has internalised the mores of "Britishness," while his compatriots have only a blind faith in it, still subject to the island thinking that maintains a faith in "British decency and fair play" and perpetuates disunity through inter-island rivalry (498-500). They believe that a multi-racial society will come about in Britain, not through their own efforts, but because of this ineffable conviction that the British will not play the oppressor forever. Effectively, he portrays the immigrants as the still-willing hands and strong backs that built the Empire patiently waiting for the benevolence of the colonialist because they are too disorganised to effectively demand their rights. Notting Hill and Nottingham stand as exceptions for the immigrant for whom "any counteraction was usually initiated by others on his behalf" (510).

Braithwaite ends on a grim note: "At present the air is troubled and thundery with bias and tension" (511). Where, in the past the black community had been hindered by the lack of strong leadership to direct collective action against discrimination, this lack might soon be filled "from the ranks of the young men and women either born into the situation or introduced into it at an early age" – in other words, the black British (511).

Braithwaite leaps effortlessly from the colonial subject to the black Briton supposedly liberated from generations of passive servility by the fact of being born, or brought up in, the heady atmosphere of the British Isles. Although he uses the term, and in fact, describes himself as one, *the West Indian does not seem to exist for Braithwaite*; he is merely a middle evolutionary stage between the British and the Caribbean descendant of slaves.

One must temper this analysis slightly with an understanding of the context of this essay. It was clearly Braithwaite's project to undermine the image of the West Indian as bogeyman, and thus he was concerned not to portray within him the aggressive potential for civil war. Furthermore, the essay has an educative aspect similar to that encountered in Selvon and Lamming. Where the two other writers have taken on the racial myths of the immigrant and sexuality or the Welfare State as part of their fiction, here Braithwaite is attempting a similar, non-fictional project that encompasses the whole gamut of racial prejudice. For example, he attributes the poor condition of the immigrant areas to the discriminatory practices of landlords and estate agents rather than an inherent slovenliness on the part of the occupants (505-7). He is also particularly clear-sighted in his condemnation of both political parties for their failure to produce a consistent

1.3 E. R. Braithwaite: The Cultural Exile

policy to assimilate the immigrant population. Black migrants are thus portrayed as the object of prejudice, rather than the cause of it.

However, in positing the black as the undeserving victim of harassment, Braithwaite assigns to him the identity of the loyal subject. His "innocence" is proclaimed by his Britishness, learned in the Colonies under the benevolent tutelage of Empire, and he appeals to the same benevolence in the white population to accept its black brothers. In doing so, he reveals his own position as a thoroughly colonised subject when he seeks approval for the immigrant by emphasising his Britishness. His rooms display "an amazingly high standard of order and cleanliness" (506), he is religious (509), a "good dependable worker" (498) and some are from "middle-class backgrounds [. . . living] frugally against the day when they could purchase their own house, preferably with a small garden" (506). Braithwaite's is thus not an exile from Guyana, but from British Guiana, and it is this aspect that sets him apart from the other writers in this chapter. Where they struggle to establish a sense of identity, Braithwaite denies it, expressing similarity rather than difference. It is this notion that will form the basis of an approach to his work.

* * *

The study of Braithwaite's fiction will be focussed primarily upon his most well-known work, *To Sir, With Love*. This text is significant for several reasons. Firstly, and most importantly, this book together with its film adaptation represents the most popularly known account of black experience in Britain to date. The novel has gone into several impressions, and the film, riding initially on the popularity of the cinema in the Fifties and Sixties, is still shown regularly on television. Although its potency has certainly receded now, the images that it presented were significant in the social perceptions surrounding the growing immigrant population.

Secondly, more than his other texts, *To Sir, With Love* deals with the experiences of the newcomer in a way similar to that of *The Emigrants* and *The Lonely Londoners* in that it relates the first shock of the "reality" of England. Here, though, the main character, Ricky, has been resident in Britain for several years prior to the main narrative. Hence, Lamming's notion of the West Indian overcoming the *idea* of England is enacted here within the text as Ricky is forced to respond to changing racial attitudes as they occur.

Thirdly, the narrative revolves around the theme of education in such a way that it echoes the cultural imperialism that both Selvon and Lamming have noted as a structural feature of colonisation. The views espoused by Braithwaite in "The 'Colored Immigrant'" have their roots exposed in the mechanics of a narrative in which a black teacher *reimports* the cultural imperatives of a colonial education to his class. The question of identity may thus be approached through the characteristics that Braithwaite assigns to Ricky as the embodiment of this education.

* * *

As noted in Selvon, the intense ties between education and social status remained in the Caribbean as a relic of the slave economy and colonial rule. Treated as units of labour power, the slaves were taught only the minimum necessary to enable the fulfilment of their duties. It may be seen that house-servants would require a greater degree of literacy than the cane-cutters, and thus the organisation of class stratification around the attainment of education, and, *ipso facto*, prestigious employment, began. By the late Nineteen-Forties and Fifties, the conflation of education and a learned Britishness was complete, as Eric Williams recalls, "'[b]e British' was the slogan not only of the legislature, but also of the school" (33). Furthermore, the cultural negotiation that Lamming recognised in the importation of English education included class-specific traditions. C. L. R. James states, "[w]e learnt, I learnt and obeyed and taught a code, *the English public school code*" (33; my emphasis). Thus, when Braithwaite introduces his character into London's East End, what becomes immediately obvious is a sense of class (rather than race) difference.

From the opening passage it becomes clear that Ricky has no sense of empathy with the working-class. Rather, there is a suggestion of condescending superiority in his description of the charwomen on the early morning bus and the "essential naturalness of these folk who were an integral part of one of the world's greatest cities and at the same time as common as hayseeds" (8-9). The text gestures towards Selvon's characters for whom the mere fact of being in London is an occasion for wonder, but

1.3 E. R. Braithwaite: The Cultural Exile

Braithwaite despises the failure of London and the majority of its inhabitants to live up to its picture-postcard image. By the time he reaches the East End streets he has become less tolerant of the real London: "I felt sick and dirtied, and only the need of reaching my destination forced me along past the shops and smells" (11-12).

The experience of racial prejudice is absent from these early scenes, described in fact as a "multi-racial jostle" (12). Ricky's sense of the familiar, though, is incurred not by the street market, but rather, in the manner of a later Moses, by the appearance on the bus of an evidently higher classed woman. She effectively refuses to sit next to Ricky and in the ensuing confrontation with the conductor is subject to the "conductor's threatening attitude [and] the pointedly hostile glances directed at her by the women in their immediate sympathy and solidarity [. . .] against someone obviously not of their class" (10). In the end Ricky defuses the situation by leaving the bus, but not before he finds his initial anger at the woman has been "surprisingly tinctured by a certain admiration for her fearless, superior attitude": she was, he says, "more than a match for the people around her" (10).

This early suggestion that Ricky empathises more with the upper-classes in Britain than the lower is then borne out through the text. The influence behind this empathy reveals itself as that of a British colonial education, which becomes clear in his courtship with Gillian Blanchard, another teacher at the school. The textual marriage of these two characters is significant in many respects. Firstly, it is very different in tone from the either tortured or bawdy relationships that feature in Lamming and Selvon. Rather, it is an asexual union based on a shared appreciation of (so-called) high culture and the mutual priggishness of outraged and outspoken respectability.

In a passage that anticipates the tone of "The 'Colored Immigrant,'" Braithwaite tackles the notion of black sexuality in the pseudo-frank language that reduces the subject to one of bodily function:

> My life in England had not by any means been ascetic [. . .] under the tensions of operational flying and the uncertainty of survival, sex became merely part of the general scheme of things and I was

no exception [. . .] the colour of my skin was not important. As a matter of fact, it helped, along with the fact that I was rather good at games – rugger, soccer, tennis, cricket, athletics. (72)

This attitude is affirmed later in the text as Ricky squirms uncomfortably at the mention of a bordello in the company of Gillian's parents (175), and is evident in Braithwaite's other attempts to relate a sanitised air of sensuality that Ramchand compares to "a parody of the panty-conscious romance of certain kinds of women's magazines" ("Myth" 14).

Secondly, Gillian's social background is made clear by the "generous personal allowance" paid by her father which allows her to keep a flat in Chelsea and to teach, "not so much for the money [. . .] but because teaching brought her into touch with people in a very personal way" (103). She is thus distinguished from the other characters in the text in much the same way that the woman in the bus was, and it is no surprise that it is to a woman of her class that Ricky is attracted. Their courtship begins with a look of shared surprise that the working-class pupils should listen to classical music with interest, and then moves on to the more intimate common interests of "books, music, the theatre and films" (61).

This ideological matchmaking is significant in the regularity with which such "types" appear in Braithwaite's fiction. The sophisticated black student, Michelle, who appears in *A Choice of Straws* (1965), parallels, as Birbalsingh points out, Braithwaite's "own irreproachable self-portrait in the autobiographical works" ("To John Bull" 78), and in terms of sophistication, beauty and wealth, is not unlike Gillian Blanchard. It is a fetishised, recurring image that owes much to the figure of the colonialist, the white ideal that dominated West Indian middle-class aspirations, and because it was no more than an image, it falls down in the reality of Britain. Ricky errs because he does not understand the class-specific nature of this image.

An important feature of the West Indian literature studied so far has been the use of dialect. There is no dialect in Braithwaite's text, apart from that of the Cockney children, and it is in this inversion of the black\white relationship that Braithwaite's misapprehension of the Mother Country becomes apparent. The point was made in Selvon that Standard English was not universally spoken in Britain and this reflected upon the notion of a

1.3 E. R. Braithwaite: The Cultural Exile

Trinidadian dialect. In Braithwaite this reflects upon class values and differentiates Ricky, as the colonial who has learned an image of these values, and Gillian, who was born into their reality.

This is first apparent in Ricky's attempts to introduce among his pupils the public school practice of addressing their male colleagues by their surnames and their female colleagues by the title 'Miss' (74-5). Miss Blanchard is reported to be "dubious about the wisdom of imposing unfamiliar codes on the children" (77), when in fact what this really represents is a concern about the loss of a linguistic signifying practice written into the maintenance of class difference. Ricky's internalisation of a linguistic norm thus reveals through the rest of the text a concomitant internalisation of ideological norms.

The imposition of these forms of address is resisted by the pupils in the text, and by one in particular, Denham. His resistance is subdued when he is knocked down by Ricky in a boxing bout, and Ricky's stock rises generally with his pupils as a result of this: "they looked at me now as if I had suddenly and satisfactorily grown up before their very eyes" (85). But it is Denham who accepts his instructions with a "[y]es, Sir" in a voice that was "shaky" but had no "hesitation or mimicry about the 'Sir'" (85). When resistance does rise again, once more it finds a primarily linguistic expression. Denham again illustrates the point in his anger after Potter is dissuaded from attacking a sadistic teacher for his abuse of another pupil: "'If I'd had the wood I'd have done the f_____r [sic] in and no bleeding body would have stopped me.' Denham was aching for trouble and he didn't care who knew it" (156). The point here is not, as is suggested by the text, that the words have any sexual connotations, but rather that they contain an expression of revolt through the recognition of their social significance.

Submission to authority, and its opposite, resistance, may thus be registered in the text on a linguistic level, derived from the existence of a linguistic norm. The fact that it is the black character that enforces these behavioural norms is an indication of the thoroughness of his colonisation. Thus, where Selvon uses correct spoken English in the character of Harris to emphasise the unity of the other emigrants' dialect, in this text Ricky's speech serves to deny West Indian-ness.

A similar comparison may be made with Lamming. Where in *The Emigrants* a "natural" sexuality is described in the islands and on board the ship, in *To Sir, With Love*, sexuality becomes a dirty word. As noted above, Ricky and Gillian's courtship is asexual, and this is shown to be the result of Ricky's class-based indoctrination. The reasoning behind the use of the term 'Miss' is explained through the rhetorical question, "is there any young lady present whom you consider unworthy of your courtesies?" (74). The implied criteria of such worthiness are then laid out, as the girls are sent off for lessons in deportment (by the Domestic Science teacher, of course) while the boys receive a homily on the nature of bravery from Ricky.

From such implicit hypostases, traditional sexual stereotyping may proceed, and terms such as "slut" (69) and its converse, "decent women" (71) flow easily into the narrative discourse. That this is a class-based moralism is easily discernable. Ricky makes reference, at one point, to "*essential* moral questions" (70; my emphasis). Such issues, however, are clearly not essential, but rather social and may thus be compared with what he indulgently describes as the "easy lewdness" of the charwomen on the bus (15). Furthermore, he shares Gillian's confidence "in the assurance of her own poise and breeding to keep her inviolate" (90). The contradiction, inherent in an immigrant's internalisation of these sexual codes, becomes apparent as the "logic" that accompanies such attitudes collides with that which underpins racist ideologies. Thus, when lesbianism becomes an issue through the character of Miss Dawes, another teacher at the school, Miss Blanchard employs the all too familiar homophobic sentiment, "[i]t's unhealthy to say the least, and bad for the children" (128).

It is clear, then, that the question of identity as such does not arise in this text. As Ramchand puts it, "the gesture towards a need for re-appraisal and re-discovery of self is made [. . .] but the new appraisal never takes place, and the need for it is quickly blotted out" ("To John Bull" 15). He notes that after the Mayfair office incident in which Ricky experiences his first real shock of discrimination, his indignation and anger give way to an "exasperating submissiveness" (24). It is also because once Ricky is in the East End his identity is in no doubt; he can play the White Man. Ricky does not question the validity of his social and moral convictions and once

1.3 E. R. Braithwaite: The Cultural Exile

placed in the position of authority over underprivileged children, the classic colonial opposition becomes inverted, and it is they who must revise their identities. This inversion affects Ricky's interaction with the whole social scene of the East End.

The opening passage of the text is again instructive as the discourse of class difference merges into that of racial superiority. Thus, as Ricky distances himself from the women on the bus and in the market scene, the images he uses to describe them are reminiscent of a Lévi-Straussian encounter with African society. The charwomen themselves are described as "thick-armed" and "bovine" with "gaudy headscarves" and their "solid legs and large feet which seemed to be rooted in the earth." "They were of the city," he says, "but they were dressed like peasants, they looked like peasants, and they talked like peasants" (7). The description of the market scene enhances this with its "open casks," "multitudes of flies" and "fetid air" and groups of young children playing on the scrubland (11-12). This inversion of the colonial as anthropologist is reiterated through the text as the relationship of teacher to (working-class) pupil displays the same characteristics as that of coloniser to colonised.

Just as Ricky can be seen to have internalised colonialist mores, so the children display the same characteristics as those assigned to black people in racist ideologies. A "loose" sexual morality, devious mind, the absence of a sense of responsibility, the prizing of the physical over the mental are all evident in the text and are the classic attributes of the "nigger." At one point, the pregnancy of a fourteen-year-old is judged in terms of her betrayal "by the combined evils of poverty and overcrowding and ignorance" (118), the appeal to which remains a regular justification for the intervention into, or continued occupation of, one country by another. The opposition here is of upper-class ideals as educated maturity against a conflation of childhood and working-class praxis. In terms of racist ideologies this is the equivalent of imperial civilisation as ontological maturity, against colonised society as ontological infancy. Ricky, in espousing British values and social mores as the indices of maturity, thus condemns colonial societies to an ontological immaturity that they must be educated out of by their imperial masters.

In the setting of the East End, then, apart from some isolated and easily smoothed over incidents, Ricky, through his association with Gillian, represents a thoroughly integrated figure. This is largely because in this context the issue of race becomes confused with that of class. Where Selvon states in *The Lonely Londoners*, "it have a kind of communal feeling with the Working Class and the spades, because when you poor things does level out" (59), in this text, the communal feeling is with the privileged classes. Ramchand condemns this successful integration of a black man into the white community because, for one group of readers, it "ministers to self-respect and diminishes the need to search consciences. For another group, a mythical success and acceptance is a comfortably flabby escape from agony, from the need of the derelict West Indian to discover and create the West Indian personality" ("Myth" 19). Birbalsingh, too, deplores the book for the way in which Ricky's unproblematised character and superlative qualities suggest "a morality that tolerates discrimination against the large majority of blacks who are neither more or less talented than ordinary men of any colour" ("To John Bull" 76).

The point clearly emerges that the absence of a West Indian personality is the result of a figure that is virtually a parody of the aspirations of the West Indian middle-class. It is this aspect that nudges the text into the fictional. Rather than regarding the constitution of Ricky's character as the embodiment of Braithwaite's own inflated ego, it should be read in the context of the prevailing attitudes to immigration at the time of its publication.

This text was the product of a period in the history of immigration in which integration was the primary social and political aim. The premises are the same as those indicated in the analysis of "The 'Colored Immigrant'"; it is a fictionalised account of how racial integration is possible if one emphasises the common characteristics of black and white, rather than highlighting difference. The close of the text with its promise of Ricky and Gillian's proposed marriage, and the narrative romance of the children's "conversion" following their appearance at the Seales' funeral, suggests the development of a new society that was the dream of the post-War years. If Ramchand and Birbalsingh note the absence of a quest for the

1.3 E. R. Braithwaite: The Cultural Exile

West Indian identity, it is because such a search was product of the time in which *they* were writing.

What this should demonstrate, as should the foregoing analyses of Selvon and Lamming, is that the fictional image of the black, his textual significance, is one that is directly linked to social change. The point has been made that the post-War years saw the establishment of the black as a legitimate sex figure and this progressive establishment may be noted in black writing. In Braithwaite, this progression does not exist, largely because the image of his blacks remains modelled upon a white Ideal; he reproduces a series of "Dicksons" who assume the assimilation of white culture will enable integration.

A different method of illustrating a sense of progression in the figure of Ricky is to look at the film adaptation. As noted in the introduction, the image presented here remains potent through its continued exposure on the television screen. What is more important is to note the way in which the cinematic representation of the black schoolteacher has been changed. This image has the double significance of not only being produced during a very different social climate from the original text, but also with the expectation of a much wider audience. As will be seen, it is not so much the image that is changed as the use to which that image is put.

* * *

The film adaptation of *To Sir, With Love* was released in 1967, eight years after the book was published and eighteen years after the time in which the action was set. Thus, the first thing to note is that there was no attempt in the film to recreate the setting of the immediate post-War. However, before any more detailed analysis can begin, certain precepts have to be considered.

Perhaps the most obvious consideration in the comparison of film and novelistic texts is the intervention of the producer, director and screenplay writer. In this case, James Clavell was responsible for each of these tasks, and as he is neither black nor an immigrant, one must question how far this text remains a record of black experience, and thus, how far the comparison would be valid. The making of the film would also be heavily influenced by its existence as a commercial project; the strictures of box-office appeal and budget requirements would affect the selection of scenes, the choice of actors and the general trend of the film. For instance, one might argue that the change of the main character, called Mark Thackery in the film, to an Americanised actor owes more to the desire of the producers to use Sidney Poitier as a box-office draw than to some shift in the ideological import of the film. The use of music and the appearance of Lulu and The Mindbenders might also be attributed to this cause.

Although these considerations have to be borne in mind, they do not necessarily detract from the analysis, but may be said to add weight to it. The project here is to expose the changing popular image of the black immigrant in Britain. If a film, being (arguably) an artefact specifically directed at popular taste, has to be selective in its choice of scenes, then that selection will be based upon popular appeal. This will necessarily be a reciprocal process, as there has to be some exchange between the media influencing its audience, and the audience influencing the media, and thus much might be derived from an examination of the popular images encoded into the cinema. In this sense, the use of Poitier may be viewed in terms of its effect rather than its cause. As will be described below, his character's Americanisation plays a very particular part in the operation of the film, and furthermore, his presence associates this film with *The Blackboard Jungle*, a similar film in which he also starred. It is the perceived effect, then, that is of the greatest importance.

As noted above, the film makes no attempt to retain the original setting of the novel. The most immediate difference that this makes to the main character is to remove his experience of Britain and his service record. There is a passing remark referring to a protracted job search in Britain, but the real emphasis is on his having come from "spending some time in California." In an early scene with Grace (Dale-)Evans which in the novel establishes his wartime experience, Mark's American-ness is emphasised through reference to his "majoring" in a subject, and his use of the term "appointment" instead of "job." This last alteration is particularly significant as in the novel it is used to associate Ricky with an intellectual discourse that Grace rejects (14), but Gillian uses, thus signalling an early sympathy between the two (18).

1.3 E. R. Braithwaite: The Cultural Exile

What is established by these changes alone is that Mark cannot be easily identified with British society. As an effective American he takes on an almost classless quality that is enhanced by the fact that he has no British counterpart in the film. Where the novel features the textual marriage of types between Blanchard and Ricky, this romance is lost in the film. This association, which locates Ricky within British class boundaries, is crucial because, although Mark displays all the same characteristics in the film as his novelistic counterpart, their social significance is lost in the absence of this association. The notion of class division is withdrawn from the film in other ways.

As early as the opening scene on the bus where the exchange between the charwomen is faithfully reconstructed, the appearance of the "superior bitch," with the different reactions that she provokes is omitted. There is a similar process to be noted in the reduction of Grace Dale-Evans' name to the more common Grace Evans. As a result, there is only one class in the film, the lower class of the East End. The picture-postcard image that was dissipated early in the book is maintained here, from the opening scenes of Tower Bridge and Big Ben, to the now fetishised Cockney backdrop.

It is easy to read these alterations in terms of current cinematic trends. Made by an American company, Columbia, this film may have been influenced by the success of the British film industry in adapting the texts of post-1956 drama and novels. In these films too, "social realism" was fetishised with the addition, for instance of the market scenes in Tony Richardson's adaptation of *Look Back in Anger* (1956, filmed 1957) and football crowd scenes in *Room at the Top* (1957, filmed 1959). The effect, though, is to shift the basis from which the opposition between Ricky and his pupils operated. Where in the novel the class-based associations gave a multi-dimensional significance to the notion of the black as teacher and to the black in British society, in the film the opposition is reduced to that of authority and revolt and is confined largely to the classroom.

The reduced scope of the film is emphasised not only by limiting the focus to the classroom, but also by reducing the pupils to two representative figures, Denham and Pamela Dare. As Ramchand notes of the book, Dare is "the hottest number in the class" ("Myth" 19); and she maintains this aspect in the film. Denham, too, is visually "upgraded," his leather jacket, black t-shirt and jeans recalling Brando's *Wild Ones* and casting him as the figure-head of rebellion. Effectively, by subduing these two characters, Mark dominates the whole class. His relationship with them is thus intensified in the film.

As noted earlier, Denham's two critical scenes in the book are the boxing bout with Ricky and the aftermath of the scene between Buckley and Mr. Bell. On both occasions it is the sense of confrontation with Ricky that is important, and it is this sense that is used very differently in the film. In the latter episode, Ricky smoothes over the incident with an absurd ease, but in the film it is a vital confrontation in which Mark loses the confidence of the children again.

It is Denham who reduces the incident to an "us against them" situation by defining Mark as the symbol of an unjust authority, and in the changed narrative order of the film, Mark does not regain effective control of his class until the fight scene. In particular, this exchange is important because Denham's line, "[i]t's alright for you, no-one tries to tell you what to do" is spoken by Seales, the half-caste in the book who says, "[i]t's easy for you to talk, Sir, nobody tries to push you around" (121). Thus, a moment that in the novel painfully recalls Ricky's racial oppression is used in the film to emphasise the theme of teenage revolt.

The boxing scene occupies a different place in the narrative to confirm the real significance of the film. Occurring much later than in the novel, it represents the climax of Denham's, and thus the class', rebellion. Faithfully adapted from the novelistic version, it is more potent due to the highly gendered role that Denham plays in the film. His physical defeat breaks the spell of his dominance, and this is signified by his subsequent change to a more conformist style of dress.

For Pamela Dare, too, there is a change in narrative order to focus the climax again upon the struggle between the teacher and the class. In the novel, Pamela's resistance is quelled after the tampon episode, and from then on her part is to play out a schoolgirl crush on Ricky. In the film, however, her opposition returns after the dispute with her mother, and is not muted until the fight has subdued Denham.

Clearly, the accent of the narrative has been changed by the redefinition of Mark\Ricky's relation to British society, and this is particularly notice-

1.3 E. R. Braithwaite: The Cultural Exile

able in the different significance of the funeral scene towards the end of each text. In the novel, the appearance of the children at the Seales' home is a strong image of hope for the future. In effectively flouting the taboos of their parents by appearing at a black immigrant's house, they enact exactly the kind of integration that Braithwaite is promoting. Importantly, it is after this that Ricky meets Gillian's parents and has to experience exactly the same kind of racism among the white upper-classes.

In the film, there is no aftermath to the funeral scene other than the end of school dance that provides a vehicle for the talents of Lulu and The Mindbenders. The textual closure has been provided through the submission of the pupils, and the only real significance of these scenes is the appearance of two younger pupils whose behaviour suggests that the next academic year will be much the same for Mark.

The theme of race is thus blotted out in the film to favour that of teenage revolt. As noted above, one of Seales' most telling lines is appropriated for Denham, and his whole role is altered to act as a virulent condemnation of "mixed" relationships. In the only scene added to the original script, Seales cries his hatred for his black father for marrying a white woman, and his continued misery with the death of his mother defines him as the unhappy product of a misconceived union.

The effect of the absence of both class and racism as effective themes in the film is to reduce Mark's role as solely that of his relationship with his pupils: the experience of racism as it survives is thus only a by-product of this drama. By subordinating these themes to those of authority and rebellion, Mark is posited as the outsider, at variance with the class associations present in the novel. The point here is that although Mark retains all of the moral and social convictions that characterise Ricky, his social isolation converts him into a symbol of classless authority. The significance of this is manifold.

It is notable that scenes of teenage violence and revolt punctuated the years immediately surrounding the release of this film. 1966 and 1967 saw the revival of weekend violence between Mods and Rockers on the English coast, while in America the news was dominated by the youth protest against the Vietnamese War. 1968 meanwhile saw the spread of student revolt across Europe. Such violence may thus be regarded as a dominant social issue of the time, and in this respect the association of this film with *The Blackboard Jungle*, which was a catalyst for the first outbreaks of such violence in 1955, becomes all the more significant.

By comparison, the question of race is clearly played down, and the emphasis on integration completely withdrawn. Again, the significance of this may be read in terms of wider social movements. The rise of anti-immigration sentiment in Britain at this time is certainly made clear in Braithwaite's essay (released in the same year as the film), and may be demonstrated, perversely perhaps, by the requirement for the Race Relations Act of 1968. The rhetoric and public emotion that surrounded the introduction of this Act demonstrates that the promotion of an integrated black character was not on the agenda for a popular film at this time.

One must ask, then, what is the narrative function of a black lead character in this film? If the notion of race has become incidental to a narrative concerned with re-establishing social order, why does the symbol of authority have to be black? One may look here to the notion of classlessness, a misleading concept of societal change that still lingered on from the "age of affluence." This is encapsulated in the film by Pamela Dare's assertion, "[w]e are the generation to be free, really free." The old symbols of authority would not be appropriate here, and added to the classless quality with which Mark is endowed through his American-ness is the idea that he has achieved his position of authority despite a similar background of poverty as the children. Much is made of his having been poor and the necessity for him to take on menial jobs in order to survive. As one of the pupils puts it, "[y]ou're like us, but you're not – if you see what I mean." The black character in this sense is a symbol of the potential of reform.

* * *

The comparative analysis has shown that in effect there are two very different texts in operation here, each very much a product of their social context, exposed in the different significance assigned to the black immigrant. In this sense, it is the *image* of the black that is of interest here. In the novel of integration he is the "insider," absorbed into British society by virtue of a colonial heritage that provided class association, and through this, social/romantic involvement. In the film he is the "outsider," his colo-

1.3 E. R. Braithwaite: The Cultural Exile

nial background overlaid by a process of Americanisation that allows him to fulfil a rather different function in an atmosphere of anti-immigrant sentiment and social disruption.

In both cases he is apparently distinguished from the characters in Selvon and Lamming who are left at the end of the final texts still subject to the proscriptions of British officialdom. For these two writers, the black person in Britain still has his life and his identity circumscribed by the perceptions of the society in which he has to live. For Braithwaite, in both texts, the black character is not only master of his own destiny, but a celebrated influence upon others. In order to achieve this position, though, the notion of a West Indian identity has been foregone, and instead different characteristics, more congenial to the biases of the time are employed. Effectively, his position is the same; the constitution of black identity remains subject to the perceptions of the white host nation.

That Braithwaite's writing is the result of the kind of mental colonisation, the learnt *way of seeing* that Lamming tries to expose is in no doubt. That this colonisation has continued in the post-colonial world in the formation of new racist ideologies is demonstrated in the adaptation of his idealised black character. The identity of exile, in this sense, remains unfixed.

PART 2

2.0 Introduction: The Second Generation

It is perhaps misleading to refer to the three writers in this chapter as the "second generation." Wilson Harris is older than both Selvon and Lamming, while Andrew Salkey (in terms both of age and time of migration) might also claim to be a contemporary of these writers. The defining factor for the purposes of this survey, however, is the moment at which they, as writers, chose to intervene in black existence in Britain. Salkey's *Escape to an Autumn Pavement* (1960) is the earliest of the texts to be discussed here, and while both he and Wilson Harris had been published prior to this year, it is the period after this date that characterises their work, and that of Linton Kwesi Johnson. In this respect, 1958 may be regarded as a seminal year in the history of Caribbean emigration.

The "riots" that occurred in Nottingham and London in 1958 did not signal the start of racism in Britain, nor were they the expression of a phenomenal rise in working-class racism in post-War society. Their significance lay rather in the way they initiated a public debate on "racial problems," the effect of which is still being felt today. Saggar's description of the events of 1958 as the eruption of simmering tensions between black and white people (100-1) is particularly apt here as, when the pot boiled over, it lifted the lid off British racism.

The press coverage of the disturbances was symptomatic of what was to come. The simple act of dubbing systematic attacks on West Indians by white mobs as "race riots," suggested an ideological link in which the presence of a black population, rather than white racism, was perceived as the essential problem. This link was then firmly established as MPs from both sides of the House, but notably Tory MPs Cyril Osborne and Norman Pannell, demanded the introduction of immigration controls as a political solution to racist attacks.

Such voices both within and outside Parliament proved to be an irresistible force. Miles and Phizacklea (35) note how once the notion of control had become common currency, it provided the news framework for all related events, thus maintaining such demands on the political agenda in the absence of any significant social developments. This self-perpetuating public clamour, coupled with the election of certain Midland MPs to the Conservative government in 1959, provided the pre-conditions for the 1962 Commonwealth Immigrations Act. While ostensibly related to the economy and labour supply, its debate in Parliament and its failure to legislate against migrants from the Irish Republic clearly identified it as an inherently discriminatory piece of legislation.

The Labour Party's opposition to the Act was based on both economic and political grounds, and they consistently accused the Government of implementing racism (Miles and Phizacklea 42). It was also accepted that they were maintaining this stance contrary to public opinion. When they succeeded the Tories in office in 1964, however, they were obliged to rethink their principled opposition. Patrick Gordon-Walker's defeat at the hands of an openly racist campaign by Peter Griffith in 1964, and his subsequent defeat in the engineered Leyton by-election were sufficient stimuli for the incoming Labour government to reform its views. The result was a political consensus with the Opposition to de-politicise race, the aim being "to defuse the possibility of one party or another making electoral capital out of the issue" (Saggar 107). The price, slightly offset by the promise of Race Relations legislation, was Labour's commitment to maintain the Tories' hard-line policy on immigration.

Labour's next two terms of office until their election defeat in 1970, may be characterised by their efforts to stay one step ahead of the immigration issue. The period is dominated still by the figure of Enoch Powell, whose nationalistic bile and rhetoric commanded more popular support than either party leader could ignore. Furthermore, Labour's desire to institute a Race Relations programme was at once undermined by the difficulty in inducing a favourable political climate in which to introduce such legislation, and fundamentally flawed by their commitment to immigration control. Roy Hattersley's now famous syllogism, "integration without control is impossible but control without integration is indefensible," encapsulates the contradiction in party policy whereby, "in order to eliminate racism in Britain, it is necessary to practice it at the point of entry" (Miles and Phizacklea 57).

Powell used the debates on Race Relations to maintain public interest in immigration. Increasingly, his rhetoric turned to nationhood and the de-

2.0 Introduction: The Second Generation

fence of a common heritage and ancestry under threat from an increasing alien population. In this, he was aided by the Kenyan Asian crisis in 1967, inducing the Second Commonwealth Immigrations Act (1968). Encouraged by his success in influencing Parliament and continued popularity after being sacked from the Shadow Cabinet for his "rivers of blood" speech in 1968, Powell began his campaign for a Ministry of Repatriation.

In the context of previous legislation, this was a logical move. Once the black presence (which, by now, clearly included the Asian community) had been identified as the "problem," and immigration had been slowed to a trickle, the only possible method of diminishing the "problem" was through a reduction of the extant presence. Duncan Sandys' warning of "the breeding of millions of half-caste children" (qtd. in Saggar 11) in 1967, anticipated the time when immigration would be less of a concern than reproduction. In this one can perceive a direct line from Powell's assertion that a West Indian or Indian born in England is English by law, rather than in fact (Saggar 113), to Margaret Thatcher's articulation in 1978 of the fear of the British people of "being swamped" by "alien cultures" (Saggar 121). As Miles and Phizacklea argue (105), to express fears about the size of the coloured population at a time when its numbers are being sustained by natural reproduction, can only lead to one logical conclusion.

While the major political parties were formulating a legislative rejection of Britain's black communities, the public opinion that had at once been inflamed by the debate in Parliament and maintained it, was finding other, more bloody modes of expression. Although the hand of neo-fascist violence was apparent in the attacks on West Indians in 1958, it was not until the late Sixties that neo-fascist parties achieved more considerable support and influence (Miles and Phizacklea 118). The most potent and visible of these organisations, the National Front, was formed in 1967, amalgamating the membership of three existing organisations, the League of Empire Loyalists, the British National Party and the Racial Preservation Society. The National Front rose to national prominence after 1972 when it gained media attention for its picket line at Heathrow Airport during the Ugandan Asian crisis. While the front only ever gained patchy support at best at the electoral polls, its policy of mounting fascist meetings and marches in areas predominately populated by blacks and Asians represented a physical enactment of the legislative confrontation set out by Parliament. Moreover, the willingness on the part of the police to defend the Front's right to speech in these areas, and to intervene (with fatal results[8]) in any counter-demonstration, emphasised whose rights the State was apparently more willing to protect.

This period of the National Front's greatest notoriety, from around the early Seventies until the end of the decade is associated with wider questions of law and order. The start of the IRA mainland campaign in 1974, the miner's strike of 1972-3 and the subsequent use of flying pickets in further industrial action, together with increasingly violent responses by the police, all combined to prompt questions of Britain's "ungovernability." With white liberals dying at NF marches, and Labour politicians (having opposed the 1971 Immigration Act) supporting the 1977 Grunwick dispute[9] as a *cause célèbre*, maintaining the image of the immigrant as a threat to society in this period could have proved difficult. Right-wing politicians and a sympathetic press thus introduced the "mugger" to racist ideologies.

As Miles and Phizacklea note (84-94), 'mugging' was a term imported from the United States to describe robbery with violence. The unmistakeable addendum to this was that it was a ghetto crime carried out by black youths against white victims. While such an assault was not new to Britain, and while such statistics as were extrapolated (relating, one might add, to a term that has no legal legitimacy) concluded that blacks were more the victims of such crimes than the perpetrators. "Mugging" became the ideological link between the black population and the law and order issue. As Miles and Phizacklea put it,

---

[8] In 1974, Kevin Gately lost his life in an anti-National Front demonstration in Red Lion Square, London. In 1979, Blair Peach died (possibly at the hands of the Special Patrol Group) in a counter-demonstration to a National Front rally in Southall (Marwick 189 and 225).

[9] The Grunwick strike began at a film-processing factory in August 1976 and lasted for over a year. The central issues were those of racial exploitation and union recognition, but these became lost in violent confrontations with the police, and the involvement of Trotskyite activists. (Marwick 227, Sivanandan 42-3).

2.0 Introduction: The Second Generation

> [t]he notion of 'waves of immigrants' overlapped with the idea of 'crime wave,' giving added impetus to the claim that 'our decent and law-abiding people, were being swamped. Moreover, what they were being swamped by was made more specific: it was not only the teeming millions,' but also young 'black' men from the 'ghetto.' (87)

While right-wingers made political capital out of this issue in the House, the police were forming special squads to apprehend "muggers." The Special Patrol Group (SPG) used the arbitrary powers of arrest under the "sus" law to effectively harass the black population in urban areas. Like the NF demonstrations, the effect of this was to translate Powellite rhetoric into the lived existence of the black community. The inevitable outcome of this increasing sense of confrontation was the 1981 riots that spread across Britain.

* * *

This sense of social and political confrontation also pervaded popular culture. As noted in the analysis of the screenplay of *To Sir, With Love*, there was a clear change of emphasis from a black teacher's struggle for acceptance in British society in the novel, to the theme of juvenile revolt and adult authority in the film. Major roles for black people in the British cinema became scarce after this, the viewing public apparently preferring to see Peter Sellers blacked up as an Indian doctor instead. This sensitivity was apparent elsewhere in the film and television industry.

The Realist dramas that had imported black characters into their screenplays to add authenticity to images of urban working-class life, found their televisual equivalent in the introduction of soap operas. *Coronation Street* experimented briefly with the theme of race in 1963 through the character of Johnny Alexander, a bus conductor played by Thomas Baptiste. The issue was not ducked here, as Johnny became the victim of racism at work and was sacked, and was furthermore involved in a racist feud with Len Fairclough. An episode of *Z-Cars* ("A Place of Safety"), written by John Hopkins the following year, also tried to depict the human consequences of a racist society on black people, and the self-conscious liberalism of the police officer involved.

These, however, were not sustained attempts to normalise black existence in Britain through the medium of the television, because public opinion simply would not allow it. Jim Pines notes the demise of Joan Hooley's well-established character in *Emergency-Ward 10* in 1964 after anxiety over an inter-racial couple kissing on prime-time television (10). Furthermore, the screening of another Hopkins drama, *Fable*, which inverted the black/white roles in an imaginary apartheid state was temporarily banned in the aftermath of the Leyton by-election, and prompted questions in the House of Commons (Pines 10).

It is thus significant that when British audiences did respond favourably to the issue of race as regular viewing, it was in situation comedy. *Till Death Do Us Part*, started in the late-Sixties, and *Love Thy Neighbour* (1972-1975), both turned on the comic expression of British racist sentiment. The use of biblical phrases for the titles aptly reflected both the central character's association with traditional social and moral values, and the contradictory way in which such values and mores were being perverted, in the name of protection, through the prejudiced and violent rejection of the black community.

The spirit of the age in which *Love Thy Neighbour* was broadcast, is apparent in Rudolph Walker's recollection of his part in the series:

> I actually laid down certain conditions, and one of the main things I said at the time was that I would only do the part if my character wasn't made into a Uncle Tom [. . .] So it was agreed that if the bigoted white neighbour called me something I would call him the equivalent back. If he hit me, I would hit him back.
>
> (Qtd. in Pines 78)

The sense of confrontation is clear, and if it can be reduced to a comic trading of terms such as 'Sambo' and 'Whitey,' then it can be trivialised and marginalised. The white racism depicted in this series, and in *Till Death Do Us Part*, was made, through the use of comedy, to appear at once exaggerated and harmless when in fact it was neither of these things.

Walker notes that after the series ended there was a significant downturn in the number of roles for black actors in British television. Horace Ové, the black film director also had his film, *Pressure*, banned from release in

2.0 Introduction: The Second Generation

1975 as the scenes of police brutality did not correspond with the current clamour over muggings (Pines 123-4). The black face all but disappeared from the television screens until the end of the decade, in concert with its political construction as an alien presence; "If we ignore them," the screen seemed to be saying, "perhaps they'll go away." July 1981 demonstrated that this was unlikely.

* * *

The three writers to be discussed in this chapter all respond in their work (perhaps not surprisingly) to the culture of violence and confrontation that pervaded British society in this period. Many contemporary reviewers felt that Wilson Harris was committing his own violent assault on the novelistic form, and did not entirely appreciate the effort. Gillian Tindall was representative of a host of mystified commentators when she described *Tumatumari* (1968) as "unusual, ambitious, probably original, but almost unreadable as a novel" (292).

Harris, though, was responding in an extraordinary way to a period that, as has been shown above, was dominated by ideological structures that passed into "fact" by their continual reiteration in Parliament and the Press. In *Black Marsden* (1972), Goodrich's trip to Namless features the self-perpetuating mentality of the Strike, and the role of the newspaper, the *Dark Rumour*, in maintaining the combative and ultimately self-destructive attitudes that sustained the conflict. This process is approached on a much larger scale in the rest of the text as Harris uses the motif of the chessboard to challenge the fixed ways of seeing which underpin societal conflict.

He continues this process in *The Angel at the Gate* (1983). The experience of the 1981 riots, the unrelenting Troubles in Ireland and the awakening concern for the global environment providing ample evidence for his thesis of a revisualisation of human perceptions. Harris does not concern himself with the existence of black people in Britain in the way that the other writers discussed here do, but his observations on British society do continually reflect back on the construction of racist ideologies.

Andrew Salkey's three London-set novels, *Escape to an Autumn Pavement*, *The Adventures of Catullus Kelly* (1969) and *Come Home, Malcolm Heartland* (1976) all appear to be firmly situated in the Realist genre which

Harris heartily rejects, and which is still associated with the West Indian novel. A defining element of each text, though, is the part fantasy, particularly sexual fantasy, played in this period of British social history.

As noted above, there was palpable relief at the appearance of a black protagonist in *Escape* grappling with his own sexual uncertainties in 1960, and rather less enthusiasm for Catullus Kelly's sexual athletics in 1969. The threat of black (male) sexuality remained a potent part of racist mythologies at this time, perpetuating the aura of lust and fear already noted in Lamming's texts. Here, Johnny Sobert in *Escape* is pursued relentlessly by his landlady; while Catullus Kelly's most challenging sexual encounter proves to be with the authoress of fascist literature. Malcolm Heartland finds that the advent of Black Power politics and the celebration of the black woman still have not purged the profound sense of prohibition that surrounds the white female body.

These texts illustrate the continued construction of black peoples in Britain as the "Other," an inassimilable mass to be kept apart as an alien threat. The question of identity (which was the focus in the first chapter) re-emerges in the recognition that two decades of immigration and existence in Britain have resulted in rejection here, and a sense of foreignness in the Caribbean. It is from this personal dichotomy that the importance of Linton Kwesi Johnson's contribution to black culture springs.

Linton Kwesi Johnson's work is a symbol of the black community's response to its continued rejection and marginalisation by white society. It was a voice of resistance, the direct result of organisations like the Caribbean Artists Movement and the Race Today Collective, providing the space to articulate an embattled existence stifled and misrepresented in the discourse of the media. Johnson's poetry is thus important because it was aimed at a black audience. His use of Jamaican dialect, and association with the emergence of the British Rastafarian movement signalled a new direction in black British culture. Confrontation, rather than assimilation was the essential theme, and the defence not just of a physical presence, but also of a cultural heritage. Furthermore, his concern with violence within the black community, as well as that directed against them by the State, signalled the start of a self-critical process that will become the subject of greater discussion in the final chapter.

2.1 Wilson Harris: Unlikely Fiction

When Wilson Harris began his published literary career with *Palace of the Peacock* in 1960 he added a completely new dimension to the growing corpus of West Indian literature. His rejection of the realist style, which had previously been synonymous with this literature, not only signalled a disassociation with the themes of identity and exile, which were the typical concerns of other West Indian writers, but began what he termed a "cycle of exploration" into the nature of human existence.

Starting from a rejection of the Realist genre as an ideological sham, he developed a literary philosophy that closely informed the content and composition of his fictional work and evolved into a highly personalised understanding of the importance of Realism in the modern age. This approach has seen his work largely misunderstood and rejected by critics who have condemned the dense unpredictability of his narrative style and pronounced it both pretentious and meaningless. In recent years, however, there has been an upsurge of academic interest in his work and Harris' proclamation by some as "the country's greatest living novelist" (Gilkes, *Literate Imagination* 9). As with George Lamming, then, some understanding of the writer's philosophical conceptions is essential to a reading of his texts.

This complex and evolving mode of thought may usefully be approached through the headings "Realism, Tradition and the Past," "Imagination, Unity and Partiality" and "Confession, Regeneration and Alchemy."

1. Realism, Tradition and the Past

In an address to the West Indian Students Union in 1964 Harris referred to what he termed the "novel of persuasion" (*Tradition* 29). This literary form he traced back to the novels of the nineteenth century, which, he said were artefacts of the process of social consolidation that characterised that age. In such novels an apparent ground of freedom and choice existed but only within certain parameters on "an accepted plane of society we are persuaded has an inevitable existence" (*Tradition* 29). In effect, an illusory freedom of choice was depicted between individuals within a frame of reference that went unchallenged.

The West Indian literature then current, he saw as belonging to this conventional mould, forming part, as it did, of the current fashion for "Social Realism." He condemned this stylised protest saying, "the novel which consolidates situations to depict protest or affirmation is consistent with most kinds of overriding advertisement and persuasion upon the writer for him to make national and political and social simplifications of experience in the world [. . .] today" (*Tradition* 29). This much has been noted in the novels discussed in the previous chapter. In Selvon and Braithwaite in particular, the kind of social education intrinsic to the texts was based upon confronting issues of racial bias as a response to the insidious propagandising of opportunistic politicking and the popular press. In the case of *To Sir, With Love*, particularly, the dangers of such a response became apparent as the "demythologised" black character emerged as a thoroughly colonised figure displaying white traits through his black skin. In all such fiction the problem has been that of a continued location within the terrain of mythologised racism. By approaching social problems through the genre of Social Realism, the writers were obliged to employ certain constructions which endorse a way of seeing, sustaining the configurations of racism in the slippage between the re-presentation of reality and the representation of reality.

As Harris developed his thoughts on realism and its promotion and effect in literature, he also used these ideas to explore lived existence. In another early essay he discusses the place of the human race in the cosmos. Our continuing survival in an overpowering and alien universe is a frail act of creation. It is, he says, frail in terms of the Universe, but authoritative in our own terms: it is all we know and it forms "the kind of world we build, the kind of living substance we realise and cherish, or the kind of dominating spirit or god we set up to chastise us" (*Tradition* 20). Ours is thus a self-made cosmos but one which is also continually evolving. Tradition in this sense is not something that may be confined to such categories as post- or pre-Columbian, Christian or pagan, ancient or modern, but should be recognised as the process in which meaning is continually generated from the past.

What Harris recognised from such a concept was the way in which notions of the real and the legacies of the past are conscripted to produce sta-

2.1 Wilson Harris: Unlikely Fiction

sis; a consolidation of the power of the dominant ideologies through the appropriation of the "real" in the age of mass communication. At this level life and text seem to merge: just as the so-called realist genre presents a distorted and circumscribed view of reality, so we are presented in our lived existence with partial histories that serve to consolidate a particularised view of human evolution and progress that obliterates or discredits the histories of other cultures. For instance, he refers to the "victor/victim stasis," the cultural legacy of conquest leading to a continual re-enactment of psychic colonisation: "Victor/victim stases are nourished from very early [. . .] in the nursery of a culture, in the school, in the cradle, in the home – these projections out, victim projecting out of himself the making of monster/victor, victor projecting out of himself the making of monstrous victim" (qtd. in Munro and Sander, "Interview with Wilson Harris" 46-7). Unlike Lamming who perceived a similar process in his Prospero/Caliban relationship, Harris goes beyond the terms of the colonial legacy and addresses the whole problem of individual existence in mass society. The perception of choice, referred to in the "novel of persuasion," he sees, in one of his more recent papers, as having been channelled into the promotion of block or uniform functions. We are all taught, he says, to operate within certain functions and not to look beyond them. He uses the example of bushmen who exercise the function of hunting and are highly skilled, but in their submersion in the task are obliged to eclipse other perceptions. In effect, they have to simplify the bush and mark their own boundaries. Harris perceives a similar process in operation in the cult of disinformation that pervades many Western societies, leading the populace to read the world, and their place in it, in a uniform manner. It is a false clarity, he says, disseminated by mass communication and paraded under the banner of the Real whilst containing the individual within mass perceptions and uniform functions (*Tradition* 15-7).

What Harris is trying to achieve in his rejection of the "novel of persuasion" is a rejection of a learned way of seeing, but in terms that far exceed those suggested by Lamming. For Harris, the novel and the imaginative writer represent a crucial space in which a circumscribed way of seeing may be challenged. Here, the "facts" of history may be confronted by its eclipsed figures, and the capacity of language to "continuously transform inner and outer formal categories of experience" set free (*Tradition* 32). The writer becomes a medium for a "lost tradition": an imaginative vessel through which that tradition may speak.

2. Imagination, Unity and Partiality

The main thrust of Harris' argument is that ideological consolidation is based upon a restriction in the flow of information: the obliteration or suspension of the already known and a perversion of the knowable. This much is evident in the notion of the block function referred to above; a restricted set of horizons are presented to the individual under the spurious banner of freedom of choice, while the indices of achievement become progressively circumscribed. In the victor/victim stasis too, self-knowledge and its attendant knowledge of others becomes increasingly derived from the oppositional images of difference, insisting on the ignorance of aspects of the relationship that do not fulfil the closure of the opposition. There are two interconnected aspects of this process that Harris confronts in his philosophy. First, he condemns what he terms the hubris of human logic and reason, and second, he attacks the illusory closure that stems from the construction of binary difference.

For Harris, human logic and reason have become the new gods in the human cosmos and our faith in them has allowed us to assume an illusory position of control over the planet. The interaction between technological progress and the natural world provides fertile ground for his arguments. Mathematics, the triumph of human abstract thinking and logic, is, for Harris, "an art, a gift of perception, of grace, of intuition" (qtd. in Fabre, "Wilson Harris" 104).

He compares the ability of humans to navigate courses through the use of formulae with that of migratory birds that achieve the same feat through instinct: "Mathematics therefore comes from some recognition in ourselves that we have lost something that the bird possesses and in losing that we enter the realm of art and science" (qtd. in Wilkinson 39). He furthermore points out that the progress of science and logic itself has in many cases sprung from "some unpredictable pool in oneself" (qtd. in Tiffin, "Wilson Harris" 24). Thus, while he does not discard the importance of reason, Har-

2.1 Wilson Harris: Unlikely Fiction

ris insists upon the role the irrational has to play in our existence and upon the necessity to attend to this realm of human potential.

It is this reliance upon logical forms that is implicit in the closure built into the modern way of seeing. In order to make sense of our cosmos and our place in it, human thought has had to drive in a singular manner that obliterates uncertainty, invests in sovereign structures and perpetuates symmetry. For Harris, though, "[w]e live in an asymmetrical cosmos, not a symmetrical cosmos. As a consequence, all the structures we erect, all the images we erect, are partial" (qtd. in Tiffin, "Wilson Harris" 27). This is a further attack on the indices of human reason. Instead of looking for the closure of binary oppositions, Harris seeks a "paradoxical unity or community of the imagination" (qtd. in Munro and Sander, "Interview with Wilson Harris" 44). There is, he says, "an unnameable centre, or unfathomable wholeness" (qtd. in Tiffin, "Wilson Harris" 24) which relates the partial image or structure; it cannot be structuralised but it does provide a certain kind of coherence as we look through the partial image towards the whole.

This is clearly Harris' own article of faith; the centre can never be materialised, an endpoint in understanding can never be achieved, and one must attend to the unconscious and the irrational in order to gesture towards the whole. This, however, is the whole point of Harris' philosophy. By recognising structures and images as partial, one can recognise the bias that is placed upon them to produce their present, apparently sovereign meaning. Closure in this respect is thus broken and in recognising partiality, one may see the potential for dialogue with other apparently alien, sovereign parts and thus to "a complex of real and genuine change in which no part assumes absolute sovereignty over the rest" (qtd. in Fabre, "Wilson Harris" 103).

This is what Harris is trying to achieve: real and genuine change through the explosion of static associations in all spheres of human existence. Real unity exists, he says, when that unity can sustain diversity within itself, rather than the strong part imposing itself upon the others (qtd. in Dommergues 95). This is a diversity that can exist between cultures (Harris' paradigm being, of course, the cultural diversity of the Caribbean and Latin America) and also in the individual mind; the recognition of an inner space, the liberation of an intuitive self from the bindings of the historical ego (Tiffin, "Wilson Harris" 24).

The clear difficulty of such a dramatic liberation from centuries of lived suppression is the task of expressing something that has been blotted out of the conscious mind. When Harris describes the necessity for a new form, he says this occurs where "new content – or 'old' content of eclipsed memory – addresses the imagination in surreal flashes or parables" (qtd. in Munro and Sander, "Interview with Wilson Harris" 45). It is important to note here that it is the content that addresses the imagination: as he puts it elsewhere, the writer is "an agent of the muse" (qtd. in Fabre, "Wilson Harris" 103). The task is thus to recognise the importance of new associations after they have emerged through the intuitive writer: "It is a question of utter obedience to intuitive clues, a question of vital concentration, a question of response to a balance of forces, apparently eclipsed voices one has been brainwashed to ignore" (Harris, *Tradition* 23).

In his fictional work, Harris approaches this element of attending to the unconscious through the use of dreams or dream-like states, automatic writing and the revision of paintings to provide the space for the unconscious to emerge. In his critical writing, Harris insists on the importance of myth as fossil, coming alive to validate the work of the imagination as part of a living substance of tradition "which nourishes us even though it appears to have vanished" (Harris *Tradition* 27). Like the revision that Da Silva's paintings undergo in *Da Silva Da Silva's Cultivated Wilderness* (1977), myth may be discovered in the imaginative work through the constant attention to intuitive clues that enter the work from the unconscious.

It is this reasoning which provides an explanation for the often-criticised difficulty of Harris' fictional texts. He indulges in free association and cites examples where he has used epigraphs or images, the "true" significance of which has only become apparent to him later. He thus lays the writer open to the same uncertainties as the reader. What gives coherence and meaning to his texts, what enables Harris to regard them as presenting in themselves a continuing cycle of exploration, is the way in which a regenerative process, rather than a retrograde chaos is achieved or suggested by the very assertion of this uncertainty.

2.1 Wilson Harris: Unlikely Fiction

3. Confession, Regeneration and Alchemy

The notion of confession is the pivotal stage where partiality turns to regeneration. The recognition of the partial (the partial sign, the partial history, the partial structure) points towards a partial knowledge or partial reasoning. In effect it is the confession of man's own partiality, of a partial existence within a greater whole that cannot be defined or dominated. Such partiality becomes most apparent in the estimation of consequences, and most pertinently in the notion of man's inability to recognise the full consequences of his actions. This aspect Harris defines most sharply in the distinction between violence and force.

Using a rather dubious metaphor in a seminar paper in 1982 ("Quest" 22), Harris compares the blow of the rapist and the "tender" blow of the bridegroom. The former is a destructive violence, while the latter is a potentially regenerative force; the two blows resemble each other but their difference is performed by their consequences. In a later interview (Wilkinson 31), he makes the same point using the image of the sculptor slicing and cutting his material: it is a violent act, but it is also an act of creation. The point he makes is that it is the ramifications of such acts that are the defining factor:

> A perception of the consequences of our actions is never immediately clear. The burden of foreknowledge [. . .] would be much too great to bear in the instant of performance. Nevertheless, a deed or act may draw upon itself a constellation of images whose strangeness [. . .] begins to prepare us for degrees of illumination and confession, degrees of comprehension and responsibility for what we have done or are still blindly doing. ("A Quest" 21)

The treatment of this subject in his fiction is based upon the illustration of the dual nature of violence and its consequences, and the implied confession that leads to a regenerative potential. This operates on both an individual and a mass scale.

In *The Secret Ladder* (1963), the surveyor, Fenwick, comes to recognise that the technology he embodies represents both progress and destruction; developing the area of the Canje he was concerned with, but simultaneously destroying the community that exists there. Fenwick as surveyor (an instrument or facet of his society) thus has to recognise the violence inherent in technological progress. In another aspect of the story, Fenwick breaks regulations and lends his hat and cape to the gauge-reader who is then killed by assassins who mistake him for Fenwick. This is the violence within; Fenwick's actions outside the dictums of his society still having their corollary in destruction.

For Harris, confession to our partiality in this kind of greater whole is our only act of redemption: "All of us are involved in action which bears consequences we cannot endure and yet, when we confess to those consequences, a doorway is opened which allows some principle to come in and restore the culture or society. Without confession there is no regenerative capacity" (qtd. in Fabre, "Interview" 7). What such confession allows is a pause in what Harris terms 'remorseless progression.' His view of history and human progress is that it is cyclical rather than linear, and it is in this sense that the concept of alchemy assumes its importance. For Harris, the three stages of the alchemical process reflect on the way the human imagination should work; the darkness of the nigredo phase being explored, leading to the illumination or dawning light of the albedo phase and moving on to the cauda pavonis or colours of the peacock phase. The important aspect for Harris is that the peacock phase leads back to the nigredo phase but on an enriched plane:

> Rather than remorseless progression, there is cyclical rebirth, a rebirth that ushers us into complete darkness [. . .] in the middle of the day. That rebirth, that complex darkness, is a miniaturisation or reductive symbol of unbearable wheels of light. It secretes a capacity for *visualisation*, a capacity to move with the indirections and mystery of interior genius, interior illumination.
>
> ("Quest" 24)

This notion of the alchemical imagination as a cycle enables what Harris terms an "infinite rehearsal" (qtd. in Fabre, "Interview" 7). Partial images or structures may be carried into a new phase but with a qualitative difference; they may thereby be approached differently and thus shatter the "tyranny of one-sided existence." This is something that Harris builds into his

2.1 Wilson Harris: Unlikely Fiction

fiction, using characters that have no sovereignty within the individual texts, and also having them resurface in other texts displaying different characteristics. It is a theme that he also extends in his critical work, pointing to the mysterious death and rebirth of human civilisations and suggesting that the dilemmas that confront our age may once have been the concerns of pre-Columbian civilisations and have led to their eclipse (Munro and Sander, "Interview with Wilson Harris" 48).

The essence of Harris' philosophy is that, on both an individual and mass scale, the human race should beware of its easy reliance on a fixed way of seeing. He addresses himself directly to the developed world, to the industrialised nations who have assumed quasi-authority over every system and structure extant on planet Earth. Nobody is innocent of this blind hubris; Harris may recognise the part ideological control plays in the maintenance of power through disinformation, but he also insists on the ability of the individual to look beyond the immediately apparent.

In the two texts to be discussed here, *Black Marsden* and *The Angel at the Gate*, this notion of individual (self-) examination may be readily discerned. The two texts complement each other through the dominant presence in each of a Marsden character as a spiritual guide for this process of examination. The decade that separates their publication dates is eloquently described in the indices of such a process.

* * *

Black Marsden was the first of Harris' novels to be set mainly outside the Guyanese landscape. Published in 1972, he had already been resident in Britain since 1959, and had had eleven novels published at the rate of one a year following *Palace of the Peacock*. His critical agenda had thus been well established by this time, and when questioned about the reasoning behind this change of location in an interview shortly after publication, Harris replied, "[t]he point one has to bear in mind is that the apparition of the landscape as it comes into the earlier novels is an apparition which I would think makes clear [. . .] that there is no absolute spiritual vessel within which the creative imagination functions" (qtd. in Munro and Sander, "Interview with Wilson Harris" 51).

He goes on to explain that part of his project is to liberate the imagination from "superstitious premises or superstitious absolutes" and suggest new juxtapositions of form that would repudiate a static way of seeing and a legacy of implacable associations. Thus, bringing the ideas and concerns formed in the Guyana novels into a European context seemed to him to be a "necessary and understandable development, triggered off by a long immersion or concentration on textures and forms" (52).

While it is clearly true that *Black Marsden* does contain the concerns and themes typical of Harris' earlier novels, what is important here is the way in which they may be read in terms of the specifically British context offered, and particularly in terms of other black writing also being published at this time.

The early Seventies was a time characterised not only by great social and economic strife in Britain, but also by a surge in black consciousness movements which, as we have seen in Selvon's *Moses Ascending*, were already claiming the works of Lamming and Salkey as powerful exponents of black culture.[10] Therefore, an interesting and significant clue to Harris' repudiation of "superstitious premises" and intervention in the current domestic debate with *Black Marsden* lies in its title.

Drawing up strict lines of allegory and metaphor is neither an easy nor desirable task with Wilson Harris, and in this text he makes a typically paradoxical start. The emphasis on 'black' in the title would seem to suggest some immediate correspondences with contemporary black literature: the rich white man takes in the poor black beggar and in the ensuing relationship, the white man comes to regain some of the spiritual strength lost in a culture dedicated for centuries to material gain. This neat correspondence falters though as it emerges in the text that Marsden is not black. In the few references to his colour, Marsden is said to be "white as chalk

---

[10] Galahad's derisive response to the idea of Moses' memoirs is accentuated by Moses' ignorance of the social and cultural role being fulfilled by the West Indian writers: "Man Moses, you are still living in the Dark Ages! You don't even know that we have created a Black Literature, that it have writers who write some powerful books what making the whole world realize our existence and our struggle" (Selvon, *Moses Ascending* 43).

2.1 Wilson Harris: Unlikely Fiction

above his bristling black beard" (31), or to have a "half-Oriental, half-Celtic" complexion (100).

What is clear then, even in this last conjunction of two ancient but widely divergent cultures, is that Harris is not going to fall prey to the predicates of emigrant literature. Instead he shifts the static associations of black and white, and in the process focuses upon other issues prevalent in the contemporary British scene from which similar block functions proceed.

The relationship between Marsden as the "Doctor of the Soul" and Clive Goodrich as a symbol of arbitrary wealth may be recognised as the focal point of the narrative. What remain less certain are the parameters of this relationship. Harris has referred to the characters he had used in earlier novels as "agents rather than sovereign devices" (qtd. in Munro and Sander, "Interview with Wilson Harris" 52). This problematised notion of character is immediately evident as the first encounter between Goodrich and Marsden is marked by the notion of each projecting from within aspects of themselves upon the other (11-2).

Through the course of the narrative Goodrich struggles on several occasions to separate "reality" from his various imaginary states, and to verify the authenticity of the existence of Marsden and his associates. The notion of Marsden as hypnotist is one of the many ways in which logical solutions to the text are presented and then undermined in the narrative. Thus, the balance of internal and external influences upon Goodrich remains enigmatic, and the reader is also invited through Harris' choice of epigraphs on the split personality to view Marsden as Goodrich's "other soul" or alter ego.

This ambiguity is important because it resists the idea that Goodrich may be viewed as the personification of the industrialised modern world being brought to book by the spectre of the ancient world for its "nightmare accumulation of wealth" (19). There is some evidence in the text to suggest that Marsden's intervention is just part of a continuing cycle of exploration for Goodrich. Harris' notion of the "infinite rehearsal" is evident here as allusions to an earlier tracing around the globe of the "contours of an implacable legend" by Goodrich (11) are recalled on the verge of his imaginary visit to Namless. Furthermore, this journey is a "*re*visualisation" and "*re*vision" (70; my italics), suggesting an earlier experience, and is itself incomplete, adding significance to Knife's remark, "[y]ou'll get to Nameless one day, Mr Goodrich, never fear. This visit or *the next*" (73; my italics).

Harris thus achieves a double significance in the character of Goodrich. On the one side, Goodrich, through his trivially acquired wealth and apparent dependence upon it as a panacea for personal and social ill, does represent a society dominated by accumulation and gain. On the other side, the very fact that Goodrich's re-sensing comes from within him (aided by the ambivalent figure of Marsden) proves that this activity is not the (dubious) privilege of the dispossessed.

This is the lynch-pin of Harris' argument; in order to achieve the revisualisation of human existence, the individual must totally revise the network of associations through which meaning and value are asserted, but (s)he must do so from within. As a textual metaphor or motif for this (self-)revision, Harris uses the binary opposition of light/white and dark/black to express Goodrich's initiation into a new way of seeing.

Harris makes his first explicit use of this motif in Goodrich's diary entry after his dream of Marsden as Camera, and his hypnotic episode in which he sees Jennifer Gorgon as a tunnel, with the light of her soul at the end of it. In this entry (written as a dialogue between the left and right hand), the ambivalent value of Light is analysed, as the light at the end of the tunnel not only acts as a guide but also as a blind, concealing the road and the self. If the light is turned on inside the tunnel the journey and the self become apparent, but the end of the road is obscured. Thus, "[w]hen freedom glares we need the deepest unravelling vision of imagination not to be stricken or deceived" (24-5).

A similar scenario is played out in Harp's account of the death of Hornby in the snow. As he relies on the light in the house to guide him back through the blizzard, he finds he has become blinded by "[a] whiteness of earth which seemed so intense it became a porous fabric of infinite darkness reaching into the sky." As he regains sight of the light in the window (thus losing sight of the road and the self), he steps through thin ice and is lost (48-9).

variation. The "blistering range of mountains" gives way to "sudden and greener" farmland (71). Signposts are marked 'TROPICAL'or 'MEDITERRANEAN' in a "family tree of contrasting elements" (72). Knife's assertion that there is a village or country or dot on the map waiting for every man suggests that the regions of Namless exist as a series of discreet enclaves, waiting to trap the individual into a hermetic landscape of the psyche (71). The notion of a chessboard landscape is affirmed by Knife as he recounts the tragedy of The Strike; "[i]t's a peculiar thing but strikes have been growing more and more into a game of chess in this part of the world. Everyone claims he is being pushed. Nobody ever does the pushing but everyone is being pushed" (73).

It is not difficult to relate the story of Namless to the domestic scene in Britain in the late Sixties and early Seventies. The idea that strikes were a major contributor to Britain's declining economic position had gained wide public credence in these years, presaging a decade of confrontation between Conservative and Labour governments and the Unions and paving the way for Thatcherism. The fact that statistics show that such a dominating concern was not warranted attests to the power of the media in shaping public opinion; a view powerfully illustrated in the *Dark Rumour*, the Namless newspaper substitute for private thinking.

To Goodrich, Namless represents the logical outcome of manufacturing capitalism; the disintegration of a society, through the greater and greater concentration upon exploitation and material gain. This is symbolised by the plight of the robot. Initially seen by Goodrich trying to pass through the eye of a needle of rock, it is described as "the collaborative nexus of sex and love, striking man and risen-up god" (76). The allusion to Christian myth reveals it as man's attempt to become God, to create a beast of burden in his own image and to take control of Nature – the triumph of technological conquest.

Goodrich leaves Namless when he has sensed its role as a model for the impulsive self-destruction of mass society. By recognising his own objective stance, he perceives that the locked binary opposition of victor and victim (the social motor from which totalitarian nemesis is generated) is not absolute. His view of the charmed circle of rocks endlessly rehearsing ritual of rise and fall (83-5) is reinforced by the spectre of violent author-

2.1 Wilson Harris: Unlikely Fiction

This last scene is recalled in Goodrich's ruminations on the Dean Bridge shortly before his imaginary trip to Namless. The two passages are related by Harris' use of the terms 'Sky' and 'Creek' as signifiers for light and dark leading Hornby to his doom (and legendary fame). The image of suicide attempts from the bridge, leaping "from Sky into Creek, sudden pouring light into inexplicable darkness," resolves itself, in Goodrich's diary (named the "Book of Infinity"), as the notion of existence as a chessboard. In this concept, the black and white squares are floating, and Goodrich comes aware of "enigmatic squares of suspended darkness and lights knitted into the pawn of himself" (51). The coincidence of the death of Mother and Harp's knits them into the same square, a square that links Doctor and Pole, and confirms the "implacable legend" that Goodrich attempted to trace in the search of the physical (seen) world (63-5).

The concept of moveable squares establishes a pattern of human existence and regeneration that evades the linear divergence of hubristic (chronological) progression:

> In the comedy of an interfused reading of the elements a capacity for genesis is born or reborn within us; a capacity to re-see our base relations, Brother Cruelty, Brother Hate – to re-shape our biased globe into moveable squares within and beyond the avalanche of greed and despair. (66)

This is an assertion of the biases within the social individual; the notion of black and white squares does not equate simplistically to the dice in global relations, but to a whole mass of experience that is denied through a learned and restricted way of seeing in a society. The blackness that Marsden thus represents is this whole mass which has been eclipsed by the light of reason. As noted in the knife and the image of the tunnel, this is not an aspect that should be embraced: Marsden is a danger as well as a treasure and to insist on the continual flux and regenerative force of the associations. Harris illustrates the notion of a static, regimented these two aspects in the "chessboard" of Namless.

The Namless landscape that Goodrich enters is not a wasteland, but an amazing and rigidly defined area

ity apparent in Knife after the enigmatic death of the double-agent (87). The compulsion towards a self-sustaining stasis is broken by the recognition of something outside it, the "deeper scrutiny or orchestration of hypothetical resources beyond that fall (of an age) so that the function of wasted lives [. . .] was transformed into an irreversible warning or motif of capacity to undermine the *hubris* of every abstract order or monument" (91).

Goodrich leaves Namless, his independent vision asserted by his rejection of Knife's interpretation of the meaning of the pipes. His self-revelations are accompanied by the "strangest chess-board of evening lights he had ever seen" (91), and he emerges as a "denuded 'I'" (94). However, just as his whole association with Marsden may be viewed as only one part of an infinite rehearsal, so his trip to Namless is only a part of that part; he has still to assert his "aloneness" with regard to Jennifer Gorgon.

Jennifer Gorgon is the archetypal *femme fatale*. Her pale and depleted lovers recall *La Belle Dame Sans Merci*, while her Gorgon ability to turn flesh into stone (or vice versa) provides the necessary duality essential to the narrative. In this context, Harris makes clear the modern root of the fascination of the Gorgon. Her first entrance looking beautiful and fashionable in a spring coat is denigrated by Marsden: "God knows how old the thing is and why it doesn't fall to pieces on her back" (13). Goodrich's subsequent hypnotic episode reveals the importance of Marsden's statement, as he recognises the female body as social garment; as a continually fetishised article in itself regardless of the fashions of the day. The reference to a "revolutionary French fashion plate," a "glossy magazine studio" and the "language of the newspapers" (14) amply identifies the source of this continued fascination.

After Goodrich's dream of Marsden as Camera in which Marsden and Jennifer stand naked together while Marsden touches her nipples, Jennifer's role in the Marsden\Goodrich relationship is to act as a point of conflict. She is the agent through which Goodrich will overlook the treasure which Marsden's teaching presents and will instead be locked into sterile and static conflict. She is also the spur that releases Goodrich into his aloneness, from falling too far under one influence. Interestingly, Jenni-

91

fer's part as the Gorgon is distinguished by the shift of emphasis from the eyes as the source of Gorgon potency, to the breasts.

As noted above, Jennifer's appearance in Goodrich's dream describes her being touched on the nipples by Marsden. Her head has been entangled in her nightdress in her haste to absorb light, and her breasts become "blind counterfeit eyes" which both cheat and fascinate Goodrich (21). If one remembers the notion of unscrewing the head of Jennifer to look into her tunnel\garment in Goodrich's first hypnotic episode, a motif for the blinded Gorgon with her breasts as substitute eyes becomes apparent.

The persona of a blinded Gorgon does not decrease Jennifer's potency. Where Maes-Jelinek and Searl suggest that the unscrewed head of the French fashion plate may make the stare of the Gorgon powerless (22), it is possible to assert that in Goodrich's various imaginary states, it is the breasts that in modern times contain the fascination of the Gorgon. Harris' reference to the threat posed to fiction by the "James Bonds of the day" (qtd. in Munro and Sander, "Interview with Wilson Harris" 45) may provide some clue to the distraction sexuality poses to a society. The reference to John Knox as being admired for his Puritanism in the nineteenth century, but condemned in the eighteenth century suggests the way in which social control may be imposed through the promotion of vicarious moral codes: "Read the times in which we live with ages past" declares Marsden (41), and Jennifer characterises the present age with the receipt of a text entitled *How To Fuck* through the post (44).

The argument that Marsden presents in the Camera dream to counter Goodrich's outrage at the sight of him (Marsden) and Jennifer naked together, is based on such moral inconsistencies. He states, "[w]e live in a penny-wise, pound-foolish age [. . .] We make a fuss about a few moral pence when millions of mortal lives are cheap" (22). Jennifer, as the suitably ambivalent "virtuous Salome," provides just this kind of distraction. As the woman in Namless (identified by the "pointed eyes of her breasts"), she is the lure that draws Goodrich helplessly onto the Namless chessboard: "Had he pushed her or had he been pushed by her?" (80). When she appears with a mud-pack on her face covering one eye, Goodrich responds as though the workings of a fantastic machine of illusion has been exposed

2.1 Wilson Harris: Unlikely Fiction

before him. He sees Jennifer now as "so many pounds of flesh"; as "[t]he hideousness of all charm, the hideousness of all compulsion" (59).

In the end, it is Jennifer who finally causes Goodrich to break with Marsden. It is an ending that has already been anticipated in the text. Almost exactly halfway through, Goodrich has a dream in which a blind woman passes her blindness onto him and warns him that he must keep a secret. Goodrich feels a "validation of identity," as though "a mysterious cycle of contrasting spaces peculiar to time had come full circle at last" (53). This sense of finality and strength falters with the entrance of Marsden, as the new vision that Goodrich has attained teaches him that he is in Marsden's debt; "[o]ver the past months he had given clothing, food, money to Marsden but it was Marsden who symbolised the Bank from which he had drawn rather than the beneficiary to whom he had given" (54).

Goodrich recognises a "dangerous hypnotic legacy" in this equation – the notion of a giving becoming a receiving is enacted in Namless where the Authorities' apparent submission to the demands of the Workers results in the Workers' greater subjugation. This sudden revisualisation demoralises Goodrich, and he again thinks in terms of violence towards Marsden as he suspects Jennifer is Marsden's agent conducting the dream scene. Marsden reasserts his power and explains Goodrich's reaction to the dream in terms of "over-compensation ritual": "You start out in the first place with a feeling of over-stimulation and then you begin to feel cheated, miserable, drained on hand, or endangered out of all proportion on the other. You are steeped in over-compensated sunset [. . .] or over-compensated sunrise" (56).

In the resolution of the text, the "secret" that validates Goodrich is that of Jennifer's pregnancy (and one may like to speculate on the correlation between this and the "upright coitus" in Namless). Her revelation to Goodrich startles him back into a facile reliance on money as a panacea, and into a position of direct competition with Marsden who knows nothing of Jennifer's condition; "[f]or this moment at least I have more of her than Marsden" (98). Goodrich's "over-stimulation" is signified by the purchase of a flame-coloured shirt (symbolising both over-compensated sunrise and sunset?), and his corresponding reaction to Marsden's knowledge of the situation is the impetuous and violent eviction of Marsden and his associates from his house and life.

For Eva Searl and Hena Maes-Jelinek, the resolution of the text presents many problems. Marsden's rejection is also the rejection of the dispossessed with whom Marsden has been associated. It also suggests irreconcilability as a potentially fruitful relationship is abruptly terminated, as it is in Namless, when greater effort could have achieved co-operation. On the other hand, "a facile reconciliation [. . .] would obviously be too easy a way out of the conflict" (29). Harris himself sees Goodrich as having come into his "aloneness" through his association with Marsden, which he clearly regards as a positive step (Fabre, "Interview" 15). Elsewhere, he describes the decision to send Marsden away as having come up through layers of the conditioned self, and breaks through still clothed in those conditions or consciousness. Marsden in one sense expects this decision and welcomes it, but is also waiting to "take Goodrich's face" (Tiffin, "Wilson Harris" 28). The ending is thus fraught with indecision and exists as one of a series of quasi-endpoints in Goodrich's journey through the layers of the self.

Harris uses the phrase, "a post-hypnotic threshold" (111), to describe Goodrich's situation at the end of the text. The altered consciousness that Marsden has helped to evoke in him could be made to appear as a dream episode out of touch with lived reality: Marsden and the others have gone and Mrs Glenwearie returns and regards Goodrich's shirt and tie with her usual prosaic manner. There is only the sense of a "strange inner tide of resolution" (111) to suggest that Goodrich has, in Harris' alchemical terms, returned to cauda nigredo on an enriched plane. In the next text to be studied, a similar process may be observed with the paradoxical twist added that, while the use of hypnosis is a declared fact, so a stronger sense of lived reality seeps through the text.

* * *

Although *The Angel at the Gate* is the next of Harris' novels in which a Marsden character figures prominently in a British setting, this text provides a striking contrast to *Black Marsden*. As Maes-Jelinek correctly notes, by this time Harris' concern had broadened from the conflict be-

2.1 Wilson Harris: Unlikely Fiction

tween groups or individuals to the plight of "imperilled humanity around the globe" ("Altering Boundaries" 147). By the early Eighties, fears for the global environment were finally gaining some public attention and, where co-operation seemed essential, Harris perceived a world characterised by domestic riots and international crises. One may thus see the significance of an altogether more beneficent Marsden character in this text, and the shift of attention from a solitary and wealthy Goodrich figure to an impoverished and divided "family of Man." The remote foreboding of Namless is replaced here by the lived crisis of fire and famine; in a sense, the deprivation of the Developing World has come home to roost. The journey of self-discovery in this text is thus not the privilege of the idle rich, but the spiritual necessity of the dispossessed.

The family unit that Harris describes is one finely balanced between crisis and Paradise. Mary Stella Holiday works for, and is treated by Father Joseph Marsden for a "physical and nervous *malaise*" (8) in which she creates separate lives for herself as Mary, the sister of Sebastian, and Stella, Sebastian's wife. As Mary she works for Marsden and presents an image of calm capability; as Stella, she is the beleaguered wife and mother who attempts suicide. Sebastian is an unemployed amphetamine addict, the latter condition being directly attributed to the former in the text, as are his violent outbursts. Harris' efforts to suggest both childhood trauma and adult deprivation as causal links to Mary Stella's and Sebastian's psychoses, add significance to the position of John, the potential "miracle child," and witness to his parents' violent decline.

Maes-Jelinek identifies Marsden's role here as the Joseph figure combining with Mary to represent the humanised parents of Christ ("Altering Boundaries 149). The continued reference to John as the "miracle-child," and the implied "immaculate conception" as Stella lives the role of Mary to absent her consciousness from her sex life with Sebastian, serve to encourage this interpretation.

Harris thus presents the family as a microcosm of "endangered paradise" (16). Choices and alternative perceptions are offered up, diverse associations and ancestry explode the myth of a fixed psychical lineage, and John is there (with his female counterpart) to represent potential regeneration or degeneration. Harris uses the motif of vision blindness as a signifier for this process and again he promotes attention to the unconscious as the essential activity for regeneration. As will be seen, Marsden's use of automatic writing as part of Mary Stella's therapy is a mechanism through which she comes to accept and recognise her unconscious self (or selves).

He validates this method with W. B. Yeats' significantly titled book, *A Vision* (1925), in which Yeats used his wife's automatic writing as a source of literary inspiration (107). At the same time, Marsden offers himself as a *tabula rasa* to accommodate and expose Mary Stella's other "fictional lives," working on the proposition that the visions of alternative consciousness should be attended to and not denied. Harris' own voice is thus more easily discerned in this Marsden despite his textual role as the "no-man's land writer" (23). He begins, though, with the blind.

The opening scene of the text is that of Sebastian reading Stella's "suicide" note. His eyes are "bright, yet curiously blind" (9), and this aspect is reiterated throughout the following pages as Mary arrives and prepares their meal. Such eyes, it is said, mirror the "veiled darkness of the community of the world" (11), and the proposition is later put forward that it was "less an outer stiffness of body and more an inner deprivation of mind that cast its scales over his eyes" (33). Sebastian is thus a representative product of his society; his violence is attributed to a need for attention whilst unemployed, as is his addiction to amphetamines and his sexual (ab)use of Stella. These attempts at self-respect and self-assertion are indicative of the indices by which Sebastian measures his life; his "blindness" is that of the block function described earlier. He has only typically masculine role-models by which to gauge his self-esteem and in "failing" to match these standards, he comes to "see" less and less in an introvert perspective which concentrates solely on immediate and short-term satisfaction: "meaningless lusts and meaningless hatreds" (15).

Sebastian's use of drugs is typical in this respect. Harris' own views on the (illegal) use of drugs are connected with his views on partiality. People who take drugs, he says, are deceived. They are taking an easy, yet false, passage to Heaven, experiencing a false "total ecstasy" that, if real, the body would not be able to endure (Fabre, "Interview" 4 and 9). Sebastian's "toilet paper diary" is of this order. He obtains amphetamines, thereby running into debt and alienating his family and doctor in the process. The

2.1 Wilson Harris: Unlikely Fiction

short-term relief that he gains yields only cryptic, self-referential messages. This may be compared with Mary Stella's automatic writing, which is a productive part of her therapy: Sebastian may have been recording "seeds of greatness [. . .] if so he was oblivious of it" (35).

Sebastian's circumscribed perceptions are made clear in the way he sees Stella. As Stella views her naked body in the mirror she reflects on the "automatic bite of Sebastian's blind, metallic eyes" (48). The aspect of blindness in the Gorgon in *Black Marsden* is reversed here: her ability to fascinate men with her body has been superseded by men's ability to make themselves blind. The "automatic bite of metallic" eyes suitably suggest the motor reaction of block function. This is confirmed in Paradise Park where the warden wears the same unseeing, metallic eyes and rattles out the automatic dictates of the park regulations and the automatic view that a "good old shooting war" would rectify a wayward younger generation (67-8).

Mary Stella's journey of self-discovery in the text begins with her sharing Sebastian's blindness. Her refusal to "visit" Stella, supposedly in hospital after her suicide attempt, expresses her refusal to accept her own psychic condition:

> Mary's eyes looked back to Stella's through Sebastian's [. . .] and looked at her with a shadow on his face that seemed to mirror all three. His eyes were deceptively open but their threaded look, threaded faces disconcerted her. Were they kind, universal eyes or cruel, universal eyes that she and Stella shared with him? Whose eyes was she seeing? (11)

This shadowy and personalised acknowledgement of shared perception is advanced when Mary surprises Anancy in Marsden's study. In the shock of discovery, Mary immediately fears rape and Anancy immediately tries to clear himself of theft as the mythical racist threat and lived reality of "the significant minority of blacks" are both enacted in this instant. Then, Mary experiences the "material and immaterial prescence of millions enfolding them," experiences "twin-memory" and her own sense of vulnerability are translated into the learned vulnerability which is the legacy of a living history of slavery and oppression: she feels "suddenly black and naked herself" (25).

That Anancy had actually entered the study in order to look at the copy of More's *Utopia* that Mary had placed there reflects not only on a whole history of enforced migration followed by rejection (from a promised Paradise?), but also on the psychic space white societies reserve to at once fear, despise and desire black populations:

> She had summoned him or he her, though when that summons, that call had gone forth was buried in layers of desire, the desire for pigmented luxuries, necessities, commodities of harsh and sweet emotion [. . .] That was the key to every white or black, schizophrenic Cupid who had afflicted her in afflicting him. (26)

This is the start of a series of experiences in which Mary Stella progressively learns to "see" correspondence rather than difference, to break out of the simplified (and thus divisive) perceptions of block function. Marsden teaches Mary to aspire to a "rainbow-bridge" on which flies the "butterfly of existence" continually reflect(ing) anew each individual history or individual body" (17). It brings one into conversation with the "family tree" between heaven and earth, transmitting like satellite branches around the globe: "The difference was [. . .] that 'family tree news' came out of parallel universes to television cocoons, universes of unfurled wings on which had been inscribed events otherwise sunken into a sea of consciousness" (17).

The "parallel universe" of televisual images is a dominant one in Harris' endangered paradise. Sebastian obtains his speed from a dealer outside the White City Television studios, and his toilet paper diary converts the drug into a "White City script" (code for prescription), and his pusher into a "producer." It is thus significant that when Stella begins to confront her beleaguered self it is in the "perceived coffin or television box" of an imaginary television studio (44). It is here that she recognises herself as Stella, a "mask Mary wears, a way of coping with truth" (44), and to identify her ancestral link with Mack the knife, Jenny Diver, Sukey Tawdrey and Lucy Brown. In supplanting the television studio with a "studio of place, studies of earth and sea and sky" (46), Mary comes to apprehend a greater reality.

2.1 Wilson Harris: Unlikely Fiction

Mary's association with Mack and the others imbues her with cross-cultural understanding. Mack, her father, is already noted as having a black antecedent (18), and it is later revealed that he has a black child from an earlier marriage – Sukey Tawdrey, the corresponding "daughter of man" to the miracle child, John (94). When Mary takes John to Paradise Park, hoping to establish Paradise through continued reconciliation with the memory of her mother (Jenny Diver), she is surprised instead by the appearance of Sukey. John steals Sukey's eyes ("unique child-creator with creatress eyes in his head," [70]) and, in doing so, he defies the lineage of grandmother to grandson (hence the absence of Jenny) and asserts the "marriageable creation" of shared perception, the "mutual genius of flower and bird" (66).

In stealing Sukey's eyes, John unites the two branches of the family of Man. John is the spiritual inheritor of Marsden's almost legendary presence; "[w]ho doesn't know Marsden of Angel Inn? Your antecedents and my antecedents were taught by him in India, the West Indies, South America, USA, Africa, everywhere" (91). His may be termed an intellectual presence; he is remembered as a teacher (and this is the role he fulfils for Mary Stella), and Mary's imaginary trip to Planet Bale reveals it as the landscape of his brain. As a dominant spiritual and global presence, Marsden's influence is coming to an end. His world has been characterised not only by the continual background references to the incidents of fire and famine (the hostage crisis, the Troubles in Ireland, the Brixton riots), but also by the notion that the achievements of civilisation, "aeroplanes, nuclear rockets, fantastic buildings, fast trains, ships, cathedrals," are an indication of that civilisation's own immaturity (37).

By wearing Sukey's eyes, John embodies the regenerative potential of new perception; "[s]omewhere in the depths of nature, brain and womb had randomly married under an elusive regime of grace to lighten and darken the human heart" (p.70). This is the beginning of the "aroused kingdom of mothers" (84) that Marsden recognises as his successors. The incident in the Park allows Mary to see common racial ancestry through Sukey Tawdrey and the significance of Jenny Diver in the "compulsive imageries of Mother Care in bleak recession" (75). It is the recognition of these two threads, or facets of her being, that presages the "success" of Mary Stella's therapy and the potential saviour of the family of man.

The care that Jenny Diver represents is the community of responsibility, the gesture towards the recognition of consequences instead of the blind progress evident in Marsden's world. From this perspective (the perspective of "curative doubt") the stain of a drunken man's vomit on the pavement is the colour of gold "to buy food for millions," reflecting the criminal wastage of the developed countries in a starving world (80). Similarly, Mary sees Stella in the street bearing the global wounds of a world where societal violence (in this case, in South Africa) is not confined to its actuation but is part of the maintenance of a global status quo (110-1). Mary watches Mother Diver protect Sebastian from imaginary prosecution by the law for possession, questioning the category of guilt and filling her with "an indescribable cosmic tenderness" (81-2). The "aroused kingdom of mothers" is one in which condemnation is tempered by curative doubt.

The lesson of cross-culturalism that Sukey Tawdrey represents is of a similar nature, but more extensive. The tale of her conception is recounted in an exchange between Khublall and Jackson, two characters that "migrate" into the narrative after Marsden's death. Sukey Tawdrey is a stage name used by generations of her female ancestors all called Josephine (a female Marsden?); she is the incarnation of "bought-and-sold peoples around the globe consenting to their new black-and-white masters" (96). Jackson's memory of her mother's strip-tease jazz and rag-time routine recalls Mary's encounter with Anancy. The shared vulnerability that exists there is echoed here, as Sukey uses her commodified nakedness as a signifier for all such perceptual fetishisms and anxieties; "her auction block strip-tease was [. . .] the echo of my nakedness rather than hers. It was a way of making me see with her body presented to me like a commodity how vulnerable I was" (95-6).

If Dickson's experience in *The Emigrants* exemplifies the fetishised black body in white society, then Mary and Anancy enact the more tortuous interplay of lust and fear in the confrontation between black and white. Sukey and Jackson, as black American and black West Indian respectively, play out a global problem in ideological perceptions which is Harris' ultimate concern. Their struggle for ascendancy within their relationship and possession of their child, Sukey, recalls Mary Stella and Sebastian's own struggle with John as their "hostage to love and fortune" (36). This continual conflict between ever-new combinations of adversaries is the lived reality of the perpetual rise and fall of the rocks in Namless; the stasis of old conflict finding new expression.

The projected union of John and Sukey is thus attributed greater significance than that of black and white, or male and female. Such categories Harris rejects, showing the difference and complexity that such crass denominations conceal. Instead, Sukey is "Jackson's animal, divine child" as John is Mary Stella's "human, divine child" (104). John's immaculate conception contrasts with Sukey's profoundly physical one. Jackson is "a good horse" beneath her mother in bed (99), while Jackson sees the animal in her mother, typically, through her eyes; "I see them as if they had fallen out of the head of a black madonna into animal's eyes, bird's eyes" (95). Sukey thus represents not just cross-cultural vision but the potential of a revisualisation linked to the animal world.

Khublall reads this potential in terms of the anomaly between the human and animal kingdoms where decoration and colour is a female characteristic in the former, and a male characteristic in the latter (100-1). This inversion is prefigured by Jackson becoming confused in his tale of Sukey's conception and upbringing. He refers to his wife as the father (103) and says, "[s]he was male [. . .] I conceived" (102). Khublall extends this reversal across the boundaries of species, reinterpreting all aspects of behaviour. Jackson's "veiled and adorned [. . .] dress of words" becomes "logically feminine" while Khublall's sober clothing becomes "animal-female" (101). It remains a question of perception, of looking beyond accepted ways of seeing. For Khublall, to overcome the division between "'fictional human divine' and 'fictional animal divine'" requires "mutual angels or daemons with a capacity to dislodge the terror of the ignorant blind, the proud blind, the terror that one may learn to see *through* each and every blind in oneself into the arts of the genius of love within" (104-5).

The blindness that Harris has been erecting and collapsing throughout the text thus emerges as one of the "dominating spirits or gods we set up to chastise us." The notion of "curative doubt" becomes a means for the suspension of (self-)condemnation and (self-)oppression because it does not suggest a new and perfect way of seeing that would conflict with Harris' notion of partiality, but would rather encourage the acceptance of the partial:

> All voices that claim to be divine are to be distrusted [. . .] Nature's crude therapy is the seal of deafness to reality, seal of blindness to reality, that it plants over our eyes and ears [. . .] When that seal lifts a little [. . .] one falls under the action of another protection, a protective grace. And even then what one begins to hear and to see needs to be accepted as partially arisen marvels of conception within still biased appearance, still biased voice, still biased sight, still biased sense, still biased nature.
> (109)

Harris ends the text on a slightly more positive note than *Black Marsden*. Where Goodrich is left feeling "utterly alone," Mary Stella is left with the realisation that to be whole is to recognise the partiality of the self and to endure the "traffic of many souls" (126). Where Goodrich had just rejected Marsden and his companions from his house, Mary Stella is reflecting on the making of a new community of the self, armed not with a "strange inner fire of secret resolution," but the awareness of curative doubt.

There is, thus, a strong sense in this text of the urgency of a new way of seeing. The ironic detail of a discarded newspaper carrying the headlines of pollution at Cramond in *Black Marsden* (62) finds its expression in this text in the backdrop of the hostage crisis and the Brixton riots, in the ready association of Sebastian, Jackson and Khublall through their unemployment and the abused sexuality of Lucy Brown, Stella and Jackson again. "Progress" here is depicted as a general decay in which parity is achieved through a slump to the lowest common denominator. Harris' easily criticised narrative style stands as a remarkable attempt to illuminate the ideological and perceptual means through which this decline is sustained. In what may be a nice piece of understated Harrisonian irony in the text, Mary sees a newspaper headline, "AMERICAN HOSTAGES HOME FOR CHRISTMAS?" and thinks to herself, "Unlikely fiction" (54). It is easy to wonder which is the more unlikely.

2.2 Andrew Salkey: The Middle Man

Andrew Salkey, like Wilson Harris, might easily have been the subject of discussion in Part One. Born in Panama of Jamaican parents, he was sent to live in Jamaica when he was two and came to England in 1952, only two years after Selvon and Lamming, to take an English Literature degree at London University. He did not, however, have his first novel, *A Quality of Violence*, published until 1959 by which time both Selvon and Lamming were comparatively well-established writers. Like Harris also, Salkey's literary output since has been prolific, but, unlike him he has received very little critical attention. *Quality* and his next novel, *Escape to an Autumn Pavement*, were both well received at their time of publication and still merit attention in most surveys of West Indian literature published since. However, there have not been any recent comprehensive studies of his work, and there remains a general lack of secondary material.

This perhaps has much to do with the timing of Salkey's work. Harris' reputation has grown with some concerted critical appreciation of his work, while Linton Kwesi Johnson must be recognised as a pioneer in black British culture. By contrast, Salkey appears to be a throwback to the tradition of Social Realism in West Indian literature stretching back to Mendes and James. What compels attention to Salkey's work, though, is his different experience of emigrant life and the different perspective that is evident in his fiction. Lamming's assertion in *Pleasures* that Salkey's work (along with several others) is "shot through and through with the urgency of peasant life" (*Pleasures* 38), was quickly betrayed in the same year by the publication of *Escape* which was to subtly extend the boundaries of emigrant fiction.

Lamming's remarks were premissed upon *Quality*. This text is set in a remote Jamaican village during the drought of 1900 and describes the growing influence of Pocomania as a response to this crisis. Apart from *Anancy's Score* (1973), a book of short stories based on the Anancy folktales, however, Salkey has not returned to the peasant theme in his subsequent adult fiction, concentrating instead on an apparently more personal source of inspiration for his fiction. As Daryl Dance puts it,

[a]fter *A Quality of Violence* (1959) his later novels generally focus on a weak, aimless, lost, ineffective middle-class young man, for all intents and purposes fatherless, unable to determine who he is and what he wants, struggling in a world that is basically corrupt, racist, evil and absurd. ("Andrew Salkey" 419)

This equates reasonably well with Salkey's own biography. One notes that he did not meet his own father, who had remained in Panama to support his family from his businesses there, until he was thirty-two. The middle-class element is important too. The hopelessness that one senses in these texts is significantly different from that expressed by Lamming when he identified a disinterested middle-class as a "push-factor" in the emigration of the Caribbean writers and artists. Salkey's characters recognise the comparative privilege of their background and education, but feel unable to convert this privilege into potency.

His third novel, *The Late Emancipation of Jerry Stover* (1968), depicts the fate of a young middle-class, depressed by the neo-colonial atmosphere of the Civil Service, seeking release in prolonged and aimless drinking binges, and toying with peasant and Rastafarian lifestyles in the absence of a meaningful social role. Johnnie Sobert in *Escape* also pronounces on the reality of his Jamaican middle-class status:

> Look! I'm unskilled. I'm puffed up with my own importance. I'm a drifter. A dreaming prig! And a coward into the bargain. A moral one at that [. . .] There are a few families who are aspiring to that sort of middle-class position. In some weird way, these are ready for it. They have the necessary trappings, the deceitfulness, the narrowness, the smugness, the holier-than-thou attitudes – all this plus a deep-rooted, working-class mentality. (47)

It might thus be said that the difference between Lamming and Salkey is that where Lamming's characters left in order to achieve something, Salkey's characters leave because there is nothing to achieve. This distinction remains with Salkey's characters throughout and is evident in the way they are removed from the emigrant community, not physically, in the manner noted in *To Sir*, but mentally isolated in the way they view them-

2.2 Andrew Salkey: The Middle Man

selves in relation to the society they live in, and, in the case of his London novels, the society they have left behind. Lamming's assertion that most West Indians of his generation were born in England, does not then apply here, as Salkey's characters fail to identify, not just with the emigrant community, but also with any social group at all.

In the three texts to be discussed here, *Escape*, *The Adventures of Catullus Kelly* and *Come Home, Malcolm Heartland*, each of the protagonists has a main preoccupation around which the plot seems to revolve; Johnnie Sobert's uncertain sexuality, Catullus Kelly's hedonistic exploration of London and Malcolm Heartland's political debate on return. Because of the centrality of their middle-class characteristics, there is some justification for regarding each of them as individual facets of a core emigrant personality. In this they would assume something of the Moses Aloetta role in Selvon's London, responding to the changing conditions of emigrant life in the metropolis, dealing with their own exile and planning their return. Malcolm Heartland's reflections on his exile and intention to return encourage a sense of closure in this last text:

> He remembered how long it had taken him to come to that decision: the years and years in London during which he hardly ever wanted to think about Jamaica or the Caribbean; the self-contempt he nurtured in order to distance himself from the anguish and solitude of under-development, which, he sensed, in his dreams and nightmares, would follow him wherever he went. Escape had been all then. He had found an uneasy spot in which to hide but it had been better than nothing, far better than struggling against the stultifying reality of home. (143)

With the notion of reality existing at home, fantasy becomes a safe harbour in exile. The different characters may be seen to be performing the most appropriate roles for escape from the society in which they are living. Something of a paradox thus emerges as the writer, who appears to be in the mainstream of West Indian realism, in fact displays the important part that fantasy plays in the construction of reality. In this respect, his association with the work of Wilson Harris may seem more comprehensible.

Writing Home

* * *

When *Escape to an Autumn Pavement* was published in 1960 it was greeted by press reviews that enthused about its apparent difference. Keith Waterhouse's reaction to *Escape* in *The New Statesman* noted earlier, was endorsed by the sleeve notes to the original edition saying, "[i]t is stimulating to find a West Indian hero wrestling with a problem like his own sexuality instead of being buried exclusively in the problems of his colour and exile" (63). Such sentiments attest not simply to a supposed weariness of the themes of identity and exile in black literature; (white) British sexuality was itself very much on trial in these years.

The Wolfenden Report into homosexuality and prostitution and the "Chatterley trial" were both signs of a society trying to contain sexual liberation and re-impose the moral order of pre-War Britain. The family unit as a site for social control was seen to be under threat from the evils of sexual transgression, a threat intensified by the racist mythologies surrounding (black) immigration. Under these circumstances it is easy to see the potential appeal of a "hero" like Johnnie Sobert.

This much accepted, however, it is perhaps surprising to note that the issue of sexuality does not arise until the end of Book One, nearly halfway through the text. By this time, the reader has traversed the familiar terrain of the emigrant novel; the bedsit, nightclub and barbers shop all feature, as do drugs, pimping, miscegenation and the full spectrum of English racism. These scenes are important because their very familiarity serves to establish Sobert in the role of outsider. Rather than blending into the emigrant community, Sobert stands apart from both the West Indian community and the black American G.I.'s who frequent the club where he works. The middle-class upbringing, which is the root of his isolation, does not bring him to Ricky Braithwaite's position of trying to assert his acceptability to white society; his is a more complete cultural isolation. Thus, when Salkey tries to establish Sobert's character in Book One, his sexuality is not important so much as his social angst. Instead he uses allusion to contemporary English literature to emphasise social dislocation before the issue of sexuality.

Sobert's disaffected middle-class identity and cultural dislocation compel comparison with John Osborne's Jimmy Porter. Salkey encourages this

2.2 Andrew Salkey: The Middle Man

association opening the dialogue in the text with Mrs Blount's question, "[w]hy are you so angry, Mr Sobert?" and then employing the clipped sentences of stage directions to describe some familiar scenes in the Trado's room in Mrs Blount's house:

> Furniture. Nice hire purchase look about it. Sexy-boy Trado is sitting in an armchair. Quite obviously reading *The Observer*. Quotes Ken Tynan in the same way a Jamaican peasant quotes the Bible. Sexy-girl Trado is playing with the handle of the old lady's vacuum-cleaner. Also sprawling in armchair number two. Carpet by the mantlepiece a trifle threadbare. (19)

Tynan was, of course, the first enthusiastic reviewer of *Look Back in Anger*.

The pervasive misogyny and theme of emasculation that accompany Sobert's relationship with Fiona in Book Two enable a continued comparison between the two characters, but there is not a strict analogy to be drawn here.[11] Sobert's antagonism ('anger' would not be the correct term) is directed as much against himself as it is against society both in Britain and in the Caribbean. This confused exchange, between failed and thwarted responsibility to the islands, is made clear in the way Sobert tries to inwardly devalue or dismiss his belief in Caribbean development and rights. His outburst to Fiona on West Indian identity and cultural disinheritance ends with the thought, "[w]hy did I talk such crap?" (49). His reverie at the club on the "success" of his exile ends on a similarly bitter note:

> Things are great. I'm a very happy man! What more could I really want? Total independence for my little archipelago of a territory? More loans for the regional governments? More enthusiasm for the publication and sale of regional books within the region? More adult education? [. . .] Of course not. I'm basically selfish [. . .] Not interested in the land, in agricultural improve-

---

[11] See Dollimore (65-8) and his discussion of the language of emasculation in Jimmy Porter's speech. A similar analysis might be applied to Sobert's misogynistic discourse.

ment and development. Not conscious of nationalism and growth and pride and independence and wealth and the rest. Used to be interested in the Yankee dollar earned on farms in the South; interested now only in the punctured pound earned by magic in industrial England. (32)

This kind of mental dialogue is a distinguishing feature of the text and it introduces an important element of fantasy into Sobert's character. This at once attests to his desire to escape the trappings of his colonial middle-class background, and his inability to do so. This is first evident after his outspoken support for the Colonial Welfare and Development schemes with Mrs. Blount when he encounters the Indian tenant, Shakuntala Goolam, on the stairs. In the narrative voice he refers to her as a "thing" and a "thick piece of curry," and then falls into further reverie speculating on her background:

> What's she, after all? A student of something or another. Law, I bet. Crazy state of affairs! Coloured territories (shameful epithet that) in the near future will be thick with wigs and gowns and silks, dear God, and not a damn' soul qualified to look after a simple thing like the land [. . .] Dirty thing, the land! Not for middle-class aspirants! Import a Scot or a Welshman. He'll make the necessary plans. Damn' good builders of bridges, canals, factories etc. (13)

The tones are those of the British Raj at its most bigoted. It is a piece of fantasy conjured up by images of Sobert's own colonial oppression and encouraged by his desire to distance himself from any colonial empathy. It is notable that when Shakuntala tries to broach the subject of Sobert's hostility, he is unable to respond decisively as it is not the individual he is reacting against so much as the colonial association (57).

A similar piece of role-playing is evident in the confrontation between Trado and Sobert over some unpaid back rent. The conflict between Sobert's thoughts and his actions are again made clear as he mentally considers two responses to Trado's increasingly racist diatribe:

2.2 Andrew Salkey: The Middle Man

> Can't let the jackass get away with all this! Might as well jump him and be over with it. Surely it's the only way to deal with a craphound like Trado. Of course there's no use behaving like a civilised chap [. . .] the way a little gentleman is brought up to behave; the way up to the bloody stars! I'll just mess his face about a bit; and as I'm about it, I might as well smash his little library-cum-castle of a room. Won't touch Mrs Trado, though. Wouldn't do to. (20)

In the end, Sobert does neither and walks unhappily out of the room ruminating at once upon his own cowardice and his means to raise the necessary cash. The role of the "civilised chap," as the letters from his mother demonstrate, is the role into which Sobert has been raised. The last sentence shows his inability to liberate himself, even imaginatively, from the dictates of this upbringing.

What Sobert is trying to escape through his exile and through the way he lives his exile, is a sense of frustrated responsibility to West Indian society. His adoption of antagonistic positions in the various episodes of Book One is a deliberate attempt to attain an intellectual detachment from his sense of guilt and frustration. It is a confused state of mind that he projects onto Ringo, a West Indian student he meets at the barber's. Ringo maintains his commitment to the development of the islands and sees his academic qualifications, gained in England, as positive attributes to take back to the Caribbean. Sobert admires this position, but he cannot bring himself to regard it as authentic:

> Must talk some more to Ringo. He has the kind of faith that I envy. A kind of vision that seems like a strength. What the hell's his vision exactly, though [. . .]? Despite the love of degrees and all that, he has a calm I envy. How did he come by it [. . .]? Must have found the calm over here, somewhere. Possibly he's that way because something's dead inside. I'll get that way in time, I suppose. (68)

When the issue of sexuality enters the text with Fiona's seduction of Sobert on the Heath, the social and ideological significance of such a liaison has already been established. Fiona's past involvement with the African, Joseph, and the overridingly sexual nature of her attraction for Sobert, suggests a participation in the myths of black male sexuality. Similarly, Sobert is sensitive to the dual significance of the white woman to the black man. Fiona's description of Joseph using her as a "beating stick for the white man's plunder of Africa" (42) maintains a significance for the way Sobert is perceived in white society. He is also keen to escape the significance of such a relationship in the Caribbean: "Shade's the thing. Could very well be the reason for my coming to England where I can get a girl a million shades lighter than myself. Just to show the Jamaican and Panamanian middle-classery where it gets off. Crap, again!" (77-8).

Salkey uses two sub-plots to suggest potential role models for Sobert's situation. In the first, the barmaid at the club, Biddy, becomes pregnant by one of the black G.I.'s, DuBois B. Washington. In the second, Larry the barber appears at the club demonstrating his new affluence with a "blonde" whom he refers to as a "piece-a-flesh" (116) and a "piece-a-excess-profit-tax" (117).

Sobert feels uneasy with both scenarios, seeing in them a fulfilment of the stereotypical roles he is trying to avoid. It is under these circumstances that the notion of Sobert's sense of empathy with Dick enters the narrative. From his first introduction to the text, Dick is recognised as a homosexual by Sobert, although in dialogue with him Sobert refuses to acknowledge this fact. His significance to Sobert grows in relation to Fiona's demands and Dick becomes another mental bolt-hole for Sobert to remove himself from reality. Just as he assumed opposing stances in Book One in relation to a series of social issues, so Sobert can be seen to be doing the same in relation to sexuality in the remainder of the text.

Book Two begins with the schizoid announcement, "[s]o I'm playing Fiona and being happy with Dick. Two months of simultaneous emotional co-starring – split enterprise" (111). This evolves into an existential suspension for Sobert, between two roles both noticeably covered in self-contempt: "I'll remain in my two minds, in my two attitudes, one ridiculous and shamed, the other blind and serving her needs" (126). It is when Fiona tries to assert her ownership of Sobert by driving Dick out of his room with the use of fascist literature that Sobert makes the decision to

2.2 Andrew Salkey: The Middle Man

take on a flat with Dick. Fiona sees this as Sobert's declaration of homosexuality, but for Sobert it is simply an escape from personal proscription, from the obligation to fulfil one role. It is a move prefigured by doubt, which he takes in order to perpetuate his sense of suspension and doubt; "[s]urely there's only one way of getting out of this mess [. . .] run like hell. Run like hell to another set of hell-like circumstances, perhaps" (128).

The notion of Hell or purgatory becomes more prevalent from this point in the text. When Sobert announces that he intends to leave the bedsit, "limbo" is one of his imagined destinations (131), and, at the start of Book Three, the club in which he works is described as "Dantesque" (145). This perhaps explains why, when the intervening weeks have been "a joy forever" (146), Sobert allows Fiona back into his life. It is inspired, paradoxically, by the tone of intense individualism that pervades the final scenes of the text, during which Sobert alienates all of his acquaintances. He goes to Larry, the closest Jamaican friend he has, with his fears over his sexuality in exactly the same way that he tells Dick about his return to Fiona's bed. The ruse works, and, where Larry had always expressed the unity of being countrymen, Sobert now becomes "the enemy" (197).

Homosexuality, or more precisely, its implication, thus becomes a mechanism for Sobert to maintain a sense of social and personal detachment. He panics when Biddy ends an argument between them with the line, "[y]ou're also bloody finished as a man. No woman in her right senses would want to know anything like you" (169). This suggests to him that he can be defined from without, that he can be seen to be something; the emigrant position that he has been trying to evade throughout the text. He thus plunges back into a state of suspension between Dick and Fiona, and this is how the text ends:

> I had a choice of lives before me. A choice of loves. And, perhaps, a choice of enemies. Fiona was waiting. Dick was waiting. And in another way, London also was. And so was I. I knew I had to wait. For the truth about Dick, about Fiona, about myself. About my next move. That and only that was worth waiting for: the truth about myself, and the courage and ability to recognize it when it came. (208)

The initial sense, that Sobert's future would depend on to whom he submits, is overridden by an insistence on truth and self-recognition; the use of fantasy to escape social definition thus seems to be coming to an end. Sobert, though, remains the object of the "truth"; he is waiting for it to happen to him rather than shaping it for himself. The notion of return is totally absent, and thus one feels that London is his purgatory, his limbo, and that in this condition of exile the truth will continually hover out of reach.

* * *

Salkey's next emigrant hero, Catullus Kelly, gives all the appearances of being a very different character to Johnnie Sobert. The Jimmy Porter-like bitterness is immediately replaced in this text with a Selvonesque description of an "enthusiastic amateur womaniser and [. . .] professional drinker"; a man "destined to drink in two hemispheres" (1-2). The text itself has the episodic style of Selvon and, with its epigraphs from Stuart Hall and Edward Kamau Brathwaite on the issues of identity and exile, might easily be interpreted as a retrospective emigrant romp. Certainly, the reviewers of the day were less enthusiastic about this text, David Haworth in *The New Statesman* typical in his condemnation of the main character as being "preposterously athletic sexually" (230).

This, again, was a sensitive time for British society. The 1968 Immigration Act remains infamous for Enoch Powell's "rivers of blood" speech and the support he received for his views after his resignation from the Shadow Cabinet. A black sexual adventurer was unlikely to be popular under such circumstances, and yet, as has been noted throughout this thesis, notions of desire may not be restricted to a Fanonian recognition of the significance of the white woman to the black man; it is the myth of black sexuality which is of equal importance. Salkey's use of Brathwaite's line, "so the boy now nigratin' overseas," as an epigraph is thus significant in the way it conflates the act of emigrating with increased racial objectification: becoming a "nigger" (all over again) by entering Britain. It is a prelude to a text that continually reveals the interplay between reality, fantasy and (learned) perception that surrounds the black immigrant in Britain.

Kelly's constitution as a character culturally displaced by his colonial education is made more apparent than Sobert's. Where, in the latter case,

2.2 Andrew Salkey: The Middle Man

glimpses of disaffected middle-class values could be discerned in the first-person narrative, in the former, the dialogue between peasant roots and an emerging class is emphasised. Kelly, is accredited with a "two-way *Weltanschauung*: his Kingston-dialect mood, and his Standard English mood" (2). Initially, this would seem to be a fulfilment of Lamming's proscription to break Prospero's contract sealed by language, in order to restructure reality for the West Indian.[12] Kelly's education in this sense should have demystified the "idea of England" and converted dialect into an empowering discourse with the capacity to redefine the self. Kelly's promotion of the concept of *négritude*, the raising of all black men to a superlative degree of Blackness (121-2), would proceed from this capacity. Once again, though, it is the fact that Kelly has had to come to London to realise his Jamaican dreams that is of vital importance. As we are told from the start, "England [. . .] foxed him. London squashed his ambition" (2). As with Johnnie Sobert, then, it is his existence in exile that proves the decisive factor.

The reality of life in the Caribbean inhabits the margins of Kelly's life in exile. His opening pronouncement on the University of the West Indies, where he took his degree, is telling; "[t]he Windies headquarters where a curious exchange is taking place: the death of the land and the resuscitation of the Civil Service" (2). The role of the Civil Service in Salkey's previous text, *The Late Emancipation of Jerry Stover*, was to take the educated elite and place them in the service of neo-colonialism. Erasmus, Kelly's landlord and mentor, pronounces similarly on Kelly's "garden" university: "You believe that the garden [. . .] really help' you to see the colonial thing round you? Or the hate thing? Or even give you a good look-see at you'self? The lovely garden surroundings doing well in exam-passing" (20). Kelly, like Sobert, is cognizant of the impotence of the Caribbean intelligensia, but he is yet to learn that the same applies in the Mother Country.

---

[12] Lamming's full remarks are, "Caliban received not just words, but language [. . .] as an instrument of the exploring consciousness [. . .] Caliban, at some stage, would have to find a way of breaking that contract, which had been sealed by *language*, in order to restructure some alternative reality for himself" (qtd. in Kent 88-9).

It is noticeable that in Kelly's first two encounters in London he is careful to use Standard English. In the first, at the offices of the White Defence League, he uses an extravagantly literate mode of discourse to embarrass a fascist who is selling books on the mental inferiority of non-Anglo-Saxon stock (10-4). In the second, his first meeting with the prostitute, Olga, he employs a "metropolitan clip" to disguise his "village innocence" and indulges in some role-playing with the images of Rock Hudson and Humphrey Bogart (14-5).

In each case Kelly feels he has scored a personal victory. The fascist ends up condemning a vast sector of the white Anglo-Saxon stock he is supposedly protecting from extinction, and Olga returns her fee, presumably as a tribute to Kelly's erotic skill. As he leaves Olga's flat, Kelly pats her car "arrogantly, heroically, like Othello before the handkerchief" (17). 'Before' may be read here as 'in front of' rather than 'prior to'; Kelly is duping himself into believing that his anglicised manner can earn him equality in Britain. As Peter Nazareth notes in his reading of this text, Olga's car is a white Jaguar, a cat that is ordinarily black ("Sexual Fantasies" 346). After these two encounters, Kelly clearly believes he can achieve a similar metamorphosis.

Erasmus is quick to quash Kelly's assumed mastery of the fascist organisation, but does not recognise the significance of sex in the colonial relationship. He himself has been in Britain for forty years and has an Irish wife, but has confined himself to the growing emigrant community. Despite his "meteoric rise in real estate" (18), he has "carefully preserved his Jamaican dialect" (19), and is thus the perfect counterpart to Kelly's colonially informed aspirations. The next "place of interest" that he suggests to Kelly is the New World Section of the Temperate Broadcasting Unit.

Here he meets two other graduate West Indians who apparently exemplify Kelly's indices for success outside the Caribbean; they have confirmed positions within Broadcasting House and from there they are transmitting cultural and current affairs to the West Indies. What Kelly actually finds, though, is rather different. The programme producers, Jonquil Merchant Georgetown and Peter Leonard Ulliphant, patronise and abuse their contributors, yet the programme that Kelly observes being recorded is no more than a summary of reviews from other sources. Their secretary dis-

2.2 Andrew Salkey: The Middle Man

misses the possibility of an active audience in the Caribbean, yet they refuse to transmit an interview Kelly records with a homosexual because they consider it too controversial. As Erasmus explains, the men are effectively obliged to submit to a further colonisation in order to maintain their positions of *apparent* power and influence in England. In this they fulfil a similar role to that of the Civil Service in the Caribbean by literally transmitting their own subjugation back to the islands (51-2).

A similar scenario is played out when Kelly takes on a teaching job at a local school. The parallels with *To Sir, With Love* are made explicit from the first, with the pupils mentioning the film version that had been released two years earlier. The familiar scenes of the teacher's gradual acceptance by both staff and pupils are played out and Erasmus notes a corresponding change in Kelly's "sybaritic" lifestyle. Kelly, however, does not have the same entrenched conformity of a Ricky Braithwaite, and the experimental trip to a museum and nervous courtship of Gillian Blanchard in the earlier text are replaced here by X-rated movies and a "riot of fornication" (70-82).

Kelly is not a thoroughly colonised subject like Braithwaite; his *Weltanschauung* is a negotiation between two discursive models, not a complete surrender to the language of the coloniser. He is thus unable to maintain his place at the school in the way that Peter and Jonquil can maintain theirs at the T.B.U., and he decides not to return after the summer break.

This decision marks a turning point in the text. Kelly has seen his intellectual *entrée* into Britain diverted, while the emigrant community he meets at the barber shop have their linguistic contribution to London exile dismissed as "the fragmentation of language, the "naming of parts," foreign parts, and a kind of *cuntish* irony" (68). Kelly senses that he is being absorbed into the (racist) reality of London and his skin tone becomes noticeably blacker while everything else "pales before his eyes" (85-9). This condition is exacerbated by Kelly's next job as a coffee-machine attendant in a coffee bar.

The owner of the bar, Martin Selby, employs his attendants as Atmosphere Men whom he expects to contribute eponymously to his business. The persona he chooses for Kelly is "Beano," characterised by a "zombie stance" and a "minimum of intelligence of expression" (100). Nazareth

115

("Sexual Fantasies" 348) correctly notes the historical significance of naming in the slave trade and the cumulative effect of this with the plantation-style decor in the bar. The effect it has on Kelly is to accelerate his sense of absorption. He tries to resurrect his feeling of alienation, of the "delight of being outside everything he touched and saw round him" (110). But it is the way he is *seen* rather than the way he *sees* that is of importance. Looking for his reflection in a shop window he finds he is "invisible but for a mere suggestion of a contour" which he cannot grasp (113). He returns to the "comforting dark presence" of the house where Dulcie is waiting for him with the light off, his sense of self now secure in the darkness (114).

"Dream, illusion and hectic fantasy" become Kelly's intended reply to his coming invisibility (114), but what he has failed to recognise is his own collusion in a wider sexual fantasy. If the first six months demonstrate Kelly's inability to express and develop himself as an educated black man, the last six months show how sexuality completely undermines the importance that he invests in his learning.

The first suggestion of this is in Kelly's sexual encounter with Martin Selby's wife, Philippa. The coffee-bar is named *The Onomatopoeia*, the pretentiously literary air proceeding most evidently from Philippa's high estimate of herself as a privately published novelist. She is surprised by Kelly's ability to quote Classical literature with her (100), and pleased with the notion of Kelly as a black reincarnated poet. Primarily, though, as her later union with Kelly shows, she fetishises his body.[13] By contrast, Kelly is trying to erase a history of exploitation, correcting "the Beano imbalance" (109), as he later calls it: "The centuries rolled back and forth for him. He was living on an extremely plush scale. The tropical light was blocked by green wooden blinds. The plantation sounds were distant. No threat. No tradition of lynching" (108). His fantasy is threatened by the "sugar-cane stem" appearance of the dressing-table leg that recalls his own

---

[13] When Catullus is indulging in his sexual reprise, he goes back to Philippa where he becomes involved in a trio with her and her friend, Tillie. Tillie exclaims, "D'you know, I've never seen one of you who didn't appeal entirely physically at a glance," while Philippa conducts a "guided tour" to display her previous knowledge of Catullus' body (170-2).

2.2 Andrew Salkey: The Middle Man

peasant roots and the heritage of slavery. Significantly, though, Philippa's flip comment on his "size" allows him to dispel his own sense of abuse as he cogitates on his innate "superiority": "He was *enormously* pleased. He promised to dazzle her *massively*" (109; my italics).

Kelly cannot so easily overcome the experience of his next encounter. Again there is a combination of intellectualism and sexuality involved, as his "favourite librarian," Penelope, or "Lope" invites Kelly to a party. Just prior to this event Kelly had been indulging his "split allegiance, schizophrenic delight" (139) by his reading of West Indian poets and his tour of minor tourist attractions in London. Sobert's sexual schizophrenia is Kelly's cultural schizophrenia as he tries to bridge his cultural divide and induce a sense of belonging. He has this process reversed on him, though, as he enters the party and is offered a "banana joint": "What's that, for God's sake?' Catullus sensed, fearfully, a passage from informed innocence on to devastating experience. How could he, from a banana-growing area, from the old agricultural world, not know about the mellow-yellow banana joint? (143).

This is indeed a "middle-passage" as he is robbed of his own certain sense of heritage by the joint and is then led by Lope into her study. Surrounded by books, Kelly tries to re-establish his sense of self. But where a quoted passage has worked on previous occasions,[14] here he is too shaken to bring it to mind. In this uncertain mood, the act of sex begins to lose its existential restoration: "Wonders were ceasing. The earth was flat. Britain was Babylon. Swinging meant sweetly sinister" (147).

This is not the end of Kelly's ordeal. Later he returns to the study with Lope and her friend, Portia, for "initiation." In this prolonged sex and smoking session, Kelly initially tries to adopt the persona of the Rastafarian and the obeah man, but the order to "give Portia love" while Lope is in the room shatters his assumed cool and his colonial upbringing surfaces: "Propriety shot through his mellow veins. His Victorian matriarchy

---

[14] I am thinking here of the episode where Catullus is trying to begin his interview with Christopher the homosexual at the TBU. He tries to fantasise about the female sound producer in an effort to calm his nerves, and when this fails, falls back on quoting Shakespeare (48-9).

screamed pink opprobrium. He was hot. His mask was slipping" (152). Before he can recover, though, the lights are switched off and he is ordered to play a game of sexual hide-and-seek. He eventually finds Portia but the sexual prize is hers, rather than his. She first delivers her conclusions on Kelly's performance in the initiation: he is "prone to ritual" and "trusting, optimistic, easy leader-fodder". Kelly is thus reduced to ontological infancy, to slave status, and under these circumstances, "Gibbon slept. And Coleridge" (155).

This experience robs Kelly of his desire to promote *négritude* and he himself uses Standard English "only when certain circumstances demanded it: during extreme Anglo-Saxon encounters: while juggling with abstractions: and whenever indulging in self-deception" (158). He feels he has found his place in London because he has ceased try to prove his special existence as the "new man" of the colonies. In this mood he can speak dialect at the barber's and visit art galleries and museums without either being existentially significant.

His final downfall, though, brings Kelly back full circle to his first encounters at the White Defence League and Othello-like performance at Olga's flat. He meets Lilith, a "tall, brooding blonde with [. . .] a predilection for the lurking potency of jet-black men" (160). With her he reaches the summits of his sexual prowess, in between time performing a sexual reprise with all of his major partners in anticipation of his return to Jamaica. He discovers, though, that Lilith is the author of the fascist book written under the name of Æthelstan Gordon-Venning that had caught his attention at the W.D.L. He finally recognises the extent of his oppression in time for his return to the Caribbean.

Kelly returns to Jamaica and a subsequent letter from his mother to Erasmus recounts the tale of his progressive madness and eventual institutionalisation. His attack on surface realities which commenced with the Beano episode is finalised in Kingston where he begins to preach the virtues of touching the surfaces of society, ultimately molesting the Governor-General's wife. In doing so, he is preaching a (presumably more authentic) alternative to seeing and being seen: his slide into insanity thus recalls Dickson's phobic reaction to being looked at in *The Emigrants*.

2.2 Andrew Salkey: The Middle Man

Salkey, therefore, does not project sexuality in itself as the mechanism for regressive racial attitudes. Kelly's relationship with Dulcie has the symbolic "plinthing scene," where Dulcie and Kelly make love in Trafalgar Square amid the architecture of the imperial powerbase. The perception of sexuality, however, is an important part of post-colonial ideology and it is this that Salkey highlights in this text. Kelly bridges the divide between Selvon's "pussy-hunters" and Braithwaite's colonial subject and in doing so, highlights the role sexual fantasy plays in continued oppression and self-oppression.

* * *

The last of Salkey's London texts, *Come Home, Malcolm Heartland* gestures strongly towards a resolution to the problems set out in the first two texts. The use of Alejo Carpentier as an epigraph prepares the reader for this: "A yearning for escape is, in fact, a search to find oneself; which is, when all is said and done, a return to oneself." Sobert's escape left him with the recognition that he was indeed trying to find himself, while Kelly's (potentially successful) quest for the self left him dramatically out of step with the society he returned to. In this text, however, we are presented with a protagonist who, from the start, has apparently made a difficult, but clear decision to return to Jamaica with the lessons he has learned from his exile. In this sense we are looking for a hero who has found himself and is ready to lead a break from the heritage of slavery and colonialism.

The main confrontation in the text is set out from the first page. Malcolm has decided to leave Britain, and a reporter from Carib News interviews him about this. Malcolm insists that what he is doing is a purely personal act, but his involvement with formative black consciousness in Britain makes this, for the reporter, a political act with specific timing and intent. In particular he points to the difference between the militancy of the new Black Power movement inspired by American radicalism, and the quest for metropolitan approval and recognition with which he associates the Caribbean intellectuals of the Fifties. For Malcolm, though, it is a choice between fantasy and harsh reality.

In the previous two texts fantasy has been shown to be at once a means of reconciling oneself to one's physical exile and also an ideological mechanism for perpetuating an existential exile. Malcolm is apparently aware of this:

> Malcolm had made up his mind to return home. He had thought about it for a long time. He had even dreamed about it, night and day, nightmare following euphoria, realistic assessment following innocent speculation [. . .] Dreaming in London was like that, he often told himself. At that time, most of his reveries in private, everything imagined or reasoned, had the quality of a shimmering dream; it strained after reality, confusing him, and even soothing him deceptively. (17-8)

London emerges as "insulation against the realities of the home struggle" (96); it removes the self from the test of development and assertion at home. Thus, the notion that the colonial subject must travel to the metropolitan centre in order to discover the reality of his cultural formation is overturned here with the overwhelming conviction that exile serves the ends of neo-colonialism in much the same way as submitting to the Civil Service in Jamaica:

> Claude was silent [. . .] Would she know that Malcolm had been trained more to take his place in London than in Kingston? Would she ever believe that he had been produced, like a unique luxury commodity, by his education [. . .] and by the hopes of the colonial elite produced before him, in order to serve the needs and the greed of an absentee authority? (98)

Claude is the main black British character in the text, and, as was suggested by the reporter above, Malcolm's decision to return home has much to do with his sense of dislocation with the new black scene in Britain. Catullus Kelly's ill-fated search for *négritude* in the last text is finally ended here as Malcolm recognises that the experience of colonialism has particularity, and is not immediately comprehensible to a new generation with its own agenda for liberation. In this respect, there are many comparisons to be drawn with Selvon's *Moses Ascending*, published a year earlier.

2.2 Andrew Salkey: The Middle Man

As noted in Part One, Moses is baffled first by Brenda's "Nordic" accent, and then by Galahad's adoption of "hip-talk." It is a signifier for the disintegration of the black community and pre-figures Moses' (and Selvon's) departure from Britain. Malcolm Heartland does not have the peasant status of Selvon's hero; he is revealed as a scholarship boy with two degrees and his use of dialect in the text is minimal. However, it nevertheless becomes clear that the new linguistic diversity of the black community in London plays an essential role in the circumstances surrounding Malcolm's attempted departure.

Claude is one of a group of black activists whose efforts to persuade Malcolm to remain in Britain provide the narrative framework of the text. She first involves herself with Malcolm under the guise of a French colonial *au pair*, mixing "lightly accented English" with the language of Black Power. (33). In the course of their next meeting, when Claude confesses to her English middle-class background, Malcolm is perplexed by an accent which is now "plainly English" and free of the "new counter-culture demotic" (49). This begins a dialogue between Malcolm and Claude and her associates in which discursive modes are variously used to appeal to Malcolm's different loyalties.

Malcolm's Jamaican friend, Thomas, is part of the group. He sleeps with Malcolm's girlfriend, Honora, in a bid to force a crisis in the relationship that would make Malcolm more susceptible to staying. When he sees Thomas subsequently, Thomas uses Jamaican dialect to disarm Malcolm's expected ire (106). He attempts a similar manoeuvre when he reveals himself to Malcolm as a member of Claude's group, using a Jamaican term in his speech. Malcolm, however, is equal to his ploy; "Thomas's 'Star Boy' was affectionately Kingstonian [. . .] Malcolm admired him for slipping it into his reply, fully realising, of course, that he had planted it there to soften him up" (141).

Malcolm is quietly appreciative of Thomas' linguistic appeal, but he has already decided that it is impossible for him to exist as a Jamaican while living in exile, "to realise his basic humanity, his plain, living everyday personality outside his island home" (82). Claude thus attempts a similar ploy in the same exchange only this time using "hip-talk":

'You can take decisions. Like most anybody can. But you have very little button control over their consequences.' She grimaced. 'That's largely true, isn't it?' She hoped for Calvino's confirmation. He merely pouted and winked, looking at her for a moment and then looking away again, in Malcolm's direction. She tried a groovy alternative. 'Some things are a rip-off and they pull out real freaky results, and that's easy; others, well aren't that straight up and down.' (142)

Such language, though, is not convincing to Malcolm. He views dialect and the language of the new black generation as a social decoy; part of what he defines as a sham existence in the metropolis. Calvino, Claude's "guru" and self-appointed source of revolutionary theory in London, personifies this existence with his Cuban records, agitprop art objects and pictures of Ho Chi Minh. Malcolm never shakes off his original assessment that "[i]t all seems so emblematic, spuriously symbolic, a kind of London political carnival escapism" (79): an assessment which hardens his conviction that the real struggle lies at home.

Salkey used sexuality in the previous two texts to signify the protagonists' continued immersion in self-perpetuating racist ideologies. It is made clear in this text that these ideologies were being successfully challenged by the growing influence of black pride in this era, and Malcolm's response to this challenge is thus an important indicator of the success of his exile and projected return. Predictably, it is here that the cracks in Malcolm's certainty begin to show.

The significance of white women is again important. Malcolm is introduced as having a long term Guyanese girlfriend, Honora, but there is something clearly insincere in her description as "his boastful asset, black and beautiful, when he needed to demonstrate that feature of solidarity on the demand of the Black communities" (18). During their first encounter, Claude challenges Malcolm on the issue of sex and white women. In the dialogue, Malcolm insists that he has no "hang-ups" or guilt about sex with either black or white women whilst in exile: "when I want to do anything about the matter, I'd just go right ahead and do what's to be done. At least, try to" (37). The last qualifying statement is important. Malcolm is no sex-

2.2 Andrew Salkey: The Middle Man

ual athlete and the narrative voice suggests that Honora's submissive availability is a greater reason for Malcolm's continued relationship with a black woman.

This unease with Malcolm's sexual politics becomes manifest when Claude comes to his room and pretends to fall asleep on his bed. He goes to touch her but is stopped by the impression given by her white blouse that she is also white:

> His hands froze. His fingers curled inwards. Like the retracted claws of an unsure predator his fists hung over Claude's breasts. They seemed white, too. They were those of some other woman, not Claude's, an intruder's. They were white. He couldn't touch them. The two mounds of flesh, because of their new reality and because of his self-imposed discrimination, were strikingly forbidden. (54-5)

This "unsure predator" might also be read as a "noble savage." Malcolm has not shed his colonial formation and the illusion of Claude's colour leads him back into a reverie about the alien and alienating aspects of his education. He remembers his first physical experience of snow after its existence as a poetic image. Feeling it was not enough, he had to urinate on the white alien substance that had "invaded" the Caribbean (59). However, Malcolm cannot extend this minor revolt to sexuality: he is not rapacious about white women, and, furthermore, Claude's "forthright behaviour" outrages his "obsolete standards of female propriety and conduct" and confirms "a false tradition of stale and received Victorian duplicity and doubtful respectability" (60).

Salkey does not, however, use sexual liberation as a signifier for a new black consciousness. Claude initially appears in a positive light compared to Honora, for whom sex becomes an act of existential validation with a fantasy self distinguished by its sexual immediacy (27-32). But Claude is also revealed as a fantasist using sexual freedom and black politics as a mode of rebellion against her middle-class parents. Sexual liberation is thus recognised here (as it is in *Moses Ascending*) as an obstacle to the black struggle. The gains of the new active role of the black woman, as it is espoused on two occasions in the text[15] being apparently outweighed by the "spread of subtle yet debilitating attacks against Black Power in London; the apolitical dilutions by both black devotees and admiring white attendants; (and) the incursion of reciprocal gains by both parties" (73).

Fantasy thus plays a far more prominent role in this text than in the two discussed above. The revolutionary polemic that accounts for much of the dialogue does not escape this implication, and one must remember that Salkey, like Selvon, also left England in the late Seventies. Like Selvon, also, he did not return to the Caribbean, but went to the United States instead. A pessimistic pattern is thus being formed: Sobert did not consider return; Kelly returned and could not re-adjust and Malcolm Heartland's return becomes an impossible fantasy.

It is significant that in the swirling confusion of allegiance and intent that pervades the conclusion of this text, the only reality issues from Clovis, the Jamaican recently arrived from the Caribbean. Throughout the text, Malcolm's internal debate on return and its feasibility has been based on reports from West Indians passing through London on their way to and from conferences on aid. Clovis' own escape and contemptuous damnation of Malcolm's plans for democratic revolution on the island dispels some of the fantasy from Malcolm's mind. The reality, however, is harsher than he realises, and having dismissed the implied threats of Claude and her associates as fantasy, it is Clovis who arrives as his assassin.

This is a bleak ending to the London exile; the fantasy of existence (integration?) in the metropolis is ultimately snuffed out by the murderous reality of home. Catullus Kelly's demise and Erasmus' reflections on the "futility of dreaming" in Jamaica (193) prepare the reader for the prospect of return, but this text suggests that London will remain a limbo for the Fifties' intellectuals, dismissed by the young black British in the text as "Black talkers who won't act" (127). The revolutionary tone of the text is undeniable, and perhaps, from the death of fantasy by reality we see the ground being laid for the Brixton reality of Linton Kwesi Johnson:

---

[15] The opening scenes with Malcolm and Thomas at Speakers' Corner include a speech on the black woman as the "uncrowned queen of the revolution" (22-3). A playscript that Calvino gave Malcolm to read is built along similar lines (103-4).

2.2 Andrew Salkey: The Middle Man

The Brixton young were not, in any way, grooming themselves to be grooved into any makeshift, interim sectors of society's handy liberalism, nor were they making themselves invisible. They were highly visible, aggressive individuals who were sharply defining themselves by way of their refreshed Blackness and by the fire of their rage and by their hatred of social injustice and brotherly treachery, and by their loathing for the fruitless political gestures of their parents' generation. (128)

2.3 Linton Kwesi Johnson: Creation Rebel

In 1981, Darcus Howe, as editor of *Race Today*, wrote:

> It is striking, that in a period of four years, we have been unable to unearth any work of art, created from within and about Britain's black community, which has the capacity to "turn the head." There is a solitary exception: the writings and recordings of the poet, Linton Kwesi Johnson. (Introduction 1)

While he pays tribute to the work of Lamming, Vidia Naipaul and Wilson Harris, Howe characterises their work as having being written "out of their past consciousness" (1). Whether or not one accepts this analysis, it is clear that Howe regarded Johnson as a voice that represented the new black identity in Britain symbolised by the nationwide rioting and civil unrest that had occurred earlier that year.

This association of art and rebellion is a defining characteristic of Johnson's work, not just in the Fanonian overtones of much of his poetry, but also in the heritage of cultural resistance that is implicit in its form and formation. This much is made clear in Johnson's biographical notes. Coming to England from Jamaica when he was eleven, Johnson left Tulse Hill Comprehensive in Brixton in 1970 and joined the Black Panther Movement, a "mass organisation of young blacks mobilised to pursue the liberation of blacks from colonial oppression in Britain" (Johnson, *Voices*, sleeve-notes). Part of this liberation was cultural; a small library of books on black issues was available to members, and Johnson recalls his response to this literature as being the spur for his art.[16] He also began to attend meetings of the Caribbean Artists Movement (CAM) at the Keskidee Arts Centre, where he began his working relationship with both Howe and John La Rose.

The riots of 1981 signified for Howe an "acceleration of the processes through which the uncertainty [of black existence in Britain] is brought to an end" (introduction 1). Black British existence prior to the mid-Seventies

---

[16] In his interview with Dread Fred, Johnson refers to *The Souls of Black Folk* by W. E. B. DuBois saying, "The book moved me so much I had to write down a response to it" (qtd. in Fred 22).

2.3 Linton Kwesi Johnson: Creation Rebel

had been defined by the ideology of integration and then by the phrase, 'cultural diversity.' In each case, the power of definition flowed from a chauvinistic white majority to a black population still unconvinced of its tenure in Britain. This changed when the influence of the Black Power movement in late Sixties America combined with the "coming of age" of the black population in Britain. The flow was stemmed as the first generation of black British fought for self-definition and the right to equal existence in their own country.

The Civil Rights movement in America had undergone a similar ideological transformation. Stokely Carmicheal's use of the term 'black power' in a speech in 1966 revealed a split between integrationists and nationalists characterised by the appeal of Martin Luther King on the one side, and Malcolm X on the other.[17] A similar process may be perceived in the impact of Johnson's poetry on black British literature. Sam Selvon's London novels may become increasingly ironic in their treatment of integration in response to a background of deepening violence and institutional racism, but the advent of British Black Power receives the same flippant treatment.[18] Andrew Salkey's literature also develops from Johnnie Sobert's tortured desire to integrate, to Malcolm Heartland's thwarted desire for return. Black Power is not established as a feasible option, as is witnessed by Catullus Kelly's universally condemned quest for *négritude*. Thus, the significance of the description of the Brixton young at the end of *Malcolm Heartland* is that they are *other* than the writer/narrator, operating from different premises than the central debates of the text and, consequently, allying themselves with a different tradition.

This practice is evident in Johnson's poetry as he draws on the traditions of rebellion and culture that is the black experience. It is black nationalism in that his poetry is not written, as Sam Selvon's novels were, for a white audience: his "dialect" is not modified. As Andrew Salkey (who was acquainted with Johnson through his activities as a founding member of the

---

[17] See chapter 4, "Malcolm X and the Rise of Contemporary Nationalism" in Pinckney for a fuller account of this process.

[18] I am thinking here of the episode in *Moses Ascending* where the American Black Panther absconds with the local branch funds (Selvon, *Moses Ascending* 114).

CAM) says in his introduction to *Dread Beat and Blood* (1975), Johnson writes to "those who share and understand a common experience of oppression and the matching language of pain, knowing implicitly that those who feel it deep down will also recognise it, and require no glossary or explanatory notes to do so" (8).

This easy recognition of an audience for Johnson's work is an indicator of the different social processes that surrounded his success. His significance as a poet and performer lies in the way he acts as a catalyst for these processes: a product of their growth and an agent in their promotion. Some discussion of these processes is thus essential, not to an understanding of his poetry, but of its significance as the new voice of the black British.

* * *

In *Race Today*, Farrukh Dhondy described Johnson's first volume of poetry, *Voices of the Living and the Dead* (1974), as having transformed the "ideal mystical lyric of the Rastafari, to the insistent rhythm of broken glass, blood and fire". He says further: "It is [. . .] the power of reggae from which the biblical fullness and the fighting imagery of blood and wound and scar have been distilled into Linton's verse" (92). The emergence of a UK-based Rastafarian movement in the early Seventies had a profound effect on black identity both as it was felt and perceived. Accompanied by the international success of reggae and the personality cult surrounding Bob Marley, it purveyed a message of essentially cultural resistance.

The Rastafarian Movement began in Jamaica as a primarily religious order but with enormous social and political implications. The deification of Haile Selassie, Emperor of Ethiopia, as the biblical King of Kings, or Christ's second coming represented the coalition of two important strands of black liberation. Firstly, by using biblical text to endorse the existence of a black Christ and to declare black people as the true and original Jews and Israelites, Rastafarian belief succeeded in separating the link between Christianity and whiteness. Secondly, it focussed notions of kingship onto Africa and Ethiopian independence as a symbol of African resistance to colonialism. As Horace Campbell puts it, this new deification replaced "the white god in heaven and his white representatives in Buckingham Palace

2.3 Linton Kwesi Johnson: Creation Rebel

with a black king and a god held to have been prophesied in Revelation 19: 11, 16" (6).

The Rastafarians became a segregationist movement determined to keep themselves remote from a colonially ordered world. In the absence of any institutional power and unable to enact their desire for repatriation to Africa, the Rastafari sought to erect a more authentic personality through culture. This took its most obvious form in the wearing of dreadlocks in imitation of the Masai warriors of East Africa, and in resistance to a society still based on skin colour and hair texture and the obligation to aspire to whiteness.[19]

A similar attitude was taken with language. A careful reading of the Bible not only offered a re-evaluation of identity and its use in a dominant white ideology, but also an understanding of the way biblical discourse had been appropriated to affirm this dominance. Rastafarians thus sought to develop Jamaican patois from a dialect subordinate to Standard English to a language in its own right. Promoted as Nation-language by Edward Brathwaite, Jah Bones designates the Rasta language as Afro-Lingua, a continually evolving discourse that seeks to undermine the principal tenets of what he describes as a "decadent" and "stagnant" language (44-5). This was not a process confined to Rastafarian thought, and Bones' exhortation that "it is imperative that I-n-I learn African languages" (51) is part of a wider appeal to Africanisation. What made the Rastafarian appeal more potent was the international success of reggae.

Important in Jamaica initially as a cultural challenge to the dominance of white American music, reggae provided a voice for social protest, carrying on the traditions of calypso and developing the sound system as a subversive space in neo-colonial society. There is some debate as to whether Rastafarianism made reggae internationally popular, or vice versa, but the result is universally recognised:

> Reggae music [. . .] played the role of linking the style and form of Afro-Jamaican street-culture to the style and form of young Afro-Caribbean blacks in Britain, and, with the rastafarian

---
[19] Campbell (12) describes the Brethren having their locks shorn during police raids in Jamaica, when all Rastafari were made subject to arrest in April 1963.

movement, gave these same youths an orientation, in that both reggae and rastafarianism (Dread), assumed together, the appearance of an overt and mutinous force or power which the state – its concerned institutions and personnel – came to regard as a threat or as potentially threatening. (Pryce 37)

Or, as Johnson put it:

> Given the anti-colonial context of blacks in Britain and the prominence of reggae music in our cultural lives, it is not at all surprising that the Rasta dominated lyrical content of reggae, replete with anti-colonialist, anti-establishment, black nationalist and other sentiments, should find ready acceptance amongst Britain's young blacks. (Rev. 21)

Rastafarianism, through the medium of reggae, effectively gave expression to cultural resistance and the notion of black solidarity to the young black British. It did not, however, instigate this drive towards an autonomous existence, as blacks activists were already starting to organise in ways that countered the ideology of integration.

As noted above, Johnson benefited from the existence of the CAM when he left school in the early Seventies. This began on an informal basis in 1966 with Edward Brathwaite, John La Rose and Andrew Salkey with Orlando Patterson, Aubrey Williams, Evan Jones and Louis James. It rapidly grew in size, responding swiftly to the specific concerns of the black British, whilst at the same time maintaining a sense of Afro-Caribbean continuity. Its use of the West Indian Students Centre as a monthly meeting place gave it an early sense of radicalism in the late Sixties: Salkey's descriptions of Calvino's lecture and the police raid in *Malcolm Heartland* probably owe much to these meetings. By the end of the Sixties, the university-dominated aspect of the CAM began to change with the influence of Donald Hinds and James Berry, and a consequent cultural shift towards West Indians living in Britain and away from the Caribbean ensued. They then moved to the Keskidee Centre where Johnson and Darcus Howe began to attend.[20]

---

[20] See Walmsley for a full account of the CAM.

2.3 Linton Kwesi Johnson: Creation Rebel

The significant element of the CAM was the way it responded to the situation of black people in Britain, shifting its original focus on creating the artistic space denied in the Caribbean, to the growing debate on Black Power. In an editorial to a special number of *Savacou*, the official organ of the CAM, in 1974, La Rose and Salkey compared black creativity and social underdevelopment in the Caribbean with the black experience in Britain where "the crucial pressures of racism and class antagonism would seem to be providing a rich mulch for some of our creative artists" (10). There is a clear sense of projecting and promoting black art within a hostile cultural environment, a sense that is also present in the establishment of two publishing houses in the mid- to late-Sixties, New Beacon Books and Bogle L'Ouverture.

John La Rose was already about to start a West Indian publishing house with Dr Sarah White when Brathwaite approached him with his ideas for the CAM in 1966. The publishing venture was an attempt to challenge the disinformation and discontinuity that they saw as characterising colonial societies:

> One of the things that strikes you about a colonial society is that there is not only a lack of information which is quite deliberate [. . .] There is discontinuity [. . .] So that, each new generation comes to the colonial situation with its long history of struggles, as though it is something new. In a society in which the population has the power to control its life, that doesn't happen. So, I saw publishing as a vehicle which gave an independent validation of one's own culture, history, politics – a sense of one's self to break the discontinuity. (Beese 82)

This is essentially the same motivation behind Bogle L'Ouverture that was formed in 1969 by a group of West Indians in Britain as a response to the Jamaican government's attempts to ban Walter Rodney's re-entry to the country. They published *The Groundings with My Brothers*, a collection of Rodney's lectures in defiance of state censorship, and went on to publish works by both Salkey and Johnson. As Howe put it: "The achievements of Bogle L'Ouverture represent an important development in the struggles of the Caribbean peoples in their quest for knowledge denied them by the colonial office nationalist governments for centuries" ("Ten Years" 117).

Howe mounted his own intervention through his membership of the Race Today Collective (RTC), editing a magazine that documented and publicised incidents of racial abuse and harassment, particularly those involving the police and judiciary. The RTC was active in the organisation of the Notting Hill Carnival after the violence there in 1976 and also launched, through Johnson's involvement with the collective, the Creation for Liberation vehicle for the promotion of black art in Britain.

One can thus see traditions of resistance in the Caribbean and Britain coalescing in the early to mid-Seventies around Rastafarianism and the cultural medium of reggae. John La Rose is careful to distinguish between religious Rastafarianism, social Rastafarianism and popular Rastafarianism. In Britain, religious Rastafarianism is, he says, in the minority and thus the language of the Rastafarians, as it is used here, signifies a different experience (25). Jah Bones describes the establishment of Rastafari in Britain as placing them at the heart of Babylon, "sitting by the River Thames and weeping and singing as they all remembered Zion" (42). In the language of the black British, Babylon refers more directly to the police and the police state, not something to seek repatriation from, but to resist. Thus, while one can recognise the importance of Rastafari as providing an identity for an evolving tradition of struggle in the Caribbean and Britain, one must also recognise that the constitution of that identity was a response to white British society.

When John La Rose was asked his views on racist violence and right wing groups in 1981, he replied: "For the black community the most serious and violent attacks come from the police. The actions of the National Front and other right wing groups complement that violence" (11). The institutional racism of successive Immigration Acts and the discourse of hate, which punctuated their debate in Parliament and the media, designated the black population (which by now clearly included Asians) as an embattled community.

As noted in the introduction to this section, this was a phase of British social history increasingly marked by civil violence. The reports of police harassment, and the daily experience of this, impregnated black existence

2.3 Linton Kwesi Johnson: Creation Rebel

in Britain with a sense of being in conflict with white society, and with civil insurrection as their only recourse. Everton Pryce's work on the organisation of the Notting Hill Carnival after 1976, notes the recognition, on the side of the Carnival Action Committee at least, that black resistance within the carnival experience was part of the essentially political nature of an ostensibly cultural event (40-42). John La Rose is more direct: "Most of the black youth and unemployed when they move against their oppression immediately come up against the state. So they're on the streets or in an insurrection like Bristol or Brixton" (111).

Three broad movements can thus be seen to be at the basis of Johnson's work; the traditions of Rastafarianism, the international success of reggae, and the emergence of a black British cultural identity encouraged by a growing sense of confrontation between the (young) black British and the State. These elements combine in his work and thus its importance lies in more than its form or content; it is a symbol of independent black expression in Britain, composed, published and sold without reference to the white majority or its cultural hegemony. However, just as in Part One, where the wider audience of the cinema demanded the adaptation and assimilation of even such a character as Ricky Braithwaite, so Johnson's poetry describes the co-option of his cultural rebellion.

* * *

The publication of Johnson's poetry grew out of his association with the CAM and the RTC. His first published volume, *Voices of the Living and the Dead*, consists of a long poem of the same name and two shorter works. According to the cover notes, *Voices* was performed at the Keskidee Arts Centre in 1973 and in this sense the notion of an audience was eased by the cultural community that had already been forming under the auspices of the CAM. Farrukh Dhondy's review of the volume is sensitive to this aspect of a poetic form that he notes as being particular to the black British situation: "one may say that it has contributed the first collective myth of English poetry for centuries [. . .] The way in which it is successful depends on whether Linton's poetry cannot only live within, but earn the love of the common people" (92).

The poem itself is instructed to be performed with drums, bass guitar and flute, and in this sense is clearly written as performance poetry but not in the oral traditions with which Johnson's work would later become associated. Written as a dialogue between the Living and the Dead with a Narrator and an Echo, it is a call to maintain a tradition of bloody resistance and rebellion in the name of black freedom. Written in Standard English, it deals with the subject in only the most general terms and within the genre of epic heroism:

> (Each time men rise up and die,
> it is a triumph for the living and the dead,
> never let it be said,
> it is the same death,
> that thoughtless tyrants die) (11)

and,

> Our singers will sing songs about you,
> Our poets will write poems in memoriam,
> Flowers will bloom on your graves. (31)

Arguably, the creation of a new collective myth cannot be achieved through a focus on gritty detail as thematic symbolism is more appropriate. Even given the potential power of performance, however, "yout rebels" were not likely to be engaged by such lines as, "Stand still you trembling hill, / my heart, I cried, / you galloping thing gone wild" (19). This poem is thus lent power by the two poems that come after it in the text, and particularly by "Five Nights of Bleeding."

When Dhondy noted the black British particularity of *Voices*, it is "Five Nights" to which he refers. Such poetry, he argues, brings "[t]he experience of locality for his own audience – Brixton, Railton Road, Shepherds, the Telegraph, Sofrano B, Neville King [. . .] what are these? Ask any young black from London" (92). One could argue that Selvon had been achieving the same feat for the past two decades with his recreation of "the Water," "the Arch" and "the Gate." The difference though is that Johnson is specifically addressing a black audience in this poem, beginning a dialogue in which he at once speaks for *and* to a black British population. He

2.3 Linton Kwesi Johnson: Creation Rebel

thus encapsulates in the poetic voice the functions of all the actors in "Voices of the Living and the Dead."

"Five Nights" speaks directly to the young blacks. The use of upper case lettering for Brixton, Railton Road, for example, does not encode a spoken emphasis for the oral performance that exists on the recorded album *Dread Beat an' Blood,* released under the artist name "Poet and the Roots" in 1978. Instead it is a challenging assertion of black British existence in a normally exclusive arena, the book of poetry. Essentially a condemnation of fighting between black sections ("Rebellion rushing down the wrong road / Storm blowing down the wrong tree"), it also implicitly acknowledges where this violence stems from. The lines "[b]*itterness* erupts like a hot-blast" and "rituals of blood on the burning / *served* by a cruel infighting" (my emphasis) describe the rebels as victims of a greater violence and their own violent responses as functions of that violence. The stanza describing the conflict with the police may end with the line, "righteous, righteous, war," but it is "the bile of oppression [being] vomited," another involuntary reaction to some internalised and alien evil. The "war amongst the rebels" may be "madness," but it is a learned madness that Johnson is trying to re-route (36-7).

"Five Nights" clearly maintained its importance to Johnson as it appeared in his next volume of poetry, *Dread Beat an' Blood*, as well as his first single and album as "Poet and the Roots." In *Dread Beat* he develops the themes of a "righteous war" and the role of an oppressive society in instigating that war. Violence within the black community remains a feature but it is always accompanied and overridden by an appeal for solidarity against a common enemy. Johnson's empathy with his audience (although this already incorporated a significant white element) is figured in this text less by the emphasis on black experience in London, and more by a general experience of police and fascist violence recounted increasingly in Nation Language.

"Doun de Road" exemplifies these developments. References to the "sus" laws, the activities of the National Front and Enoch Powell illustrate how society acts upon the black population to engender violence and "fratricide":

terror fire terror fire reach we,
such a suffering we suffering,
in this burning age of rage;

no place to run to get a gun,
and the violence damming up inside.

so in the heat,
of the anguish,
yu jus turn;

turn on your brother,
an yu lick him,
an yu lash him,
an stab him,
an kill him,

and the violence damming up inside (22)

Fratricide is declared as "the first phase" and the time come for the second phase (of violent insurrection) to show. The next poem in the volume, "Time Come," addresses white society and its goading of its black population ending with "it too late now: / I did warn you" (25).

As well as his use of dialect, Johnson emphasises a reggae-based culture as a space for unity and the voice of shared experience:

Shock-black bubble-doun-beat bouncing,
rock-wise tumble-doun sound music;
foot-drop find drum, blood story,
bass history is a moving,
is a hurting black story. ("Reggae Sounds" 56)

Oral performance using reggae backing was always Johnson's prime motivation, and he quotes Big Youth, Jah Stitch and Dillinger as his artistic inspirations (qtd. in Fred 23). He says, "my poems may look sort of flat on the page. Well, that is because they're actually oral poems, as such. They

2.3 Linton Kwesi Johnson: Creation Rebel

were definitely written to be performed in the community" (qtd. in Salkey, *Away* 8). His use of studio recording with a reggae backing does not necessarily equate with performance, but it does provide significant clues in terms of the poems that he selects for this more accessible medium.

His first single featured poems from *Dread Beat*, "Five Nights" and "All Wi Doin is Defendin," a poem which emphasises insurrection against oppression: "yu did soun yu siren / an is war now" (26-7). When the album was released in 1978, it took poems from the same volume and also two other poems that were later to appear in *Inglan is a Bitch*. As Courtney Hay notes in his review of the album, these two tracks indicate a "changing reality" as they convey collective action as an alternative rebellion (143).

"Man Free" recounts the tale of Darcus Howe's release from prison on an assault charge after his plea of self-defence had been accepted. The poem celebrates the demonstrations and unity of various black activist groups including the Race Today Collective in their demands for Howe's release (14-5). "It Dread Inna Inglan" similarly is a campaign song for the release of George Lindo, a factory worker jailed for armed robbery in Bradford. Again, solidarity is the key theme:

> Maggi Tacha on di go,
> wid a racist show,
> but she haffi go,
> kaw,
> rite now,
> African, Asian,
> an' Black British,
> stan' firm inna Inglan,
> inna disya time yah (14)

Other poems in the volume stress the same theme ("Independent Intavenshun," "It Noh Funny" and "Reality Poem"), while the violent response is problematised. "Sonny's Lettah" recounts events leading up to a murder charge as Sonny accidentally kills a policeman who was attacking his little brother. "Fite Dem Back" appears to be a call for a "countah-attack" against fascist violence, but the use of a cockney accent in the chorus suggests a lowering to their level in espousing this sentiment: "we gonna smash their brains in, / cause they ain't got nofink in 'em (20). Johnson's role as poet changes from this basis as he uses his popularity and voice to act the spokesman for the unwritten history of blacks in Britain. "Di Great Insohreckshan" celebrates the riots of 1981 as a victory "fi mek di rulah dem andahstan / dat wi naw tek noh more a dem oppreshan" (Johnson, *Inglan* 29). "New Craas Massahkah" emphasizes the efforts of the police and the press to obscure a racist motivation behind a fire in which thirteen young blacks died at house in New Cross, London also in 1981.

Gathered together on the album significantly entitled *Making History* (1984), the poems highlight the prominent space that the black British now occupied in British society and the need to assert their history as part of that society. The sense of continuity that John La Rose described is evident here, and the inclusion of "Reggae Fi Radni" eloquently describes the dangers inherent in challenging the erasure of a history of black resistance in colonial societies:

> some wi seh dat Waltah Radni,
> couldn' tek histri wait,
> soh im tek it aaf im back,
> an goh put it pan im lap,
> an goh fall in a trap,
> an soh Burham get e drap (Johnson "Some Thoughts" 59)

In terms of his own alliance of culture and resistance, Johnson had a rather different concern about the subversion of his art. By the early Eighties he was describing what he called the "Rasta trap." The success of reggae as an international music (and thus coming under the influence of the international music industry) leads to the appropriation of a revolutionary form to feed a mass market. Talking about the sudden proliferation of reggae bands, Johnson points out the discrepancy between pleas for repatriation to Africa and being accompanied by "wailing rock guitar." He says, "they see the image projected by Marley, the Rasta image, attracting a wider audience. Bob's success [. . .] made the image an attraction. Others latched onto it and fell into what I describe as the Rasta trap" ("Some Thoughts" 59).

2.3 Linton Kwesi Johnson: Creation Rebel

Johnson's particular concern was that in a burgeoning British market the opportunity to address specifically black British issues would be lost in the "constant repetition of black nationalist clichés" (Johnson, "Some Thoughts" 61). Others were feeling a similar concern in Johnson's own field of what had become known as "dub poetry." Although Johnson did not favour this term himself, preferring to be known as "the reggae poet," he is credited by many writers as influencing a similar expansion in the genre of dub poetry. Stewart Brown in his article "Dub Poetry: Selling Out" comes to the same conclusions in this field that Johnson did in reggae:

> Performers who were more amenable to the *image* demands of the record companies emerged, performers who looked the part and could play the music but essentially lacked the *licence* of the communal experience [. . .] and gradually the power leaked away. As dub poetry becomes a commercial product, as its performers, like Benjamin Zepphaniah [sic] or Mutabaruka or Ras Levi Tafari, become media *stars* and strive to entertain a mass, multicultural audience, there seems to me to be a real danger that the protest, the anger, the fire, becomes an act, while the image [. . .] becomes the real substance of the performance. (53-4)

Carolyn Cooper picks up this theme suggesting a "conspiratorial silence" between performer and (an increasingly white) audience where "the act may become an un/conscious fraud perpetrated by both performers who exploit the low expectations and ignorance of their uncritical audience, and by the perversely "liberal," patronising art establishment" (9). Dub poetry, in an increasingly diverse black popular culture, thus becomes a fetishised article to distinguish "radical" academic articles and theses, or to be played at "right-on" parties.

In his most recent album and volume of poetry, *Tings an' Times* (1991), Johnson addresses this co-option of black radical positions into the mainstream. "Mi Revalueshanary Fren" goes back to the dialogic style alternating between the narrator describing continued black oppression while his "fren" harps on the people's movements in Eastern Europe as if they hail an irresistable and organic flow to total liberation:

mi revalueshanary fren is nat di same agen,
yu know fram wen?
fram di masses shatta silence -
staat fi grumble fram pawty paramoncy tek a tumble,
fram Hungary to Poelan to Romania,
fram di cozy cyaasle dem staat fi crumble,
wen wi buck-up wananada in a reaznin,
mi fren always en up pap di same ting,
dis is di sang im love fi sing;

Kaydar,
e ad to go,
Zhivkov,
e ad to go,
Husak,
e ad to go,
Honnicka,
e ad to go,
Chowcheskhu,
e ad to go,
jus like apartied,
will av to go (57)

The narrator's lines are accompanied on the album with a steady and traditional reggae beat, while his "fren's" are backed by a South African music popularised by the white musician, Paul Simon on his *Gracelands* album. One can sense Johnson's appraisal of another national music being co-opted into the realms of the popular and thus disempowered. Consequently, "di cansequenses an implicaeshans/espehshally fi black libahraeshan" (59) become obscured as the apparent acceptance of black cultural forms acts to suggest a black liberation that has not occurred.

Johnson takes up this theme in "Di Anfinish Revalueshan" and "Tings an" Times." "Tings" reverberates with the refrain

duped
doped

2.3 Linton Kwesi Johnson: Creation Rebel

demaralized

dizzied
dazed
paralized

and considers "ow young rebels get ole" and the desire to rebel has been suppressed:

now dat wi gat wi council flat,
an wi dis an wi dat,
wi collah tee vee an all di mad con,
now dat we create some space,
an nuff a wi own a lickle place,
now dat we gat wi mp an wi black jp,
blacks pan di radio,
blacks pan tee vee,
wi sir an wi laad an wi mbe (55)

Johnson's written style has clearly developed. The broadly phonetic basis of the language in *Dread Beat* is enhanced here in "Re*value*shan," "*mad*" for mod-con and "*collah* tee vee" suggesting collar as well as colour (my emphasis). There is a greater determination in evidence to twist and make strange Standard English and to recall roots resistance in the Caribbean and Africa. "Di Anfinish Revalueshan" features surprising references to "mount zion" and "di new jerusalem" in an effort to revive Rastafarianism as a revolutionary force:

Far freedom is nat idealagy,
freedam is a human necessity,
it cyaan depen pan now wan somebady,
is up to each an evry wan a wi (61)

"Story" similarly appeals to a Caribbean past using phrases like "mi spirit get vex," "ow it craw-up," "dis smilin an skinin yu teet" and finishing with the line "si mi crawsiz?"

141

There is thus a clear sense in Johnson's most recent work of a determination to regain control of black art as an authentic voice for the black British population. His point is not one of separatism within the community as an end in itself, but as a necessary phase in a liberation that has not yet been achieved. Black art thus functions as a medium through which the desire for liberation may be communicated to a black population still controlled through white-dominated ideologies.

* * *

Something of a similar process is thus evident here, to that identified at the end of Part One. There, the constitution of the black identity, as enacted by Poitier's portrayal of Mark Thackery, remained subject to the perceptions of the host nation. By the end of this chapter, though, the host nation had a substantial black community whose sense of identity had been forged in reaction to two decades of explicitly racist activities. The celebration, and aggressive defence, of that identity was a characteristic both of the society in which it was performed, and the literature with which it was described. Thus, when Johnson regrets the loss of that aggression and sharply defined sense of self in the Nineties, one can sense something of the "*To Sir, With Love* syndrome."

As Stewart Brown notes in his article, there is a fine line to judge between the positive aspects of a more widely available access to black culture, and the ideological uses to which such exposure is put (53). Carolyn Cooper (9) points to the case of Ben Zephaniah being simultaneously considered for a Professorship of Poetry at Oxford University on the one hand, and crudely lambasted for some de-contextualised verse on the other. Black culture can lose its potential to define and liberate black identities once it becomes a commercialised commodity aimed at a mass audience. The corrective to this view will be enacted in Part Three, as the writers there assert an identity which is British by turning a critical eye on their own community.

PART 3

3.0 Introduction: The Present Generation

There is a certain significance to be found in the fact that the writers considered in this final chapter are not to be found under the 'Anglophone Literatures' section of academic libraries, but rather filed alphabetically away with the twentieth-century British fiction. Neither Joan Riley or Caryl Phillips nor David Dabydeen were born in Britain, so this cataloguing detail is perhaps symbolic of a wider social, cultural and political change.

If the 1958 riots may be regarded as enabling the articulation of public and legislative racism in Britain, then the more widespread disturbances in 1981 may be perceived as having almost the opposite effect. The Scarman Report commissioned to investigate the causes of the riots is regarded by some commentators as having initiated a wider debate into "the role and efficacy of public policy measures in tackling racial discrimination and disadvantage" (Saggar 129). In effect, after these events, the debate swung from that of immigration control to race relations.

Again, like 1958, this was not a sudden ideological departure for the Tory government, but part of a process already in place. While Margaret Thatcher's electoral success in 1979 may be partially attributed to her policy statements on immigration control, the rapid enactment of these pledges by her, through the introduction of the 1981 British Nationality Act, is regarded, by many, as having effectively silenced the debate on immigration. By "repoliticising race," Thatcher at once captured the support previously given to the National Front in the 1979 election, and silenced, thereafter, right-wing politicians by assuming control of the debate (Miles and Phizacklea 106).

Simultaneous to this policy shift to the right on immigration issues, the Conservative Party also set in train moves to capture the votes of blacks and Asians which had traditionally been associated with the Labour Party. The formation in 1976 of an Anglo-Asian Conservative Society and an Anglo-West Indian Conservative Society was evidence of this effort, rapidly mimicked by the Labour Party, to seduce the black vote. Thus, while the Government maintained its commitment to halt immigration (and the events of the summer of 1993 testify to the State's continued enthusiasm for deportations[21]), this courting of the Black vote, together with the new parliamentary mood, represented a public recognition of a permanent multi-racial population in Britain.

Clearly, this shift in debate did not herald a new period of racial harmony in Britain. Indeed, those elements of the Scarman Report which focussed on social disadvantage, racism and police aggression have been the subject of less action than those which suggested provision for a police force trained and equipped for paramilitary public order control (Northam 50-2). However, the Government's determination to interpret the riots solely as a problem of law and order, while in line with "mugging" and the criminalisation of black West Indians, had a further effect on public perceptions.

While this criminalisation originally permitted the specification of the "alien threat" as black youths from the ghetto, the last decade has been dominated by a different alien threat that has altered public perceptions of racial difference. The rise of Islamic fundamentalism, punctuated by international conflicts ranging from the Iranian revolution, the bombing of Libya, the Salman Rushdie affair and the Gulf Conflict has effectively redefined the two strands of racist ideology identified in the last chapter. As a problem of law and order, black youths have become subsumed into a generalised rise in crime and thus, an aspect of Britain's social decline. It has not been the same for the Asian community.

It should be remembered that after 1962, the impetus for further immigration legislation was provided by Asian nationality crises in East Africa, and that the British Nationality Act was worded in order to preclude any future problems of legal or moral responsibility towards other such overseas citizens. Moreover, as the calls for repatriation gave ground to debates on race relations, it was the Asian religious cultures that represented a visible and inassimilable presence. Schools became the centre of disputes as illustrative microcosms of the (white) British nation being swamped by alien

---

[21] Two cases concerning deportation were referred to the Home Office in August 1993. The first was the death of Joy Gardner who died whilst being restrained by Scotland Yard's deportation squad. The second was that of Dorothy Nwokedi who was allegedly bound, gagged and assaulted whilst being returned to Nigeria. The two stories broke on 31 and 9 Aug. 1993, respectively.

3.0 Introduction: The Present Generation

cultures. The Ray Honeyford affair received national publicity in 1986, as did the Dewsbury "strike" in 1988, articulating the same fear for nationhood espoused by Powell twenty years earlier.

As the Islamic world replaces Communism as the threat to Western civilisation, and the Salman Rushdie affair in particular identifies a Muslim community in Britain; so the Caribbean black British seem less alien, untainted by the stigma of religious separatism.[22] Sports stars and television personalities maintain a constant black presence that is identifiably British. Thus, while police harassment, racial disadvantage and social deprivation continue to exist for Caribbean migrants and their children, the term, British Asian remains clouded by fears of Islamic fundamentalism in a manner which the term black British does not invoke.

* * *

Something of this process of assimilation was also occurring in the field of art and culture by the start of the Eighties. Phillips' and Riley's inclusion into the body of British contemporary literature was reflected in a growing impatience with a fetishised idea of black art. This had nothing to do with Naipaul's rather embarrassed outburst in 1960, and more to do with two important developments in the ever-present debates on audience and identity; the emergence of a strong independent black press, and the contributions of black women writers.

The existence of a predominantly white publishing industry aiming at a largely white audience inevitably leads to the marginalisation of black writing, circumscribing the kind of black writing which does get published. Mike Phillips' description of the role of black characters in contemporary drama in this sense might legitimately be extended to a much broader field:

> Black people are always acted upon. They are always reacting. They never have any sense of initiative, and their lives are always totally bonded by the issue of discrimination. They're always confined by the responses of white people. So, if you look at any-

---

[22] Saggar refers to an "unholy alliance" between white neo-conservatives and religious separatists from Black minorities on the issue of segregation in schools (192).

thing that any white writer has written for the screen, what you see is a series of white reactions, and the space that they outline is where the black person is. The black person doesn't exist. (Qtd. in Pines 178-9)

This is a question of audience and perceptions and is confining in two ways. Firstly, because a black writer or artist is perceived to be black before (s)he is recognised for their talent, they are immediately pigeon-holed into the "minority budget" or quota. As Trix Worrell puts it, "there's always this 'one-only' mentality which says that it's OK to have one black show, but if there's more than one then there's a problem" (qtd. in Pines 187). Secondly, because the publishing house, or television studio, wants to ensure that their black slot is "properly" utilised, then the subject matter will inevitably revolve around the oppressed race theme as the expression of a self-consciously liberal white establishment.

The quite phenomenal growth of independent black publishing houses since the mid-Eighties has had a twofold effect. Firstly, without challenging the major publishing houses, they have enabled black writers to escape the "quota system" and explore aspects of black existence without the constraint of "fitting black outlines." Secondly, the existence of these presses, as exemplified by X Press in the Foreword, encourages a black reading audience who can expect the texts to have evaded Barbara Burford's "cross-cultural filter."

While this is a potentially positive development, one must be careful to avoid a cultural apartheid. Caryl Phillips, as has been noted, is conscious of his black audience but equally careful, as will be seen, not to be restricted in his subject matter by the concerns of post-riot Britain. Fred D'Aguiar is also an opponent of the term 'black British' as a restrictive and obstructive umbrella:

> The term sounds knee-capping, defining you by your race not craft or imagination, and separating you from your white artistic peers [. . .] Britain is a plural society. You can't surgically remove the black British contribution from what it means to be British [. . .] I want to opt into the intellectual combat defining

3.0 Introduction: The Present Generation

where this culture is going. Being West Indian doesn't mean you're outside it. (Qtd. in Jaggi 5)

The slight corrective to this view is the concern within the black community about the images that are presented to a white audience. This is a particular aspect of the current generation of writers who have begun to question the cultural values and social mores of their emigrant parents. The emergent black women's fiction and Joan Riley in particular, have been criticised for their negative portrayal of black men, the argument being that in a prejudiced society one should be careful not to reinforce such prejudices.

This is far from being the concern solely of women writers; Victor Headley has had to defend *Yardie* because of the criminal activity, and Caryl Phillips has also drawn criticism for his characterisation of Caribbean men. Moreover, this trend (particularly having been noted in the two most published black writers of their generation) is prey to the fetishisation of the oppressed race theme:

> publishers [. . .] tell me what they think the market requires. At the moment from black women writers it seems to require what Dorothea Smartt in a review in the New Statesman calls '. . . the pathologizing of the Blackwoman's condition,' or, as Grace Nichols puts it in her wonderful poem: '. . . a little black pain undressed.' (Burford 37)

However, the identification of Caribbean patriarchy remains an important development in the articulation of the black British identity; it is a structural feature of Phillips' and Riley's work (and is evident elsewhere[23]) as part of a reaction against a romanticisation of Caribbean society, and the emergence of a self-critical black community.

---

[23] The 1986 Conference on Caribbean Literature was disrupted by an assault on Sam Selvon by a female member of staff at the Commonwealth Institute, who "failed to recognize" the irony of the sexism in his reading from *The Lonely Londoners* (Alcorn 52).

The relationship between immigrant or black British identity and the perceptions of a white population, noted throughout this book, thus remain clearly apparent. The significance of the last decade is that it has enabled the development of debate within that black community. D'Aguiar is right to insist on being recognised as a writer, rather than a black British writer, in the same way that Burford is right to resist being confined by the specifications of a genre (Black womens' writing) which are not precisely her own. At the same time, however, the term 'black British' should maintain its legitimacy.

Mainstream British culture is not a homogeneous whole any more than British society itself. While one should not insist that black British writers fulfil only a specific function in the composition of that culture, neither should one deny the opportunity for sustained debate within the genre. Black British culture can express the concerns and reality (or realities) of the black community as long as it has the space to articulate its diversity. As Mike Phillips puts it: "We have to deal with the whole spectrum of black experience, because that is the only way we will begin to sort out what our true identity is" (qtd. in Pines 177). In this respect, it is the free expression of this diversity within mainstream culture that will signal the cultural integration implied by the library classification referred to above.

* * *

The work of Joan Riley, Caryl Phillips and David Dabydeen exemplifies the concerns of an emergent black British community. Riley's *The Unbelonging* (1985) was seized upon by The Women's Press to exploit the success of the American women writers, Alice Walker and Maya Angelou. This at once contributed to the demand for fictionalised black female misery, and drew an angry response from some black commentators for producing negative images of black men. Riley, however, was clearly undaunted, as the depiction of patriarchal attitudes remained a feature of her three subsequent texts.

In each case, Caribbean traditions are depicted as the source of these attitudes, and are set at variance with the expectations of younger, black British generation. Conflict thus arises as much within the black community, as it does as a result of racism inflicted upon it from without. In both her

3.0 Introduction: The Present Generation

first text, and the second, *Waiting in the Twilight* (1987), Riley uses memories of life in the Caribbean, prior to emigration, to allow the reader to discover the roots of that conflict in Britain. In both cases, the tragedy of the impossibility of a return to a Caribbean homeland is communicated by the character's inability or unwillingness to recognise the faults in Jamaican society.

In *Romance* (1987), Riley illustrates the reproduction of Caribbean patriarchy in Britain, both in the attitude of the men and the collusion of the women in their own oppression. Bringing an ageing couple from the Caribbean to help reverse this process provides an unusual antidote to the practice of claiming African traditions to erect male social and domestic supremacy.

Riley's later book, *A Kindness to the Children* (1992), is set in the Caribbean and again demonstrates that it is not a spiritual homeland for Britain's black population. A reality of poverty, corruption and violence provides the backdrop for a woman's lapse into insanity at the hands of a society quick to condemn women, and eager to protect men.

These themes of patriarchy and the dismissal of return, in effect the forging of the black British identity, are also evident in the work of Caryl Phillips. Starting as a playwright, Phillips' initial project was to tackle the absence of texts that might express his reality as a black person in Britain. In fact, it was his work in the theatre that persuaded Rudolph Walker to stay in the country after the downturn in black acting parts in the late Seventies (Pines 80).

Phillips' first two published play scripts, *Strange Fruit* (1981) and *Where There is Darkness* (1982), both deal with the tension between the Caribbean migrants and their British-born children. In the first, the mother's submissive struggle to educate her sons into integration leaves them existentially bereft of their Caribbean heritage. Their effort to erect a cultural heritage through black activism falters when one goes to the Caribbean and learns its reality. A converse situation is described in *Where There is Darkness* as Albert Williams maintains his attitude as an island hustler through twenty-five years in exile, and tries to breed the same ruthlessness into his son.

Phillips' first two novels continue this theme of revisiting the experience of emigration by the older generation. *The Final Passage* (1985) is written in the tradition of Lamming, Selvon and the other early writers, but, like Riley, Phillips concentrates on the female experience notably absent in the work of those writers. *A State of Independence* (1986) develops Phillips' theme of displacement and the impossibility of return, tracing Bertram Francis' experiences in St. Kitts after twenty years in exile.

In his two more recent texts, Phillips' concern to evade the circumscription of the black British writer tag, and determination to broaden cross-cultural understanding has led to an alteration in style. Both *Higher Ground* (1989) and *Cambridge* (1991), use interweaving narratives to suggest historical and social correspondences, to break down fixed and divisive perspectives.

David Dabydeen's two fictional works to date maintain the Indo-Caribbean presence in the text. His two volumes of poetry set out to restore this presence within the genre; the first, *Slave Song* (1984), using Creole to convey the brutality and tragedy of the canecutters' existence. His novels, though, like his second book of verse, *Coolie Odyssey* (1988), combines images of Guyana with a description of the immigrant experience.

The Intended (1991) and *Disappearance* (1993) both make a Harrisonian appeal to temper commitment to a materialist culture with an intuitive sensibility. Dabydeen is less obscure than Harris, though, and thus his vision of Britain as a society bound by divisive structures, and a commitment to "progress," is conveyed through images of a debased video culture and petty fraud. Using two central characters with a profound belief in the efficacy of Western education, Dabydeen asserts the value of the non-metropolitan cultures and states the case for a creolised British society.

3.1 Joan Riley: Caribbean Conversations I

When Joan Riley's first novel *The Unbelonging* was published in 1985, it was hailed by *Spare Rib* as the first by a West Indian-born woman to be published in Britain and, as such, an "historic event" (Bishop 27). It entered a literary milieu established by the publication in Britain of the Afro-American writers Alice Walker and Maya Angelou. *The Color Purple* (1983) and *I Know Why the Caged Bird Sings* (1984) had both been extremely successful, each being reprinted five times in 1984 alone. Despite the apparent similarities between the narrative content of the three texts, however, Riley was not to enjoy the same popularity as the American writers, the unease surrounding her work being expressed from the first.

Marla Bishop's discussion of *The Unbelonging* in *Spare Rib* focusses on the incidence of incest, the rapacity of the black male characters and the self-hatred of the central figure, Hyacinth. Riley, she says, "has come under a lot of criticism from black people – especially men – for washing dirty linen in public" (27). These issues also figure in both Angelou's and Walker's texts, but there are some essential differences. Most importantly, *The Unbelonging* fails to offer hope. Where Celie knows the significance of the colour purple and Marguerite knows why the caged bird sings (and indeed when Linton Kwesi Johnson's rebels are making history), Hyacinth in *The Unbelonging* is more completely dispossessed by the end of the text than she was at the start.

Furthermore, Riley's text is set in contemporary Britain. In the American texts the reader could maintain a sense of distance from the institutionalised racism of fifty years ago and see in the heroine's progress a signifier for a developing social structure. The Deep South becomes imbued with an emblematic quality akin to Dickens' London; its misery is acknowledged, but as part of a period piece. Riley's text does not permit this sense of distance and vicarious achievement and thus, when Bishop questions the effect of presenting negative images to "a society which is already too willing to focus on black people as 'problems,'" the question of for whom the writer is writing is again clearly raised (27).

While Bishop tries to insist on "the web of interrelating factors which serve to create the conditions leading to violence in the family and the abuse of children" (27), Riley is more blunt. A family split through emigration may lead to a father losing his paternal instinct towards his daughter, but the essential issue is this:

> There is a great divide between black men and women, and I think it's caused by the massive egos black men have, and by black women's conditioning [. . .] Look at Caribbean writers – very few are women. Black women have grown up in a very macho society, so there are certain images of women we're constantly fed. Although black women know they are capable of doing anything they want, they feel they have to placate men. (Qtd. in Bishop 27)

In thus addressing Caribbean patriarchy, as it exists both in the Caribbean and Britain, Riley is writing for the black community, writing a part of their history, but in a different way to Linton Kwesi Johnson. Where dub poetry and Rastafarianism may be read there as a cultural assertion of self for an embattled community, Riley's texts expose the way the same community is embattled within itself through its patriarchal traditions. The Caribbean exists in her texts as the other voice in a dialogue with the black community in Britain, speaking through that community, but interrupted by an emergent black British identity. It is this discord between accepted praxis in the Caribbean and a new consciousness in Britain that is evident in Riley's work. The Caribbean and its male-dominated traditions are rejected as alternatives to racial hostility in Britain, and the romance of return explicitly denied.

Riley's four novels to date explore a spectrum of female experience within the context of the relationship between the Caribbean and the black British. The various ways in which the main protagonists carry out their "conversations" with the Caribbean not only reflect on the romance of return, but also on the necessity to confront the influence of the Caribbean before resolutions may be found in Britain.

* * *

In *The Unbelonging*, Hyacinth's dialogue with the Caribbean through the bulk of text is a mental one, based on her childhood memories. In this respect she is an unreliable narrator, using partial and conflicting accounts of her life there. The reader, however, is invited from the start to view this as her response to a grim existence in Britain. Brutally beaten by her father, despised by her stepmother, and victimised at school by both pupils and teachers, Hyacinth's search for refuge in a rose-hued Caribbean seems entirely comprehensible. Significantly, though, there is a clear difference between Hyacinth's conscious reconstructions of Kingston and her subconscious memory. When first quizzed about her life in Kingston, Hyacinth has to make a conscious effort to override her true memory:

> A vision of the tenements with their zinc fencing and old rusting shacks, some with holes eaten right through, flashed shamefully through her mind to be pushed back hastily. 'I come from a big city [. . .] A nice big city with lots of sunshine and grass to play on at school.' (19)

She similarly tells a social worker that she lived at Mona, near the University in order to disguise her poverty-stricken upbringing (71).

Hyacinth's dreams are a similar negotiation of real memory and fantasy, gradually betraying more and more of the reality of her existence in Jamaica. The bed-wetting episodes with which the text begins are dreams about happy events such as the Independence Day parade, the excitement of which presumably leads to Hyacinth's loss of control. It slowly becomes apparent, though, that the real cause of this lies in Jamaica, as Hyacinth witnesses the death of her friend Cynthia, killed in a fire by her mad father (142-3). As reality progressively intrudes into her fantasy, the reader is encouraged to expect a resolution of Freudian self-analysis, but Riley does not allow this potential path of progress and self-awareness to reach fruition. Instead, Hyacinth's father and his incestuous intentions become interwoven with the original trauma, and Hyacinth's fantasies with regard to Jamaica only cease when she returns there at the end of the text. There she is shocked by the reality of the tenement shack and the fact that she has brought a gift for the dead Cynthia. Rather than being liberated by accepting this reality, she is oppressed by the sudden awareness that she has nowhere to belong.

Parallel to this (failed) psychic journey to a past sense of self, Hyacinth undergoes a similar travail in a present that she largely tries to obscure through her insistence on the past. Her awareness of herself at the start of the text is based on her appearance, her Blackness. When she arrives in London from the Caribbean, Hyacinth finds herself surrounded by

> a sea of white faces [. . .] all hostile. She had known they hated her, and she had felt small, lost and afraid, and ashamed of her plaited hair as she had looked enviously at the smooth straightness of theirs. She had always wanted long hair [. . .] and she wished with all her might that her prayers would be answered and she would become like them. (13)

This self-hatred is reflected onto black people generally. She hopes her father will look like a cross between Richard Rowntree and Sidney Poitier (14) (as the acceptable faces of Blackness), and when he becomes her sole and monstrous role model, she learns to distrust and reject all black individuals. Thus, when Hyacinth goes to sixth-form college later in the text, she shuns other black students, "feeling the need to establish herself as different from them in other peoples minds" and finds herself gravitating towards the Indian students; "they were not white, but they had long hair, and their noses were straight, their lips nice and thin" (81).

An essential part of this self-image involves Hyacinth's awakening sexuality. Her father's sadistic treatment of her in pre-adolescence and his attempted rape leaves Hyacinth associating men and sexuality with punishment, anger and incest. Consequently, when her attempts at improving her self-esteem with beauty treatments result in men noticing her, she is at first gratified (largely due to her diet of romance novels) and then feels panicked and ashamed by their physical advances. By attaching herself to an image of the past, Hyacinth prevents herself from coming into her womanhood and her place in the black community.

Education seems to offer Hyacinth the path to escape her past. Embarked upon initially as the means by which to return to Jamaica, her progress to University provides the few moments of triumph in the text. She is taken into care after escaping from her father's attempted rape (80-1), and thereafter her educational career is a success not only passing the exams, but

3.1 Joan Riley: Caribbean Conversations I

also in taking control of her own destiny in the face of opposition from the social services. At university she meets Perlene, who, as a radical Jamaican woman seems set to perform the Shug Avery role from Walker's text.

On arrival, Hyacinth tries to hide her history of abuse, children's homes and hostels, preferring instead to make her Jamaican fantasies real by pretending that her childhood in Britain never happened. Although Perlene can see the untruth of this, she never succeeds in helping Hyacinth come to terms with the real Jamaica and liberating her own selfhood. Even a lecture by Walter Rodney which begins to help her understand her own experiences within the context of a general black experience, is rejected by her as it subsequently intrudes on her Jamaican fantasy (116-8).

Sexually, too, the friendship fails. Although Perlene does not display any bi-sexuality herself, she does the next best thing and introduces Hyacinth to Charles, a young African who actually wins Hyacinth's trust. Hyacinth agrees to have sex with Charles in an effort to exorcise her father's presence from her sexuality, but this resolves only in Hyacinth regressing to a bed-wetting episode and in her avoiding both Charles and Perlene until she is about to depart for the Caribbean (130-2).

Hyacinth's unwillingness to accept a real and changing Jamaica is at the same time an unwillingness to accept her real self. This much is made abundantly clear when she does arrive back at her aunt's shack. Its poverty has not changed, but her expectations have, and she rejects both it and its inhabitants, running away from her bed-ridden aunt. Furthermore, it, in the shape of her friend from her dreams, Florence, rejects her as an alien, reviling her for her neglect of her aunt, and saying, "[y]u is a different person wid yu speakey spokey ways. Yu noh belang ya soh" (141).

In failing to find a Jamaican reality that she can accept, Hyacinth is unable to accept herself, as her only positive self-image is in a fantasised childhood. In this respect she is left as a "young girl, trapped and bleeding in the deepest recesses of her woman's body" (143). Ngcobo tries to broaden this experience attributing a black "schizophrenic existence" to the unwillingness of white society to allow blacks to think of themselves as anything other than immigrants (10).

This, however, does not sufficiently account for the image of Jamaican life that Riley conjures up, the Caribbean side of the dialogue that is sexual violence, madness, disease and poverty. In particular, it does not acknowledge how these aspects of Caribbean life are translated into the emigrant and black British experience. It is this theme to which Riley returned in her next novel, *Waiting in the Twilight*.

* * *

If *The Unbelonging* was an emotionally taxing text, then Chris Searle's comment on the front cover of the 1992 edition of *Waiting in the Twilight* promises more of the same: "Cry if you must, then think on what you have read and then rise." Riley herself dedicates it to "a whole generation of women, who took ship and sailed into the unknown to build a better future for their children." As a panegyric or a call to arms, though, this book provides little framework for resistance or solidarity in the clash between Caribbean patriarchal morality and British racial hostility.

As in *The Unbelonging* there is a continuous dialogue between the Caribbean and the central figure through memory. Adella is also a desperately sad character. Partially crippled by a stroke, deserted by her husband and cleaning floors in council offices, the prospect of a return to the Caribbean seems again to be the most promising scenario. Adella, though, is a more reliable narrator than Hyacinth, most strikingly so because of her absolute acceptance of, and belief in, a harsh and hypocritical moral regime. The dominant presence of men is again a central issue here.

Adella's conditioning is established at the start of the text as she remembers having to avoid the attentions of the local pastor. In Riley's later text, *A Kindness to the Children*, this assault is carried out and the girl, Jean, carries a burden of guilt for this attack. Here, Adella attempts to conceal her fears from her devout grandmother, but then is surprised to learn that her grandmother and "[e]verybady in de village know de pastor have a weakness fa de young girl dem" (33). Everybody knows, but nobody challenges his activities and it is thought best to send Adella to Kingston rather than risk an incident.

This is a patriarchal morality, in which a man's "weakness" readily indicts the girl or woman as a temptation and thereby at fault. It becomes more overt in Kingston. Adella goes to live and work as a seamstress with her cousin and his wife under the strict religious observance of the "Satur-

3.1 Joan Riley: Caribbean Conversations I

day Church." When she falls pregnant by Beresford, her cousins reject Adella and she moves into a tenement shack that Beresford rents for her. Beresford not only expects Adella to be grateful to him for this but also to repay him with sex. When she objects, he asserts the hard facts of male dominance: "Yu tink yu can jus live by yuself dung ya? Well yu betta learn dis fram now. If yu doan have a man fe proteck yu, yu gwine have plenty trouble. At least yu have me, an tru everybady know me roun ya yu gwine safe as long as dem know yu is my woman" (113). Presumably, everybody also knows that he is already married, but it is Adella who slowly loses her clients when they discover she is pregnant and unmarried. It is not until she has married Stanton that she once again feels she can attend Church and her rich clients feel they can buy her dresses.

What emerges from this part of the narrative is the complete disempowerment of women in Jamaican life, caught between the threat of physical attack from men on one side, and social censure on the other. The threat of abandonment by Beresford sufficiently cows Adella, as she is too afraid to brave life alone in the city, and too ashamed to return to her village having "sinned." Beresford does not have to beat her himself, and this is a departure from earlier Caribbean novels where patriarchy is evident in wife-beating as an accepted aspect of life. Selvon, in *Turn Again Tiger* has the entire male population of Five Rivers indulge in "[t]he-night-we-wash-the-women-with-licks" as a comic portrayal of this "activity" (90). Riley, by contrast, uses this to characterise life in exile.

In *The Unbelonging*, Riley made room to show the defeated side of Hyacinth's father as he becomes suddenly timid and respectful in the doctor's surgery (28-31). Also, as Ngcobo points out, although he drinks, he rarely goes out to do so (9). A sense is thus maintained in both these texts, and in the one that follows, that the bitterness and impotence of the black man's life in Britain encourages tyranny at home. Indeed a similar process is implied in *The Unbelonging* as Hyacinth acts cruelly towards her stepbrothers (22-4). Despite this apparent conclusion, though, Riley still configures domestic violence as a function of the older, emigrant generation that distinguishes them from a generation not born into Caribbean patriarchy.

By the time Adella joins Stanton in London, he has ceased to be the family man he was in Kingston. Adella's "failure" to provide him with a son, followed by her first stroke, which leaves her partially crippled, finally ends any sense of loyalty he had towards her, and he begins an affair with her cousin Gladys. During this time he regularly beats her, demands food that he withholds from his children and refuses to contribute towards the running of the house. When Adella finally demands that Gladys should leave their house, Stanton tries to suffocate her with a pillow and leaves. Adella thinks this behaviour is quite acceptable, even when he continues to abuse her having moved in with Gladys. Her greatest dream remains that he will return to her, because should he do so, he will restore her respectability. Ironically, Adella is obliged to have "men-friends," whose gifts help keep the household running as she struggles to keep up with maintenance costs, thus recreating the enforced prostitution that she thought she had escaped in Kingston.

Adella's children, however, do not accept their father's behaviour. Much is made in the text of Adella's different expectations of her children:

> She was determined to build a better life for her children. The ones back home would get treated like the people coming over to work, there wasn't much she could do about that. But her England-born children would be different. They were going to be just like white people. They were going to be accepted. (15)

This is borne out in the text through Carol and Audrey, both of whom have stayed in education and now work for the council. They serve as translators for Adella, speaking for her to the police and the doctors and filling in council forms. Indeed, the way in which Carol deals with the police after Adella has been mugged is almost too slick (77-80).

Adella, however, regrets her childrens' unwillingness to respect their father. She is used to being hit when Stanton feels frustrated or in the wrong, "but the children were different. They had got infected with white people's ideas" (133). They regard their father as a "goodfanuting" and try their best to dispel Adella's illusion that he will return to her one day. Their reaction to Stanton's beatings and his philandering ways is a measure both of the different praxis they have learnt as black British and of the absence of the

3.1 Joan Riley: Caribbean Conversations I

kind of patriarchy that exists in Adella's Jamaica. Adella's own reasoning of Stanton's behaviour is typical of the attitudes she was prey to herself: "A tell yu, yu father was one man. Yu caan expect a man like dat fe get tie by a cripple; and den yu Auntie Gladys did lead ihm into temptation'" (45). Notably, Stanton himself is not directly to blame, but is a victim of "temptation."

It is this sensibility that cripples Adella more surely than her stroke, and prevents her from returning to Jamaica. Stanton's infidelity becomes for her an indictment of her "own" sin with Beresford, and she knows that she would be judged on that basis if she went back:

> She had known then that she could never return. She would never be accepted with the sins she had committed. They had been sure she had driven her husband away, spoken about her life with Beresford. And even called her name in church. It had been a bitter thing, made worse by the knowledge that she would never have the money to live well in Jamaica again. (125)

When she suffers another and terminal stroke, she imagines in her final delirium that Stanton has come back to her and that the family has gathered round in a last show of respect. In this way she dies having never really left the Caribbean.

* * *

Images of the black British in *Waiting* are effectively restricted to two of Adella's children, Carol and Audrey, who accept their mother's stubborn adherence to Caribbean praxis with a mixture of tolerance and exasperation. In *Romance*, Riley focuses more intensely on a specifically black British situation using the dialogue with the Caribbean on this occasion to completely different effect.

The narrative centres around two sisters, Desiree and Verona. Like Riley's first two texts, *Romance* begins on a bleak note. Verona is duped into signing a false confession to theft at work and is sacked, while Desiree is desperately ill but receives no support from her husband, John, even when it transpires that she needs a hysterectomy. Furthermore, Verona has been raped at the age of fourteen by one of Desiree's boyfriends and, having kept it a secret, now only feels safe with (old) white men, whom she must also keep secret because of Desiree's anti-white prejudice. Like *The Unbelonging*, then, one is immediately presented with a set of problems related to a notion of selfhood that the text is expected to take on; Desiree's domestic liberation and Verona's personal liberation.

Quite apart from Verona's personal fear and loathing of black men, there is a more general dislocation from the black community apparent at the start of the text. After the dominant roles played by the first generation emigrants in the first two texts, it is noticeable here that both John and Verona and Desiree have lost their parents. While John maintains strong communications with the Jamaican grandparents who raised him, Verona and Desiree effectively lose all sense of their Guyanese heritage with the death of their father. Furthermore, John and Desiree's house, where Verona also lives with their two children, is situated in Croydon, on the absolute fringe of the south London area and significantly removed from the Brixton heartland.

This dislocation is reflected in all three characters' perceptions of themselves and the society they live in. The repressed trauma of Verona's rape has made her a compulsive eater in an effort to build up a bulky sense of protection against further assault. By the same token she takes refuge in romantic fiction and imagines herself (like Hyacinth) as the willowy blonde heroine of her various novels. Desiree similarly buries herself in domestic martyrdom to John and her two children and the continuing role of surrogate mother to Verona. John, meanwhile, is the stable provider, too aware of his own obligation to work overtime and endure racist practices at work to acknowledge any responsibilities to his wife and family beyond this function.

In each case, there is a clear sense of a character introverted from a communal awareness, particularly in terms of being part of the black British. Verona's initial response to the 1981 Brixton riots is that the black youths involved were "troublemakers" (29), while it takes the arbitrary arrest of her friend's son for theft, for Desiree to realise how she was distanced from the harsh reality of black life in the city:

3.1 Joan Riley: Caribbean Conversations I

> She wanted to say that they [the police] were oppressing the youth all the time; but she knew so little about it. Until today it had just been something on the edge of her mind, like immigration and bad housing. Somehow it had never seemed real; it didn't happen to the people she knew. She felt ashamed at how little she really cared. (125)

In this novel, the Black United Front (BUF) represents a replacement for the influence of the first generation by black British radicalism, and therefore a potential antidote for this isolation. This is a group (centred in Balham, South London) in which John was once active in a period that Desiree equates with happier marital times. It is also the direction Verona briefly takes after the 1981 riots, the accounts of police brutality exposing her romantic fiction as "cardboard unreality" (29). With Jay's arrest being personal enough to shock the family out of their insularity and back into contact with a wider experience, the episode presents a potential turning point in the narrative.

The BUF is now led by Winston, Jay's father from his first marriage to Mara. Mara and Desiree go to Winston after they receive news of the arrest to enlist the support of the BUF. Winston's initial description is suggestive of the Social Rastafarianism outlined by John La Rose in the last chapter. He has "*neat* shoulder length locks" and a "*well-trimmed* beard," and litters his previously Standard English with terms such as "downpression" and "Babylon" when discussing the BUF's involvement (118-9; my italics).

Rastafarianism as a culture of resistance surrounding Johnson's work receives a different treatment from Riley. Horace Campbell in his essay accepts that "[r]astamen need to be liberated from the myths about women and the vestiges of inequalities in the family" (18), and Johnson's poetry includes some dubious lines such as:

> de bredda dem a scank;
> dem naw rab bank,
> is packit dem a pick,
> an is woman dem a lik (*Dread* 36)

This mysogynistic bent is revealed at the BUF meeting that Verona and Desiree attend to discuss Jay's case.

On arrival, they are marginalised from the group as a "hostile-looking woman" snubs them in order, ironically, to discuss the role of the African woman (127). Then, as the discussion meanders on, Verona cuts in: she castigates the proceedings in general and Winston in particular, demanding: "As for you, Winston, if you is such a big-shot, how come Mara leave you and get more education than you?" This blow to the male ego produces the expected reaction: "'No stupid woman ain't insulting me and getting away with it!' Winston was all bluster now, jumping to his feet threateningly" (128).

'Woman' in this context becomes a pejorative term as the gender relation of the confrontation multiplies its significance. The role of the African woman, as it emerges during the course of the text, is to act as the domestic subordinate and mother, while the man fulfils the role of the hunter/provider. For Verona to challenge Winston in that situation was to upset an ideology which sought to enshrine patriarchy within a cultural identity.

This ferocious exchange is the key for much of the way the characters develop within the text. The initial condition of isolation in which the three characters are found exemplifies this ideology. John "provides," but contributes nothing other than his wages to the house. This is clearly illustrated by his almost laughably selfish response to Desiree's announcement that she must go into hospital for her hysterectomy: "You've gotta be joking! What about the football, or have you forgotten that the season don't finish for two weeks?" (85). Desiree, for her part, looks back on John's work with the BUF when she could see him as a "*real* black man," liking it when "other group members came up to ask him about 'the struggle'; *it didn't matter that she never really understood the concept*" (84; my italics). While Verona resists John's abuse of Desiree throughout the text, she cleans up the flat of one of her boyfriends (who would later attack her) on the understanding that it "really was no job for a man" (172).

In the absence of the first generation of emigrants, characterised by Riley in her first two texts (as well as by Phillips and other writers of their generation) as wife-beaters, the role of the BUF is to represent the strong-

3.1 Joan Riley: Caribbean Conversations I

est influence on the emergent black British identity. Both Winston and John are apparently vindicated during the text by the assertion they are not "beating men," but, as Mara points out, "there's more than one way to beat on a woman" (61).

It is this pervasive patriarchy that Riley attempts to counter with her "Caribbean voice" in the text. John's grandparents, Ruby and Clifford, arrive the day after the BUF meeting, John typically only warning Desiree of this the night before. Riley seems to play on her own technique of relentless and deepening misery as a plot formula by introducing the couple as a frail old man and a wheelchair-bound, rather brusque woman. Desiree immediately sees her hopes of attending college being replaced by the role of care assistant to the old couple. Perversely, though, Ruby and Clifford's function as the embodiment of the Caribbean in the text provides what amounts to a pastoral interlude at the centre of the narrative. At the risk of criticising Riley for being too positive in her depiction of Caribbean life, particularly given the fact that Clifford dies and Ruby's hip operation fails, their contribution has a romantic quality.

This becomes obvious through their immediate impact on a household previously dominated by John's domestic demands. First of all the sisters are amazed and amused at the spectacle of John being ordered around by Ruby (137), and then by Clifford's competence and easy familiarity around the kitchen (148). After the ready acceptance of patriarchal exploitation in *Waiting*, this presents a very different picture of life in the Caribbean. Furthermore, the relationship is not premised on dominance by Ruby, but on mutual concern and love. This is romance at its best, and the reader senses this during one of the more overstated passages:

> [Desiree] stood in the kitchen doorway, taken aback to see Grandpa Clifford grilling bacon and frying eggs. It was one thing to know that he looked after Granny Ruby, another entirely to see how competently he moved about the kitchen. The two of them were absorbed in each other, chattering as if they had lived through a long absence, rather than having been together for over sixty years. Granny Ruby was sitting at the table, a pile of neatly

sliced hardough bread in front of her. The old woman noticed her
first and a smile warmed her lined face. (148-9)

The couple's effect on the other characters also maintains a romantic quality. John, in particular, learns through the death of Clifford to express his fears and emotions, thus losing his autocratic attitude and effectively saving his marriage to Desiree. Furthermore, Desiree's two daughters gain a sense of a Caribbean heritage, denied them by Verona and Desiree's ignorance and begin to challenge a learnt history of black peoples in the modern world. Riley, however, does not use this reconstruction of a rose-hued Caribbean as her sole response to a black British identity being built on a misappropriated African "authenticity." As it is suggested of Verona later on in the text, "[s]he should have known there was no romance in reality" (219). Instead it is Mara who is the stronger role model.

There is the potential for Mara's transformation from the submissive wife of Winston to an independent, assertive and capable woman to be a romance in itself. Riley, however, manages to contain this in two ways. Firstly, the narrative progressively suggests a relationship blooming between Mara and Olu, the lawyer who takes on Jay's case. He "rescues" her son and is generally sensitive and supportive throughout. But as the text reaches a conclusion and Desiree meaningfully says to Mara, "[y]ou really like him, don't you?", Riley gleefully resists the temptation to write a single woman as a literary loose end, and informs us that Olu is happily married (217). Secondly, Riley reconstructs the sub-plot of Mara's own development by having Desiree and Verona live elements of her experience as part of their own liberation.

Desiree's determination to enter higher education against John's wishes is guided and encouraged by Mara's advice and experience, and sustained by her own developing appetite for politics. Her engagement with herself as a part of the black community is signalled at the end of the text by an African map clock in Mara's kitchen that "seemed to symbolise all the change Mara had achieved in her life" (218). Desiree asks for one of the same, thus simultaneously identifying her progress with Mara's and symbolically accepting an African heritage on her own terms.

3.1 Joan Riley: Caribbean Conversations I

Verona becomes pregnant by her white boyfriend, and after he beats her up, leaves to stay in a single mothers' hostel thus echoing Mara's experience after she initially left Winston with her children. The assault by a man who had been a vessel for Verona's romantic illusions also helps to dispel Verona's phobia about black men, dating back to her rape. Again, a gift from Mara acts to pronounce a new sense of the self and community. A children's book written by a black writer presents an alternative to Verona's usual fiction:

> Verona looked at the pensive face of the black child on the cover, tracing the large vulnerable eyes with her fingers. 'I suppose some of me's in you,' she told the picture, before replacing the book and bending open her other choice [. . .] Tonight she'd read romance, she decided. But tomorrow, who knows? (230)

The text concludes with Desiree musing over Ruby's assertion that "there never *had* been anything to liberate herself from but herself" (231), but this is only partially true. Desiree and Verona's (and John's) changed perceptions of themselves and their social relationships perform a liberation for their children. Mara's decision to leave Winston was stimulated by seeing her children beginning to adopt the social roles implicit in her marriage; Jay was starting to beat the girls, and Charleen decided that mathematics was not a "girly thing" to enjoy doing (57). A similar cycle of oppression is evident with Desiree's daughters, particularly through the reference to their behavioural resemblance to Desiree and Verona. By liberating themselves, Desiree and Verona also break that cycle for the next generation.

* * *

Riley's most recent novel, *A Kindness to the Children*, shifts the focus directly onto the Caribbean, setting it entirely in Jamaica. It is, however, made clear from the start that the text maintains Riley's interest in the black British and their relationship with the Caribbean. The central character, Sylvia, opens the text gazing over the Jamaican landscape and drawing comparisons between it and the images evoked by the community in Brixton where she grew up. The mention of Mostyn Road recalls Adella's house there in Riley's second book, while the line, "Sylvia thought of the years her parents had spent trying to convince her she was British," recalls both Adella and John's aspirations for their children in the last two texts (2). An effort is not being made here to suggest, as was possible with Salkey's texts, that all Riley's characters may be regarded as different facets of one core character, but to maintain a sense of dialogue with the positions reversed.

There are three women whose lives interweave to form the basis of this narrative. Sylvia, who travels to Jamaica to come to terms with the death of her husband, Winston, two years earlier; Jean, who emigrated from Jamaica, met Winston's brother Jimmy, through Sylvia and now has two children by him; and Pearl, the wife of Jean's brother, George, who lives in the house in Jamaica where the action is centred. While the network of relationships is slightly convoluted, there is an important progression evident; Sylvia is British-born, Jean is a returning emigrant and Pearl has scarcely left her village. In this sense, then, there are three voices to this dialogue.

To take Sylvia first, there is a very real suggestion at the start of the text that she has found a spiritual homeland in Jamaica. Thinking of her parents' efforts to make her British, she muses:

> If only they had realised what it would mean: to be here where no English voice intruded and most every skin was black. Where the heat and the sheer *big*ness of the empty land added haunted echoes to snatches of conversations, and gave extra meaning, even to the sound of cutlass cropping grass. No one could describe the sight, the sound, the taste of this country. This was something she had to *feel*, experience for herself. (2)

Sylvia's experience is to find, gradually, that she does not belong. There are early warnings of this, as Sylvia talks to some street traders, shortly after her panegyric on Jamaica. Here she discovers that, through bribery, there is water in George's house during the drought; that black people come to the Caribbean expecting solidarity, only to have their naivety exploited; and that Jamaica has a "scourge of mad people," who do not evoke the "abstract kind of pity" that she feels (5-11). As Sylvia becomes heavily

3.1 Joan Riley: Caribbean Conversations I

involved in Jean's mental collapse, these issues, in particular, are developed.

This becomes most evident when Jean, convinced that Sylvia is trying to take her children away from her, absconds to the city with a Rastafarian, Ras Peter. Sylvia tries to use the official channels through which the social services would deal with such a situation in England. The local policeman, however, is unimpressed with the idea of interfering between a mother and her children, and Sylvia's "foreign" ideas of child protection. He offers to help upon receipt of a thousand dollars, and Sylvia is probably less outraged by this than by Pearl and George's reaction, which is simply that Mandrake is asking too much (186-92).

Sylvia determines to find Jean on her own, but she is met, in the city, by a wall of suspicion erected against her foreign accent, and so she asks Pearl's assistance. As the women in Pearl's community give their support to the search, Sylvia feels an "illusion of belonging" (256), but this illusion is soon unmasked. While she is grateful for the support and generosity of the local women, Sylvia does not feel that they are acting out of anything more than a "gut instinct rather than a rational view of moral responsibility" (254). As she struggles with the question of whether or not to have Jean committed in England and have her children taken away from her (and what her own motivation in such a process would be), Sylvia wishes for the intellectual support of her colleagues and friends in England. Having decided that she is the best qualified to start making decisions, Sylvia sees three youths stoning the shack of a local "madwoman." She intervenes, shooing the tormentors away and is then roundly abused by Maddy for doing so; her madness appoints her as the lowest form of prostitute, allowing her to survive in a society which would otherwise let her perish. Sylvia stomps off: "'Ungrateful woman!' she thought sourly [. . .] 'She don't even have enough sense to know when somebody is trying to help her'" (260).

Sylvia eventually gives up trying to help Jean and returns to England. On the plane home she sees an item in the *Sunday Gleaner* which describes the discovery of a body, probably Jean's, in some wasteland in the city. Sylvia's decision to give the paper to a fellow passenger is a sign, not only of her severance from an intimate concern with Jean's sanity, but of her dismissal of an island she has found to be institutionally racist and corrupt.

Where Sylvia discovers that Jamaica is a country she knows nothing about and where she does not belong, Jean discovers that she has never escaped being a product of island society. There are strong echoes of Adella and Hyacinth in her story, not the least being the nagging demand for the psychotherapeutic confession that is denied Hyacinth, and the sense that Caribbean women bear the burden of guilt for a patriarchal culture.

Jean's traumatic childhood is recounted in a series of memory flashbacks. With her mother having died in labour, Jean and her two brothers are brought up by their father under the religious and patriarchal regime that characterised island society. The formative elements of John and Winston's attitude in *Romance* are evident in her father's reaction to Jean's hopes of becoming a doctor: "What! *You*? Jean, chile, leave ambition like that to your brother. You going to grow up to something fitting – teacher even, and then you can married, and raise African children to the glory of the race – just like Missa Garvey did always say" (31).

This Garveyist doctrine forbad her the enjoyment of children's books by Blyton and Milne that were rejected as "white people brainwash" (31) by her father, and by her Aunt Vi who distrusted anything that was not based upon the Scriptures. Thus, when Pastor Baker catches her reading this illicit material she agrees to accept his extra counselling as an alternative to having her crime exposed to her aunt and father. In an echo of Adella's experience in *Waiting*, this counselling takes the form of the molesting of the eight-year-old girl under the guise of "a laying-on of hands." Again, the Pastor's justification is that it is the girl's wickedness that leads him into temptation, and convinces her that the "mark of Sodom [. . .] was deep inside her stomach" (114).

This conviction is confirmed, a year later, with the death of her brother, Noel. Jean and Noel argue over some mangoes that Noel is picking, and when he is struck by lightning whilst up the tree, Jean convinces herself that it was because she had called the wrath of God down on him during their fight. The Pastor takes the opportunity at the end of the wake to rape Jean, which she accepts as the Lord's punishment for her sin.

3.1 Joan Riley: Caribbean Conversations I

Again, like *Waiting*, there is a tacit acceptance of the Pastor's activities – he goes away the following day, and Jean's bleeding is interpreted as her first period, despite the fact that it is five years before she begins to menstruate. Jean is thus a victim of a societal conspiracy to maintain its own moral façade, in which male dominance is secured by the notion of original sin. Jean's willingness to accept the responsibility for the Pastor's actions is fundamentally encouraged by the unwillingness of her society to openly condemn its own corrupt nature. In particular, it is the women's collusion in this process, procured through religious indoctrination, which is essential to this unwillingness.

Jean's emigration to Britain provides a temporary relief from this regime. She wins a scholarship to sit a degree, and on completion of that she meets Jimmy. He encourages her intellectually and sexually, and allows her to support him, and their two children, while he struggles to succeed as a writer. Part of his liberal attitude, though, is a rejection of marriage vows. This fans Jean's insecurity in Britain, particularly when Jimmy starts to become successful, and, more importantly, denies her a possibility of reconciliation with the Church. She turns to drink, while in England, to escape her sense of rejection; but incipient alcoholism there, resolves into complete mental breakdown when back in the moral climate of Jamaica.

Jean continues to find solace in drink and casual sex in her home community in Jamaica. She tries to escape this cycle by returning to the Church, but this is the same Saturday church whose harsh moral regime was an element in Adella's downfall in Kingston, and it vilifies and rejects Jean for her unmarried status. After her humiliation there, Jean turns to the Sabbath church, where she is made more welcome and confesses to her sins, entering into a period of evangelical righteousness and self-conscious piety.

Although this conversion is always fragile in its intensity, its demise is an indication of stasis in Jamaican society. Jean's new Deacon offers to arrange special guidance for her from Pastor Simmonds. Almost inevitably this resolves into a repeat performance of her childhood sessions; the pastor is clearly under the impression that Jean's confession to her sexual history casts her as a willing recipient of his own lust. She flees and sinks into a drinking binge, which collapses into madness, and during which she absconds to the city with her children and a Rastafarian, Ras Peter. Her last attempt to explain her sudden change from piety to depravity is cut off by George in by now familiar tones: "Pastor Simmonds is a man with not one single blemish to his name, *whatever bad-minded* people saying, so a hope you not intending to bear false witness" (171; my italics).

Once in the city, Jean not only spirals into insanity, she is also inexorably reclaimed as part of the city. Her discussions with Ras Peter convince her that her abuse of the children is simply an effort to bring them up in "the disciplined ways of old Jamaica" (146). As officialdom and the slum-dwellers impede Sylvia's search, Jean's Standard English speech becomes progressively superseded by Jamaican dialect, and when she is finally found and taken to a doctor, he recommends her to the psychiatric hospital. Having been thus pronounced as one of Jamaica's "scourge of mad people," she escapes to the streets; there to be adopted, abused and finally killed as just another "Maddy."

Pearl is very much the success story of the text. Initially she presents an analogous figure to Desiree at the start of *Romance*. Instead of requiring a hysterectomy, she suffers from post-natal depression, but her husband, George, maintains a similar domestic presence as John's; and Pearl's limited spatial horizons imbue her with mental limitations which echo those noted in Desiree. However, where Desiree is isolated from a sense of cultural identity, Pearl is very much part of the society which Sylvia rejects and of which Jean falls foul.

As with all of Riley's work, the importance of the children as the next generation is of prime significance. It is easy to regard Jean's children as being the most central to the narrative, given their mother's abuse of them, but the text actually opens with the effect of Pearl and George's continual bickering on their three children. The essence of their dispute is domestic responsibility. Pearl's struggle to bond with the infant Kaona leads her to demand help from George, but his position has been firmly established by his father, and he expresses the same sentiments that oppressed Jean in her childhood: "Pearl, don't start up your foolishness again, is your job to look after Kaona, just like is my job to provision the family" (128). Pearl's experience in the text demonstrates that this is not solely an ideological means by which women are physically restrained, but also a means by

3.1 Joan Riley: Caribbean Conversations I

which they are restricted in their sense of social and personal value and potential.

Initially, Pearl's circumscription is evident in the differing ways that religion affects her life, and George's. Pearl's beliefs are described as "more routine than deeply held" (77), and this idea is evident in the daily task of waking her children for early morning devotion, and as she absent-mindedly sings along to morning worship on the radio whilst performing the household chores. George, by comparison, has the sanctimonious zeal of a late convert and takes every opportunity to bring religious justification into his actions and ideas. There is a rank hypocrisy here. While George is loudly condemning Jean for shaming him with Ras Peter, Pearl is all the time aware of his practice of visiting another woman when her husband is away (78). By comparison, Pearl is unable to practice a similar assertiveness, hypocritically or otherwise, as "years of conditioning" convince her that such behaviour on her part would be interpreted (by men) as "unnatural and anti-woman" (210-1).

The correlation between Pearl's physical and mental restraint becomes clear when Sylvia wants to go to Kingston to find Jean and the children. Pearl is too scared to accompany her as her fear of the unknown is fed by rumours of violence, exactly like her children's fear of Maddy. Sylvia's belief that Pearl can help her overcome the suspicion that her English accent raises in the city helps Pearl decide to break out of her circumscribed world, thus implicitly bringing a new influence upon her children as well. First, though, she determines to climb to the provision ground as the first symbolic step towards liberation.

The provision ground lies above her house, cut off by a steep slope. Although Jean and the domestic help, Mauvia, both can make the ascent, George had always convinced Pearl that the climb was beyond her capabilities. The symbolism is clear. Pearl's inability to reach basic staples, such as limes, demonstrates that her dependence on George is not merely economic, and the continual need to cajole him into fetching such staples reinforces this dependence. Thus, in reaching the top, Pearl breaks new ground, both literally and metaphorically, and in the sense of freedom that she experiences there is a liberation from the boundaries of patriarchy.

After this episode Pearl progresses quickly. She is able to help find Jean and to bring back the children, and she then goes on to get a part-time job, all in spite of opposition from George. Her final exchange with him illustrates her ability now to avoid bickering confrontations through an assertive self-belief, rather than trading accusations and grievances (309-10). Jimmy, who arrives rather belatedly to take charge of the children, delivers the final reflection on the events of the narrative: "Men over here have the exact same attitudes as their fathers and their fathers before them [. . .] Just goes to show that nothing will change in Jamaica, unless the women cause it" (310). Such sentiments would not have been out of place at the end of *Romance*, but Sylvia's contribution demonstrates that, for Riley, it is for the women in their own communities who must recognise their own circumscription for change to be effected.

3.2 Caryl Phillips: Caribbean Conversations II

When Caryl Phillips' first novel, *The Final Passage*, was published, its title was intended to situate the post-war emigration from the Caribbean within the historical of the slave trade: the final stage, as Johnson puts it, "of a long journey from Africa to Britain via the Caribbean" ("Searching" 2). It was a passage in which Phillips himself participated, being carried to England while only a few weeks old by his mother in 1958. However, it has been in evidence throughout this study that this stage of emigration was rarely the *final* passage, as the issue of return or of a renewed involvement with the islands becomes a characteristic of a literature increasingly concerned with the racial hostility of British society. Phillips' own body of work exhibits a similar progression, but instead of seeing the Caribbean (or Africa) as repositories of cultural identity, Phillips' migrations take a different route.

Notions of identity and displacement pervade not only Phillips' fictional work, but also the material that surrounds it. In the introduction to his collection of essays, *The European Tribe* (1987), Phillips recounts his schooldays in predominantly white areas of Birmingham and Leeds, commenting, "[i]f the teaching of English literature can feed a sense of identity then I, like many of my black contemporaries in Britain were starving" (2). Going to Queen's College, Oxford served to at once maintain Phillips within white-dominated surroundings, and also to exclude him from the emergent black radicalism important to the artistic development of Johnson and other writers. He began to travel to Notting Hill to get a feel for the black communal experience, an activity that served to alienate him from the traditional concerns of Oxbridge literary studies, and to emphasise the dearth of material that addressed that experience.

The Caribbean did not immediately present an alternative model of identity or experience; as he said in a later interview, "St. Kitts was in my mind as somewhere my parents were from" (qtd. in Johnson, "Searching" 6). Rather, it was the British urban experience that he empathised with, being affected more by the portrayal of "class and cultural dislocation" evident in writers like Braine, Storey and Sillitoe, than by novels dealing with Caribbean life (Birbalsingh, "Interview with Caryl Phillips" 45). In the apparent absence of black British literature, it was the American writers Richard Wright and Ralph Ellison who provided the impetus for Phillips to feel he could "express the conundrum of my own experience" and fill this gap with his own writing (*European* 8).

This conundrum is essentially one of displacement. While wanting to explore his own sense of alienation, Phillips has not sought a sense of solidarity in either the "yout scene" or Caribbean roots. His first play, *Strange Fruit*, dealt with the problems of black British identity in terms of the cultural interface between the colonial heritage in Britain and in the Caribbean, but it is his reaction to its reception that is interesting. The view of one critic that Phillips had "pillaged the white man's theatre knowledgedly" (qtd. in Phillips, *Shelter* 11), demonstrated to him the preconceptions which haunt black British writing: "In Africa I was not black. I was a writer. In Europe I am black. I am a black writer" (Phillips, *Shelter* 12). This is similar to Barbara Burford's assertion that "the expectation that angers me most is that all writing by Blackwomen is autobiographical" (38). The point here is that, although Phillips wants to explore the colonial and post-colonial experience, he does not intend that this should contribute to a consolidation of difference.

There is thus, in the progression of Phillips' writing, a clear determination not to become limited by the theme of rage, but to be "seen as a writer *per se*" (qtd. in Birbalsingh, "Interview with Caryl Phillips" 44). Thus, where his first two novels deal with issues relating to the post-War emigration to Britain, two of his later works present a strong divergence from the theme of emigration that has characterised most of the fiction dealt with so far. Phillips sees himself as being in the unique position of exploring both Caribbean and British society, placing on him a special responsibility: "I can see historical connections between the two societies, and I can see contemporary reverberations between them [. . .] I can build bridges and help to cross-fertilize the two" (qtd. in Birbalsingh, "Interview with Caryl Phillips" 46). Evidence of this endeavour may be noted in the technique in two of Phillips' earlier texts, where he writes them as a novel in three parts, thus insisting on this kind of historical cross-fertilisation.

In seeking to explore and examine a whole range of political and social subjects bound by the history of colonialism and slavery, Phillips is pursu-

3.2 Caryl Phillips: Caribbean Conversations II

ing the formation of a collective identity going beyond the post-war experience. The "Caribbean conversation" in his texts will thus be seen to reverberate with manifold voices.

* * *

Phillips wrote *Strange Fruit* before making his first return trip to St. Kitts since his initial "migration." Set in contemporary urban England, it explores the theme of the black British identity in terms of the conflicting influences of life in Britain and an uncertain Caribbean heritage. This conflict is played out through Errol and Alvin, two black youths who have been brought up by their emigrant mother under a regime of integration. Both have rejected this path and are involved in black radicalism, when the eldest, Alvin, goes to the Caribbean to represent the family at his grandfather's funeral.

As the character that remained in England, Errol is representative of Alvin, before the trip, as well as himself. Having been brought up by a mother who has discouraged a positive sense of black identity, Errol emerges as a character trying to build a sense of self from Black Panther-inspired images and pseudo-intellectualism. His confusion is noted from the start in the stage-direction description of him; "he dresses untidily, knowing it is the mind that matters, but he will occasionally pin on a badge of protest only to remove it a few days later thinking that he's 'sold out'" (18-9).

Although this ritual with the badge is not illustrated in the action of the play, it remains an integral part of Errol's character. He enters just as his white girlfriend, Shelley, and his mother are looking through the family photograph album. Shelley has just said that Errol would dismiss such an activity with the phrase "Pictures negate progress," and Errol duly obliges (18-19). Such formulaic responses are part of Errol's radical politics, but their glib utterance suggests they are important to Errol more for their effect than their meaning.

This aspect is emphasised through Errol's use of Caribbean dialect. When Alvin returns, Errol presses him for "a bit of the lingo. You know, add a bit of authenticity to the banter" (62). Clearly, even if Alvin did provide him with some phrases it would not be "authentic" but simply another discursive badge to wear. Predictably, Errol makes most use of dialect in his efforts to oppress Shelley, to maintain her exclusion in a relationship that bears the hallmarks of the "black man holding the white world to hostage" scenario. This becomes most marked after the sex scene where Errol quickly gratifies himself and throws Shelley out with a slap and phrases such as "[p]ut your fucking clothes on and watch you don't mess up the woman's settee, you raas clart" (44).

Africa is the other important symbol in Errol's life. At the end of the text, when he has found out that Shelley is pregnant, he leaves with her, saying that they are going to Africa to join the freedom fighters. The unreality of this ambition is compounded by his passport application, which apparently has his nationality as African and his place of birth as "The Dark Continent" (99). Africa exists as a mental space for Errol, a reflection (not unlike Hyacinth's) of a harsh reality in Britain: "I'm gonna sit out in the sun all day listening to the drums till I'm black as coal. I'm gonna sit there and feel fine 'cos everywhere I look they'll be as black as me. I'll find myself a family. A new family" (44).

Alvin, as noted above, clearly shares these concerns with Errol until his trip to the Caribbean. They have been planning a robbery to fund the Black Front, and Alvin sees his trip to the Caribbean as a prelude to "the mother country – Africa" (78). What he discovers, and what he subsequently wants Errol to discover, is that they had been building their identity on a pastiche of popular images that do not correspond to reality. The "diseases of decolonisation" have not shaped the Caribbean (and Africa) into homelands of black solidarity, awaiting the return of the prodigal sons of the diaspora; instead it has rendered them liable to violence, corruption and unemployment (69).

When Alvin goes to the Caribbean, he is rejected, not only by his biological relations, but also by the mythical family of black people that never existed. As such, he loses the sense of self that had sustained him thus far, and he experiences the same sense of unbelonging evident in Riley's text: "What am I supposed to do [. . .] Live on a raft in the middle of the Atlantic at a point equidistant between Africa, the Caribbean and Britain?" (99). He ultimately decides to train as a social worker, thus signalling his com-

3.2 Caryl Phillips: Caribbean Conversations II

mitment to becoming a part of British society rather than seeking an escape.

Alvin blames his mother for failing to guide him in his Blackness. Her policy of dissociating herself and her children from their Caribbean past is strongly reminiscent of John's attitude to his daughters in *Romance*, and equally motivated by the notion that if the children regard themselves as an undifferentiated part of the population, then the converse will be true. This is a hangover from the years of integration, as Mother accepts any amount of prejudice being directed towards her, but for her sons things should be different:

> VERNICE: You should be grateful that the pair uh them managing to keep themselves outa trouble with the police and thing.
>
> MOTHER: Should be glad of what? Grateful for what! . . . My children are qualified, they have 'O' levels and 'A' levels and have both been to college, and you're telling me that I should be happy they are managing to keep out of trouble. (10)

This emphasis on education, quite apart from its significance in the islands, is a demonstration of the idea, noted in the first chapter, whereby 'integration' effectively means 'become like.' For Phillips, though, the lesson that is learnt by the second generation is that white society will not accept black people as a legitimate part of the British population. Alvin's appearance as described in the stage directions is again significant. He has smartened up after his re-evaluation in the Caribbean and he is now "too casual to be important, yet too smart to be bullied by the police (at least on a first glance)" (56).

Phillips' contention is that British attitudes towards black people since the post-War emigrations have changed from "curiosity, then hostility" to "almost hostility distilled" (qtd. in Birbalsingh, "Interview with Caryl Phillips" 41). Since Phillips also refutes the possibility of repatriation or return as a response to such attitudes, this conundrum represents the central problematic of his writing. The play ends with Mother committing suicide and Errol and Shelley off on a misconceived mission to produce a "leader in the promised land" (96). One feels that the last gesture of conciliation by

Alvin demonstrates Phillips' voice in the play. He comes back to collect a picture of his mother, and, thinking her asleep, kisses her as he leaves. As Alvin says, he is surrounded by people either "too busy playing white or too busy playing black" (88).

This negotiation between integration and confrontation is another aspect of the Caribbean conversation evident in Riley's work, in the continual interplay between the experience of the Caribbean, the first generation of emigrants and their children. Phillips explores this interplay from a different angle in his next play, *Where There is Darkness*. Here the emigrant experience in Britain is thrown into relief on the eve of Albert Williams' return to the islands after an exile of twenty-one years. His initial emigration and life in Britain are described through a series of flashback scenes, revealing a character that uses the ethos of integration in pursuit of personal advancement. Phillips describes him in an interview as a hustler, an opportunist who uses the politics of race relations in order to achieve material goals in Britain (Johnson, "Searching" 7). This much is made evident in Albert's explanation of his choice of career:

> They [i.e. the white Establishment]) like black social workers, you know, is why I decide is not law or medicine or any of those things I going try for [. . .] I decide is social work for me for I know they like nothing better than having black people explaining black people to them. (25)

This frank opportunism is not a response (as may be argued with the domestic violence in Riley's males) to racial prejudice in Britain; Albert freely admits to fathering Remi on the basis that his father-in-law would then finance the emigration of his family to Britain (25). His life in exile, instead of encouraging a sense of solidarity with the black community, simply adapts to the new circumstances. Thus although he says, "black people in this country must act and feel like a tribe" (22), we nevertheless learn that he has used his (first) wife's money to set up an illegal club with another emigrant, Vince, whom he then leaves to face gaol when the club is burned down.

In essence, Albert maintains his island attitude in Britain; the notion of a "black family" as it exists in *Strange Fruit* again being debunked, this time

3.2 Caryl Phillips: Caribbean Conversations II

in favour of opportunism. Phillips declares that Albert does not represent a substantial section of the black community and that he should be pitied, rather than grappled with as a self-destructive figure (in Johnson, "Searching" 7). He does however anticipate Michael's character in *The Final Passage*, and, as an island hustler, recalls the point made in *A Kindness to the Children*, that black people returning to the Caribbean are easily dismayed by the inhabitants' willingness to cheat them. Significantly, though, it is in his relationship with Remi that his island values are most evident.

Initially, Albert's determination to raise his son (after Muriel leaves him in an orphanage and returns to the Caribbean) seems atypical; both generally and as a recurring theme in Phillips' work. Certainly in *A State of Independence* and, to an extent, in *Strange Fruit* one can detect a similar correspondence between an absent father figure and a lost, aimless son, to that noted in Salkey's fiction. Here, Albert's aspirations for his son are based on his own adapted techniques of island success. Thus, where Tiger, in *A Brighter Sun*, saw literacy as a signifier for manhood; for Albert, Remi's degree holds a similar significance: "you done nothing and you are nothing till I see a degree in front of me" (24). Albert, though, is not dazzled by this sign of literacy. He is not interested in "becoming like" as ontological maturity; for him, material success is the essential measure of a man: "You think I get where I am today, Executive Social Worker and Magistrate, by being a boy? You think I have this house, two cars and a flat by being a boy? You think a boy can afford to throw parties like the one I throw [. . .] Well? Well?" (27).

Remi, though, as the next generation, has not his father's predatory instincts or single-minded attitude to exploiting life in Britain to the full before returning to the Caribbean. Thus, when he reveals that Sonja is pregnant and that he intends to marry her, leave University and get a job, he is signalling (rather like Alvin) his sense of himself as a part of British society. Significantly, Sonja is an orphan, so in her union with Remi there is a clear sense of dislocation with an unacceptable Caribbean heritage. Albert's pervasive misogyny is accentuated by the idea that his plans for Remi are to be thwarted by a woman, after he has casually (ab)used women for his own ends:

ALBERT: Boy, you still don't know the difference between a white woman and a black woman [. . .] Tell me about this woman, then. She have any form? Fast finisher, firm ground, like a heavy jockey, or maybe the bitch tell you is she first time out.

REMI: She's not a bitch.

ALBERT: How you know is your child?

REMI: It is.

ALBERT: And even if it is – which is never definite – how is it you can't let she go to work and you finish off your education?

REMI: We need money more than we need a piece of paper.

ALBERT: And I bet you she need a man more than she need a baby. (24-5)

While Remi is torn between allegiance to Albert and his own sense of morality, Sonja has no such split allegiance. Albert's attempts to intimidate her meet with a different response to those he has grown used to: "You're like all black men, think the world owes them a favour so they can behave how they like, whether it's throwing bottles and bricks at the police or smashing women in the face" (58). Sonja is clear that she wants her baby to inherit a "stable and well-ordered past" (55), and thus it is incumbent on Remi to order the past that has been crowding in on Albert through the flashback cameos that have punctuated the action. In effect, Remi's childhood is akin to Alvin and Errol's. His Caribbean heritage has been shielded from him through Albert's (misinformed) determination to secure his future. In these terms, Albert plays both black and white with a conviction only in winning a personalised war. In the last scene, when Albert and Remi are left alone, both are overwhelmed by the past as Albert slips into an illusion of being back in the Caribbean (in order to escape the ghosts of his exile) and Remi is apparently reduced to childhood:

3.2 Caryl Phillips: Caribbean Conversations II

ALBERT: Is good to be back home and have to make these little decisions. First mango or swimming? Son, you just watch me clothes like a man.

(He starts walking down the garden).

REMI: Dad, please. I don't understand. I'm frightened. (63)

In his first two plays, Phillips has the mother committing suicide in the first and Albert edging towards a different kind of self-destruction in the second. The conflict with white society that these representatives of the first generation have suffered, though, is played out in the margins of the text while the central confrontation is between them and their children. In writing thus, Phillips is not attempting to erase the self-perpetuating aspect of racist ideologies, but to broaden the identity of the black British from one that is simply reactive to those racist structures. He thus stays with the experiences of the first generation emigrants in his first two novels, recovering the Kittican experience at either end of the migratory venture, and providing a black British continuum that is liberated from the British experience.

* * *

After receiving the royalties for *Strange Fruit* in 1980, Phillips returned to St. Kitts for the first time since his involuntary migration in 1958. This visit, he says, "fired my curiosity about myself, about England, about the Caribbean," and it was here that he began his first novel, *The Final Passage* (Swift 91). Although a tale very much in the tradition of *The Emigrants* or Collins' *Jamaica Migrant*, both Phillips and Louis James (in his review of it), felt it was important that someone of Phillips' generation should be tackling the subject. Since the work of Selvon, Rhys and Lamming, as Louis James puts it, "there has been a blank in the communal memory of the second-generation Black British writers" and *The Final Passage* marks for him a "'coming-into-consciousness' of important areas of history" (33).

As noted above, it is possible to view the central male character, Michael, as a precursor to Albert. Although Michael's activities in Britain are not fully explored, his determination to succeed and willingness to forfeit any sense of personal responsibility and loyalty in the process, is strongly reminiscent of Albert's doctrine. Again, Phillips insists that Michael is not a typical Caribbean male, and points to Michael's friend Bradeth as a textual alter ego who develops into a "hellishly responsible man" (Johnson, "Searching" 8). Despite this, however, Phillips (like Riley) is clear on the existence of Caribbean patriarchy and the way this is played out in interpersonal relationships and domestic situations.

In an interview in 1986, Phillips speaks of the Caribbean as a "very male, macho society" in which women "seem to have much more of a responsible role in the family – perhaps because men are far more irresponsible." He also refers to "a long tradition of wilful or unwilful neglect or absence on the part of men" (qtd. in Saunders 44-5). Thus, part of the "coming-into-consciousness" that James refers to is the insertion of the female experience of emigration that was largely absent in the work of Lamming and his generation, but is clearly evident here.

Leila, the central character of the text, is strongly reminiscent of Adella in Riley's *Waiting in the Twilight*; Adella's moral bindings are Leila's social bindings. As a light-skinned and educated girl in the compact island society of St. Kitts, her expected partner is the "steady" Arthur, who leaves for the American training that will establish his future (and hers) as prime movers in the island's development. Instead she marries Michael, the island "bad boy," in a ceremony made public by the spectacle of a union that defies social hierarchy.

In marrying Michael, Leila is signalling her desire to escape the limitations of island life; his motorbike and irresponsibility are symbols of freedom and imagination diametrically opposed to, and more potent than, Arthur's education and dreams of the future. For Michael, capturing Leila is akin to owning the motorbike; it is an outward sign of non-conformity in a society too static to provide scope for revolt. Having achieved his goal, he immediately loses interest in Leila, throwing his drink in her face after the ceremony and then leaving to stay with his lover Beverley and their child (54-5).

When Michael walks out after the wedding ceremony, Leila's mother also walks away, signifying her subsequent dissociation from Leila's life.

3.2 Caryl Phillips: Caribbean Conversations II

With the significance that Phillips places on family relationships as metaphors for social development, this can be seen as Leila's point of severance from the island. There is an intervening period, during which Leila's mother migrates to England and Leila indulges Michael's irresponsible behaviour in a way that, like Adella's, stretches credulity. Michael returns just often enough to conceive a child with Leila, and to be thrown out of Beverley's house for taking that child there six weeks after he was born. A pattern of inequality is thus established in the Caribbean section of the text, a description of patriarchy from which the experience of emigration provides a potential release.

Phillips opens the text with Leila on the harbour queuing up to board the ship bound for England; it is a section significantly called *The End* which bears little resemblance to the corresponding journey described in *The Emigrants*. There, the passage maintains the communal aspect of Caribbean life and provides a space for the islanders to re-sense their identity in anticipation of the racist structures awaiting them in Britain. Here Leila is locked into an isolation that confirms her in the role of the Caribbean woman, rather than heralding her release. Michael is taken ill and has to be nursed by Leila throughout the voyage, as well as the daily task of washing Calvin's nappies and guarding them from theft whilst drying. There is none of the inter-island debate that characterised Lamming's voyage, as Leila's few moments of personal time are spent thinking of her mother who has already emigrated. She becomes, then, more circumscribed by the family, being confirmed into the role described by Phillips above. Michael, by comparison, spends the passage reconciling himself to the notion that if he is to exploit his time in Britain to the full, he cannot expend time and energy on trying to maintain his marriage.

So, where Munro notes the preponderance of interior scenes that characterise the emigrants' life in Britain in Lamming's text, the voyage establishes the onset of Leila's isolation. She and Michael rent a house in a white working-class area, and as Michael progressively withdraws from her in pursuit of his own ambition, her mind begins to fail and she begins to cling to the idea of return. Significantly, the one chance she has of attaining an independent presence in Britain is thwarted when she collapses on her first day as a bus conductor through a combination of hunger and early pregnancy.

Louis James describes Leila in his review article as "a recognizable figure in Caribbean literature – the personality broken by a defective social reality" (33). This is the Caribbean reality; both Michael and Leila are struck by the aimlessness of an island "overburdened with vegetation and complacency" (20), but react differently to their exile. For Michael, England was more than he had "dared hope for" (169), and he consciously puts behind him those parts of his island existence which cannot help him in England. Leila is unable to do this and thus becomes trapped in a twilight world populated by hybrid figures from her past and present and, in her incipient madness, "leaves England behind" (198).

* * *

Phillips' next novel, *A State of Independence*, describes the journey that might more properly be regarded as the final passage, as it relates the return of scholarship boy Bertram Francis to St. Kitts after an absence of twenty years. In taking on this subject, Phillips was aware that he was running counter to the expectation that his work would continue to deal (as Riley's did) with the black British situation. *The Final Passage* does leave significant gaps in the exploration of Michael's experience and there is certainly no sense of resolution, as Leila is left receiving a blank Christmas card. There is a clear connection, though, between this text and *Strange Fruit*, as Phillips adds his own experiences to the trauma of return.

As noted earlier, it was not until after his first play that Phillips himself made the return journey to the Caribbean, and thus the experience of return was couched mainly through the politics of the "yout scene." By the time he came to write this text, though, Phillips had resolved to address the Caribbean situation as much as the British one. This text is therefore different from those that describe the experience of return; there is a clear effort to establish Bertram as a character encountering the Caribbean as a lone figure. In this regard, it is notable that in both *Moses Migrating* and *A Kindness to the Children*, other characters and situations that influence their experience of the Caribbean join the main protagonists. Indeed, for Sylvia, in Riley's text, the drama that follows her from England prevents her from

3.2 Caryl Phillips: Caribbean Conversations II

undergoing the voyage of discovery that she had set out for. Bertram lands alone: the brief, dismissive account of his life in Britain, and uncertain ambition to remain on the island, act as a testimony to the relative insignificance of his life there.

Bertram, however, does not land in St. Kitts completely unencumbered by twenty years of exile. In *Where There is Darkness*, Sonja says that the tragedy of the immigrant is that they "change faster than the countries they have left behind and they can never go back and be happy" (47). Phillips is thus concerned to describe a change of consciousness akin to Moses' overdeveloped British patriotism, but based upon the experience of institutionalised racial hostility.

The text opens with Bertram's plane circling above St. Kitts preparing to land. After his long absence, Bertram is already full of apprehension about being a stranger in his own land, and tries to convince himself that he knows that what looks like a "neat and tropical Versailles would seem little more than a sprawling mess when on the ground" (10). He lands, and the taxi-ride that he takes from the airport to his mother's house provides the textual space to re-encounter the physical reality of the island.

The sense of lethargy and complacency, which was a characteristic of the St. Kitts in the previous text, is again evident here. The posters which proclaim the imminent day of independence have already had their colour sucked out of them by the sun (14), and their state is echoed by the "slack sea," "stove-weary mothers" and cane-cutters who "walked like condemned men with neither hope or desire" (17-8). Bertram's struggle of consciousness begins here, as he is struck by these images of hopeless poverty and tries to see in his reaction some part of the "liberal guilt that he had always despised in some English people" (19). This struggle becomes confrontation as, in a scene reminiscent of Hyacinth's arrival in the Jamaica slums with a bag full of expensive gifts, Bertram arrives "home" and is dismayed at the "absurdity of his luggage [. . .] for the two suitcases took up most of the floor area" (27). This journey and arrival at his mother's house is essentially a prelude to a more serious confrontation between the past and the future of the Caribbean. Bertram's return to the island has been precipitated by the prospect of its independence, a prospect potentially more significant to the exile than the islander, as Bertram, like Alvin, arrives with a heightened consciousness of the black\white divide.

Bertram's vision of the future revolves around a vague plan to open up a business on the island, convinced of the notion that "the only way the black man going to progress in this world is to set up his own shops and his own businesses independent of the white man" (51). Such plans are met with derision by the people he meets, who are entrenched in the lethargy of the island and point to the stagnant shops and bars, still unchanged in Bertram's lifetime. The economics of colonialism and its modern aftermath are clear to Bertram after the heightened experience of exile, but not so to the islanders. It is a reassertion of Lamming's exiled perspective from 1960 that "the West Indian has learnt, by sheer habit, to take the white presence for granted. Which is, precisely, his trouble" (*Pleasures* 33).

Bertram's encounter with unchanged island attitudes is no less profound than his encounter with the change that independence will bring. Phillips has expressed his concern that "the Caribbean is now, to some extent, culturally an extension of the Florida Keys" (qtd. in Swift 102), and the independence that Phillips describes here is the facilitation of a greater submission to the United States. Bertram searches out his childhood friend, now government minister, Jackson Clayton, to discuss his plans for settling back on the island. Jackson, though, has little time for Bertram's Garveyist economics: "We living under the eagle and maybe you don't think that is good but your England never do us a damn thing except take, take, take" (112).

The independence that Bertram has returned for is thus something that will never exist, and, in his duel with the old colonial masters, he has failed to notice the opportunistic sale of the island to America by its political leaders. This is the battle of consciousness that he returns to, as he is unable to accept the resigned poverty of the rural masses on the one hand, or the enthusiastic adoption and exploitation of American culture on the other. Jackson gives him the inevitable advice to return to Britain and there is some ambiguity at the end of the text whether or not this is what he has resolved to do. The future that he has returned to is, however, made clear.

When Bertram left the island he was also unwittingly leaving behind an unborn son. Bertram's inability or unwillingness to recognise that he is the

3.2 Caryl Phillips: Caribbean Conversations II

father is a signifier of his own effectual detachment from Caribbean society, while the boy, Livingstone, now in his late teens, exemplifies the new colonial product. Working as a gardener in a big American hotel, and aping American fashions, the new age explorer is clear where his mission will lead him: "I think I prefer America [. . .] New York, Yankees, Washington Redskins, Michael Jackson, you can't want for more than that. The West Indies is a dead place [. . .] Too small in size, too small in the head" (103).

* * *

Phillips' overwhelming perception of St. Kitts after the independence celebrations, which formed the basis for *A State of Independence*, was that the island was already "completely infused with American colonialism." "It didn't strike me," he says "that there was going to be any intervening period where an indigenous Caribbean cultural form of expression could flourish" (qtd. in Saunders 45). In the text itself, he articulated this idea through Patsy, Livingstone's mother, when she says: "Nothing in this place ever really falls into the past. It's all here in the present for we too small a country to have a past" (142). The twin concepts of culture and history, which have been the recurrent concern of Caribbean writers since Reid's *New Day* (1949), thus re-emerge as part of the final passage for black British writing.

After *A State of Independence* was published, Phillips embarked on a trip from Morocco to Moscow in order to "explore the European Academy that had shaped my mind," feeling that a "large part of finding out who I was, and what I was doing here would inevitably mean having to understand the Europeans" (*European* 9). These travels formed the basis for *The European Tribe* in which Phillips' increasing preoccupation with historical perspective is evidenced in some strong echoes of writers featured earlier in this book. Phillips concludes the text with the reflection: "I was raised in Europe, but as I walked the tiny streets of Venice, with all their self-evident beauty, I felt nothing [. . .] Nothing inside stirred to make me rejoice, 'Ours is a rich culture,' or 'I'm a part of this'" (128). One is immediately reminded of Johnnie Sobert's anguish in *Escape*: "I walk around London and I see statues of this one and that one. I see litters of paintings in your museums and galleries. St. Paul's and the Tower. All of them [. . .]

And do you know how I feel deep down? [. . .] I feel nothing, I feel nothing at all" (46). This in itself is reminiscent of Baldwin's *Notes of a Native Son* and Lamming's discussion of this sentiment in *Pleasures* (30-3).

Phillips is touched, then, by a need similar to that of earlier writers: to research, provide and maintain an absent sense of cultural history. The role of the writer which he has impressed upon him in Soviet-dominated Poland, bears a strong resemblance to Lamming's *houngan*:

> I had learnt that in a situation where history is distorted, the literature of a people often becomes its history, its writers the keepers of the past, present, and future. In this situation a writer can infuse a people with a sense of their own unique identity and spiritually kindle the fire of resistance (Phillips, *European* 99).

It is from this basis then that one should approach Phillips' next two novels, *Higher Ground* and *Cambridge*.

* * *

Higher Ground is written almost as three short stories; describing events in an African slaving port in the first section; the prison letters of an American black radical in 1968 in the second; and the experiences of a Jewess, a refugee from Poland to Britain before the War, in the last. The clear link between the three is the theme of displacement and alienation that has already emerged as a characteristic of Phillips' work, but it is the juxtaposition of these three apparently variant historical moments and their reassessment in the text that fulfils the writer's role.

The first part, "Heartland," approaches the slave trade in terms of its corrupting and debilitating effect on the human mentality. The central, and nameless, character has been taught English by the slavers, initially, to bargain with tribal elders for their slaves, and presently, to aid the process of splitting up tribes and families in the coffles in order to induce isolation and forestall rebellion. This invidious role is epitomised when the brutal Price takes him to a nearby village to procure a girl on whom to practice his sadistic lusts. The Elders acquiesce to the demand, but focus their hatred on the hapless interpreter: "They blame me because I am easily identi-

3.2 Caryl Phillips: Caribbean Conversations II

fiable as one who dwells with the enemy. But I merely oil the wheels of their own collaborationist activities" (24).

After her ordeal the girl is rejected by the tribe and saved only when the interpreter, obsessed by the thought of her, returns to the village and is allowed to take her back to the fort. Thereafter, both interpreter and girl are abandoned by their tribes because of the use to which the slavers have put them. The interpreter's relationship with the girl reminds him of how much he has already forgotten about the ways of his people. The misery of his existence teaches him the "art of forgetting – of murdering the memory" (24).

The slavers similarly forget or abandon their world. Price revels in the absence of social control, the authority of the Governor being completely nominal:

> We stand at the edge of the world. The rules that bind normal men have no place in this land [. . .] if I return to your world of silks and fine wines there you might reproach me, but here sweating in this hellish climate [. . .] there comes a point at which your rank and order must fall away and be replaced by a natural order.
> (31)

The sadistic Price rises to the top of that order, while the humanistic Governor dies of a fever. This brutalising process is played out through Lewis, one of the soldiers at the fort. He begins the tale as the interpreter's only source of compassion, but degenerates into drunkenness and when he discovers the girl hidden in the interpreter's quarters begins to use her himself. Finally, he betrays the couple to Price, condemning them to the ordeal of the middle passage.

His victimisation by the guards and the other (white) prisoners is an attempt (not unlike the practise in the slave trade of splitting up tribal and dialectal groups) to rob him of his sense of identity. In this isolated state, Rudi's only points of reference are with the radical literature he studies and the letters that he exchanges with his family.

Under these conditions, Rudi's black radicalism becomes characterised by extremism, illustrating some of the contradictions that informed Errol's politics in *Strange Fruit*. Certainly, the curriculum vita that he sends to a "Defense Committee" is reminiscent of Errol's passport application:

Name: Homo Africanus.
Occupation: Survivor.
Age: 200-300 years.
Parents: Africans captured and made slaves . . . (91)

He also insists on Africa as a heartland, which does not admit to the collaboration evidenced in the previous section. He looks towards settling in Ghana, "the mother-country of African independence. They have made it clear that there is plenty of land for us all, and the admission price is 'soul'" (70). His revolutionary fervour is directed, in his letters, at his mother, father and sister, as he tries to educate them into black radicalism. In his isolation, though, where "the enemy" is easily recognisable, his exhortations become part of his prison as he alienates each of his family in turn. His brutal assessment and rejection of his mother for baptising his sister is followed by a similar rejection of his father for failing to attend night school, and then his sister for becoming pregnant. Each rejection is followed by a determination to make an ally of the next family member in his war against American society. As no one in "ordinary" life can maintain this sense of embattlement, so he is condemned to increasing abandonment and eventual madness. His last letter is written to his now dead mother in the persona of a plantation slave writing back to Africa.

In these first two sections Phillips has taken two seminal aspects of black history and shown how alienation and dispossession can come about. In the first case, unwilling service for the white slave traders entailed rejection for the interpreter, and in the second, the violent refusal to interact with the white majority results in the same rejection. Clearly, this cannot be read as an indictment of the black peoples, but as an attempt to capture two individual casualties of broad historical movements that go beyond the structures that typify those movements. In this sense, the story of Irina in the final part is less unlikely than it first appears.

Part One, named "Higher Ground," describes the story of Jewish refuge in Britain during and after the Second World War. Irina's father has sent her away from Poland during the rise of anti-Semitic feeling in Warsaw.

3.2 Caryl Phillips: Caribbean Conversations II

She never hears of the fate of her parents and sister who intended to follow her, and she is quickly separated from the other refugees who have made the journey with her. The photographs that were her only link with her family also get lost as she is moved between hostels. She is thus completely dispossessed, a state deepened by the corruption of her name to Irene when she goes to work in a munitions factory, a sign that she must now become another person.

Bereft of her roots, though, Irene has only Jewish fatalism to fall back on; "*Harginnen.* 'They're going to kill us'" (192 and 218). Thus, when her joyless marriage fails with the pregnancy that demanded it, she tries to commit suicide and is taken instead into psychiatric care. She is released and given a temporary job in a library, but her existence in England is blighted by her inability to master the interpreter's art: "She could not spend another winter in England staunching memories like blood from a punched nose. She could not afford a memory-haemorrhage, but to not remember hurt" (180).

On the last night before she is re-admitted into care, she meets Louis, a West Indian emigrant who has already decided to return to the islands after only ten days in England. After the other lives in the text, where misery and suffering were countered by the determination to retain dignity and self-esteem, Louis recognises that he must return if he is to maintain this: "he knew that it was better to return as the defeated traveller than be praised as the absent hero and live a life of spiritual poverty" (197).

There is, thus, a strong corrective in Irina's tale; it demonstrates that the "wretched of the earth" do not come solely from the African continent and also that the misery of the slave trade, or the Holocaust, was not played out solely in the plantations or concentration camps. This does not belittle such suffering but it does provide a means through which such violence can be used to create mental links, rather than consolidate difference.

In his next novel, *Cambridge,* Phillips attempts a similar juxtaposition of voices, this time more closely intertwined in terms of time and setting, but still relating discrete voices and experiences. Set largely on St. Kitts in the period between abolition and emancipation, the first and longest part takes the form of a travelogue written by the daughter of an absentee landlord on a trip to his estate. Whilst there, she is courted by the brutish estate manager, Mr. Brown, and miscarries his child after he is murdered by one of the slaves.

Although this is a fairly sombre end to the tale, Phillips insists that Emily grows in the text and that her suffering is part of the "displacement ticket" (qtd. in Swift 102). There is certainly a clear difference in Emily's attitude to the black slaves from her "undisguised revulsion" upon landing (21) to her closing lines about her maid, who is now "her friend. Stella. Dear Stella" (184). For all this, though, Phillips does not depict a person shocked into emancipationism by the barbaric spectacle of plantation life. Instead there are descriptions of an existence "which the average English labourer might consider luxurious" (67), including Sundays off, in which to dress up and go to town, or cultivate produce on their personal plots.

In this respect, though, Emily is an unreliable narrator as her sense of propriety clashes with her tentative liberal instincts. Thus, she will, at one moment, question a society which would not prosecute a white man for killing a slave (107), but at another, indict women slaves for their concubinage: "I had been sufficiently alert to realise that it is sometimes the custom for white men to retain what they term 'housekeepers.' These swarthy dependants elevate their status by prostrating themselves" (75).

The course of Emily's seduction into the slave owners' rationale is reflected in her affair with Brown. When she first arrives, she dismisses him as a social inferior whose habit of whipping the slaves himself leaves her shocked and distressed. By the end of the text, though, she is waiting for Arnold to "dispense his justice, being confident that whatever decision he reaches will most likely be the correct one" (120). It is only his death that prevents her discovering more of Brown's brutal methods from the more liberal estate-manager, Wilson, whom he had ousted from the estate prior to her arrival.

Emily is redeemed by her suffering at the end of the text and by her ability to show affection for Stella. It is also clear that in making this progress, she has made herself unfit for life in England:

> England. Emily smiled to herself. The doctor delivered the phrase
> as though this England was a dependable garment that one simply
> slipped into or out of according to one's whim. Did he not under-

3.2 Caryl Phillips: Caribbean Conversations II

stand that people grow and change? Did he not understand that one day a discovery might be made that this country-garb is no longer of a correct measure? And what then? (177)

In the second narrative of the text, that of Cambridge, a slave on the plantation, a converse journey is made. Cambridge's tale, clearly based upon *Equiano's Travels* (1789; ed. Paul Edwards), tells of his capture and sale to the slave factors in Africa and subsequent Christianisation in England.

As David Henderson, he is allowed to marry his master's servant, with whom he goes on a missionary tour of England after his master dies. His wife dies of pneumonia through want of shelter during the winter and when he then embarks on missionary work in Africa, he has his money stolen by the ship's captain and is sold into slavery on Emily's plantation. Like Emily, he now feels alienated from the other slaves, being convinced, still, of his Christian faith, and waits for God to release him from his "unChristian labour" (160).

Cambridge's narrative provides a parallel account of Brown's brutality and his abuse of Christiania (the female slave whom Cambridge regards as his wife) and of how he came to be involved in a struggle with Brown that resulted in his death. But the true value of his account is in the multiple ironies that make up his tale. He and Christiania are thrown together on the plantation because of their difference from the other slaves; Christiania, though, is isolated as an obeah-woman. It is then Cambridge's efforts to make Brown recognise Christiania as his wife, which end in Brown's death and in Cambridge's execution.

In effect, he exchanges sensibilities with Emily; his last testament, in which he describes his life, begins with a reference to "my dear England" (133), and ends with a plea for forgiveness for his "heathen behaviour" (167). Cambridge's experiences at the hands of the Christian world have not shaken his learnt values, while Emily appears permanently displaced by her trip to the estate. In modern terms, both characters remain ambiguous. As Phillips says, "in modern parlance [Cambridge] would be regarded as an Uncle Tom" while there is something "small and somewhat unpleasant in the context of 1991 to find a woman expressing some warmth and affection for her black maid" (qtd. in Swift 99). They are both, though, like the characters in *Higher Ground*, marginal figures who serve to highlight detail in the broad sweep of history.

* * *

In the introduction to his interview with Phillips, Graham Swift suggests that it would be "facile [. . .] to assess either Caz's (Phillips') work as a whole, or his heroine, by any crude cultural or racial analysis" (99). Certainly, it has been Phillips' purpose throughout to approach his material in a way that reconsiders the issues of colonialism rather than simply adds inches to the library shelf marked "Black Writers." Like Riley, his work does not forgo integrity in favour of solidarity, and thus it includes collaborators, hustlers, bigots and fools. This is not an innovation in Caribbean or black British literature. As noted in chapter 1, Selvon's Londoners were a similarly mixed bunch, but the intended audience has changed.

Phillips, like Riley, has come under attack for the portrayal in his work of the black male in particular, and for failing to write more about the black British predicament. Phillips, though, feels he is addressing an absence in black cultural and social fields where "the critical tradition just hasn't developed" (qtd. in Saunders 52). He thus addresses a black British audience in this spirit of critical awareness. By comparison, the final writer in this study, David Dabydeen, who is both author and critic, uses his work to turn that critical tradition onto British society; to similarly re-sense the issues of colonialism, and promote the marginalised figures of the colonial relationship.

3.3 David Dabydeen: Caribbean Conversations III

While David Dabydeen has not been as prolific a writer as either Phillips or Riley, his poetry and two novels maintain an important presence within the genre. In what has been a largely self-selecting body of works in terms of the writers and texts studied, Dabydeen not only follows Braithwaite and Harris as the Guyanese writer in each chapter, but also, and more importantly, follows Selvon and Harris as the Indo-Caribbean writer in each chapter. As noted in the Foreword, the use of the term 'black British' can become problematic when discussing writers of Asian origin, and so a study of Dabydeen's work can answer some important questions with regard to the sustainability of black British literature as a generic term. Dabydeen was born in 1955 into a family that, like Selvon's, had not maintained strict adherence to Hindu or Moslem traditions. Unlike Selvon, however, he was not brought up in a cosmopolitan atmosphere thriving on a mixture of races. Instead, his early childhood was disrupted by the violence between the Indians and blacks that marked and marred the negotiations for Guyanese independence. Living in the predominantly Afro-Caribbean New Amsterdam at the time, his family were regularly obliged to move back to the Indian villages in rural Berbice to escape the rioting.

This experience, he says, intensified "one's nascent sense of Indianness" (qtd. in Birbalsingh, "Interview with David Dabydeen" 94), not in terms of a revived religious commitment, but in a deep identification with the land. The metropolitan existence, he says, is non-West Indian as the people who undergo it imbibe metropolitan values, rather than West Indian ones (112). There is a certain Guyanese specificity about this statement. The Guyanese interior is a unique space in terms of the Caribbean, and this, coupled with a comparatively undeveloped tourist industry, has encouraged a cultural stability less affected by the process of Americanisation identified in Phillips' work. Furthermore, the migration from rural areas by former plantation slaves to the metropolitan centres, and their replacement by indentured labour from India has led to an intimate relationship between the Indo-Guyanese population and the shape of the land. Dabydeen can thus refer to the "whole setting of cows, and houses on stilts, and savannahs and paddy fields" as a specifically Indian contribution to the landscape (qtd. 111).

The intention here is not to erect and maintain cultural barriers in the Caribbean, but to insist on the Indo-Caribbean contribution to a literature and language that had been overcome by the emphasis on African retentions. Thus, his first volume of poetry, *Slave Song* (1984), sought to reassert a "continuum of slave and indenture experience" (qtd. 112). Essential to this task was the use of Creole.

Dabydeen's use of Creole and his provision at the end of the text of notes and translations to the poetry are indicative of certain developments in the genre. On one level it was a response to nationalistic calls for Creole to be recognised as a distinct language that would require translations. On another level, it was a response to the notion of audience. Where Selvon in the Fifties was seeking to build his dialect voice into British society, Dabydeen was trying to resist the critical which, as has been noted elsewhere, was thriving "upon the expression of poverty or of dispossession" (qtd. in Binder 77). The poems manage to balance the brutality and suffering of existence on the plantation with a redemptive vulgarity indicative of an irrepressible human spirit. Creole is a "naturally tragic language," a "natural gush from the gut" (*Slave Song* 10), and Dabydeen uses this potential for the language as a sensual and immediate response to elicit the physicality of plantation life. Using a language that, he says, "cannot achieve a certain level of abstraction" (qtd. in Binder 76) aptly reduces life on the plantation to one of physical presence and bodily function.

This conception of the language facilitates Dabydeen's intention to explore the "erotic energies of the colonial experience" (*Slave Song* 10). He notes the construction of the (female) black body as the site of unconstrained sexual fantasy, of "dominance, bondage and sado-masochism, of sensual corruption and disintegration." This corruption enters the language, and lyricism becomes vulgarity, and fantasy, obscenity. Thus, the celebration of a slave's unbroken spirit in "Slave Song" becomes a celebration of his uncolonised sexuality being played out through fantasy on the slave-owner's wife. In "Canecutters' Song," this fantasy degenerates into a desire to defile the woman and in "Nightmare" is articulated by the slave as rape being the white woman's secret fantasy.

Thus, although Dabydeen uses the broken and savage aspects of Creole discursive patterns as a linguistic embodiment of life on the plantations,

3.3 David Dabydeen: Caribbean Conversations III

there is also a real sense in which the language circumscribes life and thought there. Benita Parry in her reading of these poems is troubled by the way in which the rage of the slave or canecutter is "spent in fantasies of abusing and mutilating the white woman" ("Between" 6).

* * *

Dabydeen's first novel, *The Intended*, bears some strong resemblances to Riley's *The Unbelonging*. The story of a boy brought to England by his father, and then left in care while he struggles to get into University against a backdrop of violence, adolescent sexuality and a developing sense of self in an alien country, forms a familiar pattern. A steady dialogue between memories of his younger boyhood in Guyana and experiences in London maintains the correspondence. The similarities, however, end here as Dabydeen addresses a different audience.

As a poet and academic critic, Dabydeen recognised the appropriation of his work into the oppressed race theme, and continued dilemma of the exiled writer "writing home" to an audience which, as in Hyacinth's delusory narrative, may not exist:

> I am almost saying that an immigrant in Britain lacks genuine audience. What is your audience? You don't have an audience in Guyana because you have moved away and are reconstructing Guyana fictionally, perhaps falsely, because of your absence from the place. You are forced to address Whites, and you address them on issues that have to do with dispossession, and they are such personal experiences that to have the Whites consume them is painful and shameful. It is almost like saying, "I am naked before you." (Qtd. in Binder 78)

This understanding of his probable audience differentiates Dabydeen from Riley's persistent critique of Caribbean patriarchy and Phillips' literary *houngan*. In addressing a white audience, Dabydeen revives the aspect of emigrant fiction noted in the first chapter with the crucial difference that he is educating white society about itself. By illuminating the residual social and historical myths of colonialism, he argues his own case for bringing marginalised cultures to the centre of the British identity.

The theme of education is a quite literal one in the text. The narrator's progress, through secondary education to his acceptance at Oxford, is monitored by the professorial coaching of his friends through the English 'A' Level syllabus. In the course of these sessions, Dabydeen (as the inscribed critic in the text) ironically schools the reader in ways to approach his text:

> There was also another standard trick, that of 'the theme of appearance and reality.' All great works of art had this theme thing [. . .] In fact, the surest way of identifying what was a work of art from what was just popular literature was to keep a sharp eye out for the theme of appearance and reality. Once you spotted it, you knew you were on the right track. (95)

This "theme" is a structural part of the text, operating on levels to illustrate the narrator's attempted cultural migration into the metropolis. At the most basic level, appearance and reality in the text refer to the power of the perceptions of white society to conscript individuals into a group identity. The fear of being seen, which has been a recurrent theme in the texts studied so far, is similarly potent here. The narrator, an Indo-Caribbean boy, finds himself enacting a "regrouping of the Asian diaspora" when he starts school in London (5). He and his new friends all *appear* Asian (although they are aware of differences in shade) but they have divergent Caribbean, British, Pakistani-Muslim and Ugandan-Hindu backgrounds. This is the reality of their lives, but in the playground, as in British society as a whole, they are marginalised and disregarded as "Pakis."

The narrator's determination to become assimilated into the colonial centre makes him keenly aware of how he is seen in public, and how he may be associated with other minority groups. When a car whilst trying to escape from a racist attack knocks down his friend, Nasim, the narrator finds himself in a hospital ward when Nasim's relatives arrive en masse:

> I was embarrassed for all of us, for the several Asians wrapped in alien, colourful clothes who whispered to each other in a strange tongue and crowded protectively but belatedly around their beaten son. No doubt they presented a right sight to the white pa-

3.3 David Dabydeen: Caribbean Conversations III

tients and guests who kept eyeing them. I was sure I could hear a few giggles. I knew then that I was not an Asian but that these people were yet my kin and my embarrassment. I wished I were invisible. (15)

The desire for invisibility forces a chameleon identity onto the narrator, as he tries to escape being seen as an immigrant. Thus, when the narrator goes to Nasim's home, he can see the grace and dignity of a sari in that "protected environment" (25). Furthermore, when he is surrounded by boisterous black youths on a bus later in the text, his sense of cultural identity changes again: "I'm like the whites, we both have civilisation. If they send immigrants home, they should differentiate between us Indian people and those black West Indians. I was glad to be sitting next to Shaz, one of my own, with brown skin and straight hair" (178). This confused sense of identity proceeds from the indiscriminate acceptance of Britain, and its inseparable Whiteness, as the imperial purveyor of cultured civilisation:

I suddenly long to be white, to be calm, to write with grace and clarity, to make words which have status, to shape into the craftsmanship of English china, coaches, furniture, harpsichords, wigs, English anything, for whatever they put their hands and minds to worked wonderfully. Everything they produced was fine and lasted forever. We are mud, they the chiselled stone of Oxford that has survived for centuries and will always be here. (197-8)

Such monumental glory was not cheaply bought. The capital raised through the colonial venture paid for the stately homes of England, and was invested in its cultural institutions. The Tate Gallery from the Tate and Lyall sugar empire; the Booker Prize from Booker's Guyanese sugar estates, "foster[ing] the illusion," as Dabydeen puts it, "whilst [. . .] profiting from the reality" (*Slave Song* 10).

This literary illusion of a cultivated colonial centre and a debased and savage colonial hinterland is reinforced by the narrator's enthusiasm for his studies. His attempted seduction of Janet, and continued failure to overcome his sexual shyness with her, is read with reference to Troilus and

Criseyde (121). Janet, having come from a Kentish background and unsullied by the multi-cultural metropolis, is viewed as an English rose to be protected and revered in the traditions of chivalry (244). The narrator's own self-image, his "coon condition" (230), is maintained by reading *Heart of Darkness* and the thematic association of animal images (with which the Congo natives are usually described) with "moral ugliness, indecency and the like" (94).

The narrator's uncritical acceptance of these associations is echo of Lamming's notion whereby Caliban learns language as an instrument of the exploring consciousness; the narrator learns the language, and thereby limits his consciousness. Dabydeen emphasises this process through the character of Joseph Countryman, a totally uneducated, young black Rasta whom the narrator meets at the Boy's Home. Joseph's intuitive understanding of the operation of language as a system of social signifiers allows him to expose this system as a limit to the consciousness. The literary rules with which the narrator learns to understand poetry become a means by which "[y]ou turning all the room in the universe and in the human mind into bird cage" (95). Moreover, Joseph understands the extension of this signifying practice into social perceptions: "When I was in borstal I was rumour. They look at me and they see ape, trouble fist [. . .] all the time they seeing you as animal, riot, nigger, but you know you is nothing, atoms, only image and legend in their minds" (101).

Joseph brings the theme of appearance and reality to a dramatic conclusion in the text. His original intention to film a revised *Heart of Darkness* on his stolen video camera, becomes supplanted by a fascination with the space between things; with "nothingness, colourlessness, the sightlessness of air, wind, the pure space between trees" (133). Joseph is trying to escape (or grasp) the invisible system of associations by which he has been locked into his own coon condition. Ultimately, he sees himself locked in by a word:

> It's me, all of that is me [. . .] here is C and this one here is O and another C and two more O's, and then N [. . .] Look! C is half O [. . .] it nearly there, but when it form O it breaking up again, never completing [. . .] A is for apple [. . .] B is for bat, C is for

3.3 David Dabydeen: Caribbean Conversations III

cocoon, which is also coon, N is for nut, but it's really for nuts, N is for nothing, N is for nignog. Can't you see, all of it is me. (194-5)

Joseph escapes his condition through self-immolation. Through this act he transforms himself; the appearance of black flesh becomes reduced to a human reality of white ashes.

Joseph's visionary aspect casts him as a perennial alien in Britain. His institutionalised past prepares him only for imprisonment in the future, and he is street-wise enough to know that criminalisation is the lot of alternative voices and counter-cultures in Britain; "[i]f you talk peace, they think you only smoking weed. Is a dangerous thing to preach feelings and oneness. They prefer you to hang around cars" (87). By comparison, the narrator's two friends from school, Shaz and Patel, embrace the ideological morality of the British market economy with zeal. Shaz becomes a pimp and collaborates with Patel, who uses his father's corner shop business to finance and front drug-dealing and an amateur pornographic video industry. As Patel puts it: "All they [the whites] have over us is money [. . .] and any monkey can make money, once you learn the trick" (245).

Parry argues that the two boys' consequent facility in "the inert jargon of Business Plans or the brutalised vocabulary of sex magazines," ("David Dabydeen's" 87) condemns them to the margins of British society. One might argue, however, that such discourse is no more marginal than the language of literary analysis that the narrator goes to learn in the "guarded walls of the library where entry is strictly forbidden to all but a select few" (195). In fact, both boys, by participating enthusiastically in the culture of supply and profit, are participating thereby in the master culture. Moreover, they recognise that in so doing, they are forfeiting their ancestral culture. As Patel says; "Oxford has only got money, but the Asian community made you rich" (231).

The narrator's memories of Guyana are clouded by his determination to shed his colonial condition, and thus he is unable to identify these riches. His recollections, however, while they convey an impoverished and violent society, both in urban New Amsterdam and rural Albion Village, represent a counter-cultural voice akin to Joseph's in the text. The spontaneous generation of popular myths, a language rich in metaphor and a strong undercurrent of communal superstition all illustrate a society free of a gridlock mentality. Thus, his Auntie Clarice's parting comment, "You is we, remember you is we" (40), haunts the narrator in his efforts to join a British society based on division and delineation.

The narrator's quest for assimilation is, perhaps bizarrely, recognition of these divisions. He does not want to become "a lump of aborted, anonymous flesh" (198), but rather take on the finely chiselled features of Academia; his appearance will be outweighed by an academic reality that commands respect. His immature dream that when Janet returns from three years studying in Australia, he "will have become something definite, my education compensating for my colour in the eyes of her parents" (245), is somehow vindicated by the position from which he writes his retrospective account; "I am no longer an immigrant here, for I can decipher the texts" (195). In the process, though, he has developed a "dark shadow [a] dark self" (196), which, like the society he has embodied, will not go away.

* * *

If there is an echo of Wilson Harris in the conflict between a master culture premised on a gridlock mentality and a marginalised intuitive imagination in *The Intended*, then this echo resounds more thoroughly in Dabydeen's most recent text, *Disappearance*. Dabydeen quotes from Harris' *The Secret Ladder* in an epigraph that prepares the reader for a text which revolves around just this conflict: "All at once he leaned down and splashed the liquid extravagantly on his face to clear away all doubt of a concrete existence." Again, Dabydeen centres the narrative upon the acquisition of a western education (in this case, the narrator's training as a civil engineer) and then questions its efficacy. In so doing, he once more interrogates the authority of the master culture as the purveyor of progress.

In a text that maintains the format of a first person narration interrupted by memories of Guyana, there are two immediate differences from *The Intended*. Firstly, the narrator is of African-Caribbean, rather than Asian origin. Secondly, the action in England is set away from the metropolis, in Dunsmere, a coastal town in Kent. This enables Dabydeen to describe cul-

3.3 David Dabydeen: Caribbean Conversations III

tural conflict and confusion as not being confined to the journey from the periphery to the centre, but intrinsic to the centre itself.

The narrator's description in *The Intended* of Janet's home village in Kent as a stable and secure community, the people there as somehow responsible for his own disordered existence (168), seems to be in agreement with Caryl Phillips' construction of Sneddington in *Playing Away* (1987): "The heart of England has nothing to do with the inner cities," says Phillips, "I mean the power in Britain is located in those awful places, in Suffolk and Kent and Sussex" (Johnson, "Searching" 9). Dunsmere seems similarly set, as the narrator is struck by the cottage in which he lodges as a symbol of a "venerable England" (8), and by the wealth of historical data that accompany his geological plans. This documentary evidence of an ordered past, though, does not position Dunsmere as the enduring seat of authority and control implicit in those other texts. Instead, Dunsmere is steadily crumbling into the sea, its inhabitants mostly retired and its atmosphere, moribund.

The narrator's arrival in the village is thus that of a potential saviour not only from sea erosion, but also from a spiritual decline, a loss of vitality. In particular, this role is prepared for him by his landlady, Mrs Rutherford. There is much in this relationship that compels comparison with Teeton and the Old Dowager in *Water With Berries*. Mrs Rutherford is an elderly woman, but her youthfulness is quickly established by her mental acuity, regular jogging stints and taste in modern fashion. There are strong sexual overtones to the relationship, too. The narrator, like Teeton, is quickly associated with, and compared to his landlady's absent husband. The language becomes similarly sexualised: she has "lover's eyes" (38), an "agile and passionate hand" (67), can point her toes "coquettishly" (139) and imbue a picked wildflower with the qualities of a "lover's memento" (108). She takes in a lodger, she says, not for the money, but for "a bit of excitement" (13).

The narrator appears to embody the characteristics evident in Teeton (and Dickson), in that he combines a cultivated and civilised demeanour, with the potential for an unfettered sexuality attached to black men in racist mythologies. It quickly becomes clear, though, that the narrator has schooled himself out of any attachment to a roots culture. Instead, he is grateful for an absence of his own history: "As a West Indian I had no cause to anticipate the future nor to fear death because I had cultivated no sense of the past. I was always present, always new" (10).

The narrator's sense of the new, though, is dominated by the icon of technological progress held up as a means of dominance over the encroachments of Nature. This, like the narrator's belief in academicism in *The Intended*, is inseparable from his Anglomania. When six years work in Demerara is wiped out by an overnight storm, the narrator goes to England to gain "greater skill, greater knowledge of the latest techniques and machinery" (18). His instructor there is Professor Fenwick, who had been his principal at the Guyana Technical College. Fenwick not only imparts technological knowledge, but also becomes a role model for the narrator. His austere existence in the hubbub of Georgetown profoundly affects the young narrator who tries to mimic his personality, finding it a clear contrast to the students' "creole ways" (82).

Mrs Rutherford's African artefacts and masks thus disturb the narrator's attachment to an identity based upon an image of civilised England. Collected during her time there with her husband, setting up schools in the post-colonial era, they threaten to rob the narrator of his confident association with a tradition of empirical control and superiority. The presence of the masks testifies to a tribal culture that was crushed, rather than failed from its own inherent weakness. Mrs Rutherford describes the masks' ability to project the imposed silence of the colonial venture:

> It's odd that these masks rob strangers of speech, because the African world was created by speech. The world began with an egg, and the egg only hatched birds and animals and humans when god spoke. His Word gave birth and motion to every living thing, like our Christian god. When the missionaries came with their Bibles bearing strange words, they killed off the African god and reduced the Africans to a pathetic silence, by making them speak alien words. (12)

The narrator does not need to reflect on Africa to identify this process. Coming from a rural village to Georgetown to study, Professor Fenwick's influence sees the narrator's character change. This becomes evident when he is takes on the "pharaoh's authority" over coolie labour preparing sea defences in Guyana. The narrator comes into conflict with Swami, a charismatic labourer who becomes the labourers' unofficial spokesman. The narrator's reported speech contrasts sharply with Swami's Creole, the same Creole that the narrator spoke as a boy in his village. Swami displays that same kind of uneducated vision as Joseph in the last text, is similarly acute in identifying the cultural, spiritual and mental exchange that is inherent in the narrator's training: "All-you people is straight-line folk, all-you does live along ruler's edge. The white man who used to rule you so fulsomely left you with a plastic ruler to rule you" (36). The narrator starts to wonder whether he has lost the ability to work the land as his forefathers had done, whether all he had were the "trappings of white people's ideas" (37); but when Swami dies in an accident, and there is no (super)natural response to this event, the narrator returns to his graphs with greater zeal.

Mrs Rutherford tries similarly to appeal to the narrator's (absent) sense of a colonised consciousness, and tries to school him in the iniquities of the history of British civilisation. Thus, where the Old Dowager's control over her garden may be read as a symbol of her lingering colonialism in Lamming's text, Mrs Rutherford maintains her garden to remind her of the thin veneer of civilisation that is Britain: "I've kept the garden, I suppose, to remind me of the English, of their cruelty. It's the most English thing I can do. As you say, it's all order on the surface" (158).

Mrs Rutherford uses the narrative of the events leading up to the commissioning of the sea defences in Dunsmere, to enable the narrator to "make up the story of England, to interpret it with the same abandonment with which we described and dominated your lot" (159). A sub-narrative read as a summary of a collection of newspaper cuttings and quoted phrases from a pamphlet, the tale recalls *Heart of Darkness*.

A local pressure group calling for the construction of sea defences is led by Mr Curtis. This anglicised Kurtz, the potential "leader of an extreme party" (149), propels the ordinarily inert villagers into a campaign against the council through reference to Britain's past glories. The sea defences enter the tradition of resistance to invasion; become a potential monument to arrest an appearance of national decline; and represent a Victorian ethos of protecting England for future generations. Amidst this jingoistic rhetoric, it is the council bureaucrats who are associated with savages (148), and Curtis' lay opponents who inhabit "the most far-flung moral wastelands" (154). This tale, though, does not end in horror, but in a "whiff of scandal" (155). The narrator cannot retell it in the "cruellest language of [his] tribe" (159), as Mrs Rutherford wants, because all he can find in the pervasive inertia of Dunsmere is a "seedy narrative of adultery and civic squabbles" (155). Curtis wins the battle for the sea defences to be commissioned, and returns to obscurity in his cottage: the narrator's pursuit of him through rumour never arriving at some vibrant presence.

In the end, the narrator returns to Guyana. The "seedy narrative" closes with the revelation that Fenwick has himself been defrauding the council with false accounting and ordering, and the narrator drops his plans to stay on and undertake further research. He recognises Dunsmere as a symbol of a stagnant consciousness, rejecting the unfamiliar, rather than being the embodiment of the "new" with which the narrator identifies: "It would take centuries for me to grow into the English landscape, as it took centuries for a hybrid flower to evolve, slowly transformed by pollen from the east, brought back by Crusaders and merchant venturers" (131). Until then, he would be invisible: "It was not just that they would ignored me, it's just that there was nothing to acknowledge" (132).

The narrator's mental dependence upon the efficacy of the straight lines thus becomes supplanted by a belief in cities as "random, chaotic places, allowing people to dissolve into each other" (131). They possess a regenerative capacity like the Guyanese climate, which devours and rots its relics through humidity, or bleaches its records in the sun. The Britain of Dunsmere thus maintains its façade of civilisation by denying the savagery of its tradition as a "civilising" nation. Simultaneously, it denies the presence of a population that stands as a testament to that savagery. "Guyana," thinks the narrator, "had its own legacy of deceit and cruelty, but there was space to forget" (179). It is clear for Dabydeen, what the (white) British people need to do: remember.

* * *

The debate on the use of the term 'black British,' as it was outlined in the introduction to this chapter, can thus be seen, at the end of it, to continue to

3.3 David Dabydeen: Caribbean Conversations III

revolve around the interconnected concerns of identity, audience and perception. Joan Riley and Barbara Burford both seem to insist on their right to a body of literature that reflects and addresses the reality and concerns of their community. Caryl Phillips and Fred D'Aguiar, by contrast, do not want to have their work pigeon-holed and marginalised in advance, by being placed in the "Black Literature" section of bookshops, libraries and readers' minds. Dabydeen argues for a culture and society drawing its strength from difference and tolerance.

In each case, the essential question is this: will black writing in Britain be defined by the intentions of its authors, or by its reception within mass (white) perceptions? The tragic irony of this debate is the realisation that the inestimable value of this literature is in the new perspectives it has given on multicultural Britain. None of the texts discussed in this book have been solely about black people in Britain; they have been about Britain, about its history and its modern society. As Dabydeen puts it, "when I say I want to belong [to British society], I mean I want them [the white British] to recognize that" (qtd. in Binder 72).

Black British literature can maintain its specificity, and the term will only remain knee-capping so long as it, like the black population itself, is regarded as a branch to be severed or an enclave to be ghettoised. Auntie Clarice's voice from Dabydeen's rural Guyana reverberates throughout: "You is we, remember, you is we."

Bibliography

ALCORN, Maggie. "Conference on Caribbean Writing: A Report." *Wasafiri* 6-7 (Spring-Autumn 1987): 50-2.

ALLEN, Walter. Rev. of *The Faces of Love*, by John Hearne. *New Statesman* July-Dec. 1957: 542.

ALLNUT, Gillian, et al., eds. *The New British Poetry 1968-88*. London: Paladin, 1988.

BAUGH, Edward. "Friday in Crusoe's City: The Question of Language in Two West Indian Novels of Exile." *Language and Literature in Multicultural Contexts*. Ed. Satendra Nandan. ACLALS Fifth Triennial Proceedings. Suva, Fiji: Univ. of South Pacific, 1983. 44-53.

BEESE, Barbara. Interview with New Beacon Books. *Race Today* 9.4 (June-July 1977): 82-4.

BERNHARDT, Stephen A. "Dialect and Style Shifting in the Fiction of Sam Selvon." *Studies in Caribbean Language*. Ed. Lawrence D. Carrington, Dennis Craig, and Ramon Todd Dandare. St. Augustine, Trinidad: Society for Caribbean Linguistics, 1983. 267-76.

BERRY, James. *Chain of Days*. Oxford: Oxford UP, 1985.

___. "The Literature of the Black Experience." *The Language of the Black Experience*. Ed. David Sutcliffe and Ansel Wong. Oxford: Basil Blackwell, 1986. 69-106.

___. *News For Babylon*. London: Chatto and Windus, 1984.

BINDER, Wolfgang. Interview with David Dabydeen. *Journal of West Indian Literature* 3.2 (1989): 67-80.

BIRBALSINGH, Frank. Interview with Caryl Phillips. *Caribbean Quarterly* 37.4 (Dec. 1991): 40-6.

___. Interview with David Dabydeen. *Kunapipi* 12.3 (1990): 104-32.

———. "Samuel Selvon and the West Indian Literary Renaissance." *Ariel* 8 (July 1977): 5-22.

———. "To John Bull, With Hate." *Caribbean Quarterly* 14.4 (1968): 74-81.

BISHOP, Marla. Interview with Joan Riley. *Spare Rib* (July 1985): 27.

Blackboard Jungle. Dir. Richard Brooks. MGM, 1955.

BONES, Jah. "Language and Rastafari." *The Language of the Black Experience.* Ed. David Sutcliffe and Ansel Wong. Oxford: Basil Blackwell, 1986. 37-52.

BOXILL, Anthony. "Wilson Harris." *Fifty Caribbean Writers.* Ed. Daryl Cumber Dance. Westport, Connecticut: Greenwood, 1986. 187-97.

BRAITHWAITE, E. R. *A Choice of Straws.* London: Bodley Head, 1965.

———. "The 'Colored Immigrant' in Britain." *Color and Race.* Spec. issue of *Daedalus* (Spring 1967): 496-511.

———. *Paid Servant.* 1962. London: NEL, 1968.

———. Rev. of *A Quality of Violence. Bim* 8.31 (1960): 219-20.

———. *Reluctant Neighbours.* London: Bodley Head, 1972.

———. "Roots." *Bim* 10.21 (1963): 10-21.

———. "Sir Galahad and the Islands." *Bim* 7 (July-Dec. 1957): 8-17.

———. *To Sir, With Love.* 1959. London: NEL, 1970.

BROWN, Stewart. "Dub Poetry: Selling Out." *Poetry Wales* 22.2 (1987): 51-4.

BRYAN, Beverly, Stella DADZIE, and Suzanne SCAFE. *The Heart of the Race: Black Women's Lives in Britain.* London: Virago, 1985.

BURFORD, Barbara. "The Landscapes Painted on the Inside of My Skin." *Spare Rib* (June 1987): 37-9.

CAMPBELL, Horace. "Rastafari: Culture of Resistance" *Race and Class* 22.1 (1980): 1-22.

CARR, Bill. "A Complex Fate: The Novels of Andrew Salkey." *The Islands in Between*. Ed. Louis James. Oxford: Oxford UP, 1968. 100-8.

CARTER, Trevor. *Shattering Illusions: West Indians in British Politics*. London: Lawrence and Wishart, 1986.

CATHOLIC COMMISSION FOR RACIAL JUSTICE. "Rastafarians in Jamaica and Britain" *Roots* 3.1 (1982): 9-15.

COBHAM, Rhona, and Merle COLLINS. *Watchers and Seekers: Creative Writing by Black Women Writers in Britain*. London: Women's Press, 1987.

COOKE, Micheal. "A West Indian Novelist." *Yale Review* (Summer 1973): 616-24.

COOPER, Carolyn. "Words Unbroken by the Beat: The Performance Poetry of Jean Binta Breeze and Mikey Smith." *Wasafiri* 11 (Spring 1990): 7-13.

DABYDEEN, David, ed. *The Black Presence in English Literature*. Manchester: Manchester UP, 1985.

___. *Coolie Odyssey*. London: Hansib/Dangeroo, 1988.

___. *Disappearance*. London: Secker and Warburg, 1993.

___. *The Intended*. 1991. London: Minerva, 1992.

___. "On Writing 'Slave Song.'" *Commonwealth* 8.2 (Spring 1986): 46-8.

___. *Slave Song*. 1984. Oxford: Dangeroo, 1986.

___, and Nana WILSON-TAGOE. *A Reader's Guide to West Indian and Black British Literature*. Kingston-upon-Thames: Rutherford, 1987.

D'AGUIAR, Fred. "Wilson Harris in Conversation with Fred D'Aguiar." *Wasafiri* 5 (Autumn 1986): 22-5.

DALPHINIS, Morgan. "The African Presence: Similarities Between West Indian Creole and African Oral Literature." *Wasafiri* 2 (Spring 1985): 15-7.

DANCE, Daryl Cumber. "Andrew Salkey." *Fifty Caribbean Writers*. Ed. Daryl Cumber Dance. Westport, Connecticut: Greenwood, 1986. 418-27.

___. *New World Adams*. Leeds: Peepal Tree, 1992.

DAVIES, Barrie. "A Sense of Abroad: Aspects of the West Indian Novel in England." *World Literature Written in English* 2.2 (1972): 67-80.

DAVIES, Joan. "George Lamming: The Novel and Revolution." *Stand* 4 (1960): 52-8.

DEVONISH, Hugh. *Language and Liberation: Creole Language Politics in the Caribbean*. London: Karia, 1986.

DHONDY, Farrukh. Rev. of *Voices of the Living and the Dead*. *Race Today* 6.3 (Mar. 1974): 92.

DOMMERGUES, Andre. Interview with Wilson Harris. *Commonwealth Essays and Studies* 9.1 (1986): 91-7.

DURIX, Jean-Pierre. "Talking of *Moses Ascending* with Sam Selvon." *Commonwealth* 10.2 (Spring 1988): 11-3.

EDWARDS, Adolph. *Marcus Garvey 1887-1940*. London: New Beacon, 1972.

EDWARDS, Paul, ed. *Equiano's Travels*. London: Heinemann, 1967.

FABRE, Michel. "From Trinidad to London: Tone and Language in Sam Selvon's Novels." *Literary Half-Yearly* 20 (1979): 71-80.

___. Interview with Wilson Harris. *World Literature Written in English*. 22.1 (1983): 2-17.

___. "Moses and the Queen's English: Dialect and the Narrative Voice in Samuel Selvon's London Novels." *World Literature Written in English* 18 (Nov. 1982): 385-392.

___. Wilson Harris Interview. *Kunapipi* 2.1 (1979): 100-6.

FRED, Dread. "Dread Fred Interviews LKJ." *Race Today* 9.1 (Feb. 1977): 22.

FRYER, Peter. *Black People in the British Empire: An Introduction.* London: Pluto, 1989.

___. *Staying Power: The History of Black People in Britain.* 1984. London: Pluto, 1987.

GILKES, Michael. "An Infinite Canvas." *Caribbean Quarterly* 21.4 (1975): 47-54.

___, ed. *The Literate Imagination: Essays on the Novels of Wilson Harris.* London: Macmillan, 1989.

GILROY, Beryl. "The Woman Writer and Commitment: Links Between Caribbean and African Literature." *Wasafiri* 10 (Spring 1989): 15-6.

GREY, Cecil. "Mr Salkey's Truth and Illusion." *Jamaica Journal* 2.2 (1968): 46-54.

HALL, Stuart H. "Lamming, Selvon and Some Trends in the West Indian Novel." *Bim* (Dec. 1955): 172-88.

HARRIS, Wilson. *The Age of the Rainmakers.* London: Faber and Faber, 1971.

___. *The Angel at the Gate.* London: Faber and Faber, 1983.

___. *Ascent to Omai.* London: Faber and Faber, 1970.

___. *Black Marsden.* London: Faber and Faber, 1972.

___. "Character and Philosophic Myth." *A Sense of Place: Essays in Post-Colonial Literature.* Ed. Britta Olinder. Göteborg: Gothenburg UP, 1984. 124-30.

___. *Companions of the Day and Night.* London: Faber and Faber, 1975.

___. *The Eye of the Scarecrow.* London: Faber and Faber, 1965.

___. *Explorations.* Ed. Hena Maes-Jelinek. Aarhus: Dangeroo, 1981.

___. *Far Journey of Oudin.* London: Faber and Faber, 1961.

___. *Fossil and Psyche.* Austin: African and African and American Studies and Research Center, U of Texas, 1974.

___. *Genesis of the Clowns and Da Silva Da Silva's Cultivated Wilderness.* London: Faber and Faber, 1977.

___. *Heartland.* London: Faber and Faber, 1964.

___. *History, Fable and Myth in the Caribbean and Guyana.* Georgetown: National History and Arts Council, 1970c.

___. *Palace of the Peacock.* London: Faber and Faber, 1960.

___. "A Quest for Form." *Kunapipi* 5.2 (1982): 21-7.

___. *The Secret Ladder.* London: Faber and Faber, 1963.

___. *The Sleepers of Roraima.* London: Faber and Faber, 1970.

___. *Tradition, The Writer and Society.* London: New Beacon, 1967.

___. *Tree of the Sun.* London: Faber and Faber, 1978.

___. *Tumatumari.* London: Faber and Faber, 1968.

___. *The Waiting Room.* London: Faber and Faber, 1967.

___. *The Whole Armour.* London: Faber and Faber, 1962.

___. *The Womb of Space: The Cross-Cultural Imagination.* Westport, Connecticut: Greenwood, 1983.

HAWORTH, David. Rev. of *Escape to An Autumn Pavement*, by Andrew Salkey. *New Statesman* Feb. 1969: 230.

Bibliography

HAY, Courtney. "Rev. of *Dread Beat an' Blood.*" *Race Today* 10.6 (Sep.-Oct. 1978): 143.

HOWE, Darcus. "Ten Years of Bogle L'Ouverture." *Race Today* 11.5 (Nov.-Dec. 1979): 116-8.

___. Introduction. *Race Today Review* 14.1 (Dec.-Jan. 1981-1982): 1.

JAGGI, Maya. "On Being Here." *Guardian* 6 Aug. 1993: 4-5.

JAMES, C. L. R. *Beyond a Boundary.* 1963. London. Stanley Paul, 1986.

___. *Minty Alley.* 1936. London. New Beacon, 1971.

JAMES, Louis. Rev. of *The Final Passage*, by Caryl Phillips. *Wasafiri* 4 (Spring 1986): 32.

JOHNSON, Linton Kwesi. *Dread Beat an' Blood.* 1975. London: Bogle L'Ouverture, 1980.

___. *Inglan is a Bitch.* London: Race Today, 1980.

___. Rev. of *A Rasta In A Babylon - A Documentary Film by Howard Johnson. Race Today* 111.1 (Jan. 1978): 21.

___. "Searching for Answers: Caryl Phillips in Conversation with Linton Kwesi Johnson." *Race Today Review* 17.4 (1987): 6-9.

___. "Some Thoughts on Reggae." *Race Today* 13.1 (Dec.-Jan. 1980c): 59.

___. *Tings an' Times.* Newcastle: Bloodaxe, 1991.

___. *Voices of the Living and the Dead.* 1974. London: Race Today, 1988.

KENT, George E. "A Conversation with George Lamming." *Black World.* 22.5 (1973): 4-14 and 88-97.

KING, Bruce, ed. *West Indian Literature.* London: Macmillan, 1979.

KLINKOWITZ, Jerome. "Wilson Harris' Intertextuality: The Angel at the Gate." *Hambone* 6 (Fall 1986): 143-5.

LAING, Stuart. "The Production of Literature." *Society and Literature 1945-1970*. Ed. Alan Sinfield. London: Methuen, 1983. 121-72.

LAMMING, George. *The Emigrants*. 1954. London: Allison and Busby, 1980.

___. *In the Castle of My Skin*. 1953. Harlow: Longman, 1970.

___. *Natives of My Person*. Harlow: Longman, 1972.

___. *Of Age and Innocence*. 1958. London: Allison and Busby, 1981.

___. *The Pleasures of Exile*. 1960. London: Allison and Busby, 1984.

___. *Season of Adventure*. 1970. London: Allison and Busby, 1979.

___. *Water With Berries*. Harlow: Longman, 1971.

___. "The West Indian People." *New World Quarterly* 2.2 (1966): 64-5.

La ROSE, John, and Andrew SALKEY. Introduction. *Savacou* 19.10 (1974): 10.

La ROSE, John. *The New Cross Massacre Story*. London: BPM, BYM and RTC, 1984.

LEE, Robert. "The Novelist in Caribbean Politics: An Interview with George Lamming." *Race Today* 10.3 (Mar. 1978): 66-9.

Look Back in Anger. Dir. Tony Richardson. Woodfall Films, 1958.

MACFARLANE, L. J. *Issues in British Politics Since 1945*. Harlow: Longman, 1981.

MAES-JELINEK, Hena. "Altering Boundaries: The Art of Translation in *The Angel at the Gate* and *The Twyborn Affair*." *Hambone* 6 (Fall 1986): 146-56.

___. "'Inimitable Painting': New Developments in Wilson Harris's Latest Fiction." *Ariel* 8.3 (July 1977): 63-80.

___. *Wilson Harris*. World Author Series. Boston: Twayne, 1982.

___. "The Writer as Alchemist: The Unifying Role of the Imagination in the Novels of Wilson Harris." *Language and Literature* 1.1 (1971): 25-34.

MARWICK, Arthur. *British Society Since 1945*. 1982. Harmondsworth: Penguin, 1986.

MILES, Robert and Annie PHIZACKLEA. *White Man's Country*. 1984. London: Pluto, 1987.

MITTELHOLZER, Edgar. *Kaywana Blood*. London: Grafton 1986.

___. *A Morning at the Office*. Harmondsworth: Penguin/Hogarth 1950.

MORRIS, Mervyn. "People Speech: Some Dub Poets." *Race Today Review* 14.5 (1983): 150-7.

___. "A West Indian Student in England." *Caribbean Quarterly* 8.4 (Dec. 1962): 17-29.

MUNRO, Ian H. "George Lamming." *Fifty Caribbean Writers*. Ed. Daryl Cumber Dance. Westport, Connecticut: Greenwood, 1986. 246-75.

___, and Reinhard SANDER. Interview with George Lamming. "Kas-Kas: Interviews With Three Caribbean Writers in Texas." Ed. Munro and Sander. *Occasional Publication of the African and Afro-American Research Institute*. U of Texas at Austin. 1972. 5-22.

___, and Reinhard SANDER. Interview with Wilson Harris. "Kas-Kas: Interviews With Three Caribbean Writers in Texas." Ed. Munro and Sander. *Occasional Publication of the African and Afro-American Research Institute*. U of Texas at Austin. 1972. 43-56.

NAIPAUL, V. S. Rev. of *The Last Enchantment*. *New Statesman* July-Dec. 1960: 97-8.

___. Rev. of *Turn Again Tiger*. *New Statesman* July-Dec. 1958: 826-7.

NASTA, Susheila. "The Moses Trilogy: Sam Selvon Discusses his London Novels with Susheila Nasta." *Wasafiri* 1.2 (Spring 1985): 5-9.

NAZARETH, Peter. "The Clown in the Slave Ship." *Caribbean Quarterly* 23 (June-Sept. 1977): 24-30.

NAZARETH, Peter. Interview with Sam Selvon. *World Literature Written in English* 18 (Nov. 1979): 420-37.

___. "Sexual Fantasies and Neo-Colonial Repression in Andrew Salkey's *The Adventures of Catullus Kelly*." *World Literature Written in English* 28.2 (Autumn 1988): 341-56.

NGCOBO, Lauretta, ed. *Let It Be Told: Essays by Black Women in Britain*. London: Virago, 1987.

NICHOLAS, Tracy. *Rastafari: A Way of Life*. New York: Anchor, 1979.

NORTHAM, Gerry. *Shooting in the Dark*. London: Faber and Faber, 1988.

PARRY, Benita. "Between Creole and Cambridge English: The Poetry of David Dabydeen." *Kunapipi* 10.3 (1988): 1-14.

___. "David Dabydeen's *The Intended*." *Kunapipi* 13.3 (1991): 85-90.

PARRY, J. H., and P. M. SHERLOCK. *A Short History of the West Indies*. London: Macmillan, 1983.

PHILLIPS, Caryl. *Cambridge*. 1991. London: Picador, 1992.

___. *The European Tribe*. London: Faber and Faber, 1987.

___. *The Final Passage*. 1985. London: Faber and Faber, 1989.

___. *Higher Ground*. Viking, 1989.

___. *Playing Away*. London: Faber and Faber, 1987.

___. *The Shelter*. Ambergate: Amber Lane, 1984.

___. *A State of Independence*. London: Faber and Faber, 1986.

___. *Strange Fruit*. Ambergate: Amber Lane, 1981.

___. *Where There is Darkness*. Ambergate: Amber Lane, 1982.

Bibliography

PHILLIPS, Mike. "Invisible Ink." *Guardian* 29 June 1993: 3-5.

PINCKNEY, Alphonso. *Red, Black and Green: Black Nationalism in the United States*. Cambridge: Cambridge UP, 1976.

PINES, Jim. *Black and White in Colour: Black People in British Television Since 1936*. London: BFI, 1992.

POET AND THE ROOTS. *Dread Beat an' Blood*. London: Virgin Records. 1978.

POUCHET PAQUET, Sandra. *The Novels of George Lamming*. London: Heinemann, 1982.

___. "Samuel Dickson Selvon." *Fifty Caribbean Writers*. Ed. Daryl Cumber Dance. Westport, Connecticut: Greenwood, 1986. 439-49.

PRITCHETT, V. S. Rev. of *In the Castle of My Skin*. *New Statesman* Jan.-June 1953: 460.

PRYCE, Everton. "The Notting Hill Carnival: Black Politics, Resistance and Leadership 1976-1978." *Caribbean Quarterly* 32.2 (June 1985): 35-52.

RAMCHAND, Kenneth. "The Myth of *To Sir, With Love*." *Voices* 1 (Dec. 1965): 13-20.

___. "Sam Selvon Talking: An Interview with Kenneth Ramchand." *Canadian Literature* 95 (Winter 1982): 56-64.

___. "Song of Innocence, Song of Experience: Sam Selvon's *The Lonely Londoners* as a Literary Work." *World Literature Written in English* 21.3 (Autumn 1982): 644-54.

___. *The West Indian Novel and its Background*. 1970. London: Heinemann, 1983.

RAMRAJ, Victor. "Selvon's Londoners: From the Centre to the Periphery." *Language and Literature in Multicultural Contexts*. ACLALS Fifth Triennial Proceedings. Ed. Satendra Nandan. Suva, Fiji: U of South Pacific, 1983. 297-306.

REDCAM, Tom. *Becka's Buckra Baby*. Jamaica. Jamaica Times Printery, 1903.

REID, Victor. *New Day*. 1949. London. Heinemann, 1973.

RICHARDSON, Maurice. Rev. of *The Emigrants*. *New Statesman* July-Dec. 1954: 333.

___. Rev. of *The Lonely Londoners*. *New Statesman* July-Dec. 1956: 846.

___. Rev. of *Ways of Sunlight*. *New Statesman* Jan.-June 1958: 546.

RILEY, Joan. *A Kindness to the Children*. London: Women's Press, 1992.

___. *Romance*. London: Women's Press, 1988.

___. *The Unbelonging*. 1985. London: Women's Press, 1988.

___. *Waiting in the Twilight*. 1987. London: Women's Press, 1992.

ROHLEHR, Gordon. "The Folk in Caribbean Literature." *Tapia* 2.1-3 (1972).

___. "Samuel Selvon and the Language of the People." *Critics on Caribbean Literature*. Ed. Edward Baugh. London: Allen and Unwin, 1978.

___. "Sparrow and the Language of Calypso." *Savacou* 2 (Sept. 1970): 87-99.

Room at the Top. Dir. Jack Clayton. British Lion Films, 1959.

ROTHFORK, John. "Race and Community in Sam Selvon's Fiction." *Caribbean Quarterly* 37.4 (Dec. 1991): 9-22.

SAGGAR, Shamit. *Race and Politics in Britain*. London: Harvester, 1992.

SALKEY, Andrew. *The Adventures of Catullus Kelly*. London: Hutchinson, 1969.

___. *Anancy's Score*. London: Bogle L'Ouverture, 1973.

___. *Away*. London: Allison and Busby, 1980.

___. *Come Home, Malcolm Heartland*. London: Hutchinson, 1976.

___. *Escape to an Autumn Pavement*. London: Hutchinson, 1960.

___. *Georgetown Journal*. London: New Beacon, 1972.

___. *Havana Journal*. Harmondsworth: Penguin, 1971.

___. *In The Hills Where Her Dreams Live: 3 Poems for Chile, 1973-1980*. Havana: Casa de las Americas, 1979.

___. Introduction. *Dread Beat an' Blood*. By Linton Kwesi Johnson. 1975. London: Bogle L'Ouverture, 1980. 7-9.

___. *Jamaica*. London: Hutchinson, 1973.

___. *Land*. Sausalito, California: Black Scholar, 1979.

___. *The Late Emancipation of Jerry Stover*. London: Hutchinson, 1968.

___. *A Quality of Violence*. London: Hutchinson, 1959.

SAUNDERS, Kay. Interview with Caryl Phillips. *Kunapipi* 9.1 (1987): 44-52.

SEARL, Eva, and MAES-JELINEK, Hena. "Comedy of Intensity: Wilson Harris's *Black Marsden*." *Commonwealth Newsletter* 4 (July 1973): 21-9.

SELVON, Sam. *A Brighter Sun*. 1952. Harlow: Longman, 1979.

___. *A Drink of Water*. London: Nelson, 1968.

___. *Eldorado West One*. Leeds: Peepal Tree, 1988.

___. "Finding West Indian Identity in London." *Kunapipi* 9.3 (1987): 34-8.

___. *Highway in the Sun and Other Plays*. Leeds: Peepal Tree, 1991.

___. *The Housing Lark*. London: MacGibbon and Kee, 1965.

___. *I Hear Thunder*. London: MacGibbon and Kee, 1963.

___. *An Island is a World*. London: Wingate, 1955.

___. *The Lonely Londoners*. 1956. Harlow: Longman, 1972.

___. *Moses Ascending*. 1975. London: Heinemann, 1989.

___. *Moses Migrating*. London: Heinemann, 1983.

___. *The Plains of Caroni*. London: MacGibbon and Kee, 1970.

___. *Those Who Eat the Cascadura*. London: Davis Poynter, 1972.

___. "Three into One Can't Go – East Indian, Trinidadian or West Indian? Samuel Selvon Discusses the Question of an East Indian Identity." *Wasafiri* 5 (Autumn 1986): 8-11.

___. *Turn Again Tiger*. 1958. London: Heinemann, 1979.

___. *Ways of Sunlight*. 1957. Harlow: Longman, 1985.

SINGH, Sidney. "A Bibliography of Critical Writing on the West Indian Novel." *World Literature Written in English* 22.1 (1983): 107-42.

SIVANANDAN, A. *A Different Hunger*. 1982. London: Pluto, 1987.

SKED, Alan, and Chris COOK. *Post-War Britain: A Political History*. Harmondsworth: Penguin, 1986.

STEWART, Robert J. "Linton Kwesi Johnson: Poetry Down a Reggae Wire." *New West Indian Guide* 167.1 & 2 (1993): 69-89.

SWIFT, Graham. "Caryl Phillips Interviewed by Graham Swift." *Kunapipi* 13.3 (1991): 96-103.

THIEME, John. "The Legacy of Conquest: An Interview with Wilson Harris." *Caribbean Contact* 7.10 (1980): 17-8.

TIFFIN, Helen. "The Tyranny of History: George Lamming's *Natives of my Person* and *Water With Berries*." *Ariel* 10 (Oct. 1979): 37-52.

___. "Wilson Harris: An Interview." *New Literature Review* 7 (1979): 18-29.

TINDALL, Gillian. Rev. of *Tumatumari*. *New Statesman* 1968: July-Dec.: 292.

To Sir, With Love. Dir. James Clavell. Columbia Pictures, 1967.

WAKEMAN, John, ed. *World Authors 1950-1970*. New York: HW Wilson, 1975.

WALMSLEY, Anne. *The Caribbean Artists Movement 1966-1972*. London: New Beacon, 1992.

WARNER-LEWIS, Maureen. "Samuel Selvon's Linguistic Extravaganza: *Moses Ascending*. *Critical Issues in West Indian Literature*. Ed. Erika Smilowitz. Parkersburg I.A.: Caribbean Books, 1984. 101-11.

WATERHOUSE, Keith. Rev. of *Escape to an Autumn Pavement*. *New Statesman* July-Dec. 1960: 63.

WATSON, Jack. *The West Indian Heritage: A History of the West Indies*. London: John Murray, 1982.

WILKINSON, Jane. "Interview with Wilson Harris." *Kunapipi* 8.2 (1986): 30-45.

WILLIAMS, Eric. *Britain and the West Indies*. London: Longman, 1969.

WOOD, Anthony. *Great Britain 1900-1965*. London: Longman, 1978.

Series Subscription

Please enter my subscription to the series **Studies in English Literatures**, ISSN 1614-4651, as follows:

☐ complete series　　　　OR　　☐ English-language titles
　　　　　　　　　　　　　　　　☐ German-language titles

starting with
☐ volume # 1
☐ volume # ___
　　☐ please also include the following volumes: #___, ___, ___, ___, ___, ___,
___
☐ the next volume being published
　　☐ please also include the following volumes: #___, ___, ___, ___, ___, ___,
___

☐ 1 copy per volume　　　OR　　☐ ___ copies per volume

Subscription within Germany:

You will receive every title on 1st publication at the regular bookseller's price incl. s & h and VAT.

Payment:
☐ Please bill me for every volume.
☐ Lastschriftverfahren: Ich/wir ermächtige(n) Sie hiermit widerruflich, den Rechnungsbetrag je Band von meinem/unserem folgendem Konto einzuziehen.

Kontoinhaber: _____ Kreditinstitut: _____
Kontonummer: _____ Bankleitzahl: _____

International Subscription:

Payment (incl. s & h and VAT) in advance for
☐ 10 volumes/copies (€ 319.80)　　☐ 20 volumes/copies (€ 599.80)
☐ 40 volumes/copies (€ 1,099.80)
Please send my books to:

NAME_____ DEPARTMENT_____
ADDRESS _____
POST/ZIP CODE_____ COUNTRY _____
TELEPHONE _____ EMAIL_____

date/signature_____

Please fax to: **0511 / 262 2201 (+49 511 262 2201)**
or mail to: *ibidem*-Verlag, Julius-Leber-Weg 11, D-30457 Hannover, Germany
or send an e-mail: ibidem@ibidem-verlag.de

ibidem-Verlag
Melchiorstr. 15
D-70439 Stuttgart

info@ibidem-verlag.de

www.ibidem-verlag.de
www.edition-noema.de
www.autorenbetreuung.de